THE
SCOTTISH
THIRTIES

AN ARCHITECTURAL INTRODUCTION

"WELL, ANYWAY, THE PEOPLE WHO HAVE TAKEN IT SEEM TO BE THE USUAL SHAPE!"

THE SCOTTISH THIRTIES

AN ARCHITECTURAL INTRODUCTION

CHARLES McKEAN

1987

SCOTTISH ACADEMIC PRESS

Published by
Scottish Academic Press Ltd,
33 Montgomery Street
Edinburgh EH7 5JX

ISBN 0 7073 0494 6

Cover and design concept by Roger Emmerson
Artwork by Dorothy Steedman
Printed and bound in Great Britain
by Bell and Bain, Glasgow

CONTENTS

INTRODUCTION

In 1937, Scotland was enjoying the only real boom year it was to experience between the wars. New employment, created by rearmament programmes and service industries, enticed chain stores north from England, fuelled a further wave of pavilions, dance halls, cinemas and pubs, and financed an accelerated proliferation of private houses and bungalows. Though hunger marches leave little tangible trace, virtually every other Thirties activity is recorded in the architecture that it required.

Probably the most significant examples are those buildings realised between the summers of 1936 and 1938. Although generally uncharacteristic of both the decade and the inter-war period as a whole, they represent the manifestation of ideas that had been debated and developed *ad nauseam* during the previous ten years without the resources to carry any of them out. In those two years, Scotland moved visibly from the old to the new: new materials and structures led to new architectures appropriate for the programmes of social welfare, of housing, and of state intervention in the economy, with which the country intended to tackle possibly the worst economic, overcrowding, and health record in Europe.

This book is founded upon the perceptions of the Thirties held by the Scots of that time – as recorded in books or recollected in interview. It cannot be definitive, since so much remains to be investigated, and each new interview cast doubt upon its predecessor. Yet it is all held together by the architecture. So this book is primarily about architecture: those who commissioned it and those who built it. Originally conceived as an architectural reconnaissance of a dormant period, it broadened inexorably into a study of the period as a whole, as it could be inferred from what had been built. It would have been seriously incomplete if it did not enquire into what lay behind the enormous quantity of building that took place, some of it of an unexpected adventurousness. It would have been insufficient to judge cinemas, for example, purely on the grounds that many people found them vulgar: there had to be a reason for their appearance. They, like bungalows, factories, garages and hotels all required the evolution of an unfamiliar architectural language appropriate for what were (in many cases) new structures for new activities.

The Thirties are characterised by a fascination with the idea of the "new". Books, journals and interviews conveyed belief in an ever-improving future, and a determination to achieve it in Scotland. They had a fervour that nowadays is only found in Japan. The Scots of the Thirties – even in the heat of the "renaissance" – did not reject the past; neither were they going to use it as a convenient retreat from the present. They used that cultural legacy to create a future that was as modern and as adventurous as could be found in all Europe – but nonetheless Scottish. They were not encumbered with our debilitating notion that being "Scottish" was something necessarily adorned with tartan carpets, nodding deer and wall-to-wall Macmusack.

Entirely unexpected has been the number of ironic and rather eerie coincidences between then and now. How ironic many of the Thirties luminaries would find the daily debate in our newspapers about the purchase and removal from Scotland of our native industries: for it happened then. How unsurprising they might have found the recent reports that Scotland is still close to the bottom of the European league in terms of health, housing and economy. As we jettison free school milk and perhaps parts of the planning system, we forget the desperate battles supported by a broad range of Scots to introduce them in the first place: it might be salutary to examine what it was that encouraged so many people to campaign for their introduction.

Fifty years ago, Scots awaited the Empire Exhibition, due to open in Glasgow in May 1938, with growing anticipation: so do we, for the Glasgow Garden Festival. But examine the difference in aspiration. At current prices, the Empire Exhibition had an investment over six times the size of the Garden Festival, and a target audience of around four times.

Those Thirties buildings that survive are now approximately 50 years old. With the exception of houses and flats, most are either neglected (and lacking that brilliantly white or coloured imagery that was so central to Thirties architecture) or brought up-to-date in ways that harm the original aesthetic. That is the principal reason why so many illustrations in this book are drawings: for it is only through drawings or contemporary photographs that we can appreciate the style and flavour of what they were trying to do. Some particular monuments to Thirties society are decaying or derelict: an emergency list of these would probably include the India of Inchinnan factory (1930), the Infectious Diseases Hospital, Hawkhead, Paisley (1934), the Maybury roadhouse, Edinburgh (1935), Paton and Baldwin's extension, Alloa (1935), the Portobello Swimming Pool (1936), Glasgow University's Garscadden Pavilion (1936), St Cuthbert's Co-operative store, Bread Street, Edinburgh (1937), the Seaforth Canteen, Hillington (1938) and the Frances Colliery Pithead Baths, West Wemyss (1939). Many other significant buildings still seem to provide good service, the "open air" schools well represented by Tullos, Aberdeen, industrial welfare by Weir's amenity building, Cathcart, cinemas by the Cosmo, Glasgow, and hotels by the somewhat under-appreciated Beresford, Glasgow (now a Hall of Residence). Houses and flats provide a key to the period, but in most cases are surviving the transition to their second wind reasonably well.

Acknowledgements to the immense number of people who have contributed to, or assisted, this book are made at the rear. Their help has been invaluable. One significant result has been the addition of over 2000 drawings and photographs of the Thirties to the RIAS Collection, which may be viewed at the Royal Commission on the Ancient and Historical Monuments of Scotland at 4–6 Coates Place, Edinburgh. A special section of the RIAS Library has been formed around the books, interviews, notes and other material from this study. The book, however, could not have been completed without the acquiescence and encouragement of my family, the RIAS and its staff, to both of whom I owe great thanks. I would like also to thank David Walker, Ian Gow, Alan Reiach and Neil Baxter for their particularly unstinting help; and Bruce and Douglas Mickel, whose financial support made the colour photographs possible.

Charles McKean
January 1987

Empire Exhibition 1938. The Cascades and Tait's tower.

1▮ THE STATE OF SCOTLAND

Scotland has been in recent years an increasingly unprofitable sphere in which to conduct various businesses, and the alarming effect is, of course, cumulative. The way to check this tendency is to inspire the people of Scotland not only with confidence and faith in their own country but with a determination to face the facts.

Sir James Lithgow.
Daily Record 20th October 1932.

The architecture of the Thirties is best examined against the social and economic context from which it arose. We are looking at the buildings of a country in a worse economic state than any other country in Europe, and yet in the midst of a cultural revival; of a country undergoing immense social change, yet retarded by its preponderant Victorian inheritance of grim, overcrowded industrial workplaces (scarcely deserving the dignity of "town"); of a country using nationalist sentiment to extract greater concessions from the elephant (i.e. England) with whom it was reluctantly bedded. There are many uncomfortably recognisable parallels between the Scotland of the Thirties and that of the Eighties.

One's perception of the Thirties economy depended upon whether or not one had work. Those still employed enjoyed a rising standard of living since real costs continued to decline, and consumables—irons, washing machines, radios and cars—became cheaper with mass production. There was an expansion in the light engineering, food and service sectors, mainly in the centre and the east. The heavy industry to the west had become dependent upon the whim of government policy. The Base Rate dropped to 2% in 1932, and cheap money brought cheap mortgages.[1] Land was available for urban expansion,[2] and a large bungalow in King's Park, Glasgow cost as little as £25 down and 21/- per week: and sold like ice creams in a heatwave. Mactaggart and Mickel established a world record, or so they claimed, with the sale of 134 such houses within a 24-hour period in 1930.[3] Those with money to spare after their new house and car could satisfy their craving for the Talkies in the new super cinemas, for dancing in innumerable "Palais" and "Pavilions" and for the better things in the smart new shops in Edinburgh and Glasgow and in the new chain stores—C & A, Burtons, Marks and Spencer—emerging over Hadrian's Wall from the south.

Those without a job experienced a different reality. They were likely to be concentrated in the old industrial centres, some of whose communities experienced complete economic failure. Scotland's economy is now thought to have begun collapsing about 1910, saved only by the armaments and shipping programmes of the First World War. Much of central Scotland's mineral wealth had become exhausted, and the west was over-dependent upon heavy engineering and shipbuilding for which the peacetime market was shrinking. Most northern European countries suffered a slump immediately after the War but Scotland was the only one whose production continued to fall after 1922.[4] The Depression which began in 1929 and reached its nadir in 1932 merely accelerated a Scottish economic decline already well advanced.[5] Some of Scotland's economy drifted south to a

[1] Professor Roy Campbell: paper to RIAS Thirties conference 1984.

[2] Agricultural land prices slumped from 1917, and many landed estates found their way onto the market following the deaths of heirs in the Great War.

[3] Interview with Douglas Mickel. Also Mactaggart and Mickel advertisement in *Bulletin*.

[4] Between 1907 and 1930 production in England rose by 20%. Scottish production fell by 12%. George Malcolm Thomson: *Scotland that Distressed Area* (Porpoise 1935).

[5] Thomson op. cit. p.46.

Ross's Dairy, its clean lines symbolising the drive for better health through nutritious milk products.

Strathclyde Archives

warmer climate—banks, motor cars, calico printing and even the printing of the Scottish telephone directories.[6] The move to Corby by Stewarts and Lloyds of Mossend in 1934, accompanied by 1000 Scots workers, was regarded as proof that Scotland was being abandoned. "An economic blizzard", wrote A G Macdonell "was sweeping icily over Britain, and England was prepared for her own safety to sacrifice Scotland. The mask was off, and little Red Riding Hood was alone in the forest with the wolf. Within a few years, Scotland was shorn of her railways, her banks and most of her shipping".[7] To make matters worse, the Government reacted to the economic crisis by withdrawing council housing subsidies in 1931 for three years, causing crisis in the building industry.[8]

Comparisons with the condition of England only served to support the nationalist arguments of people like Macdonell. Whereas the proportion of English unemployed averaged between 1931 and 1932 about 20%, the Scottish proportion was 7% worse.

In 1932 the unemployment rate in Edinburgh—Scotland's least affected city or town—was never less than double the London rate. In 1935 over 25% of Scots were still dependent upon poor relief.[9]

The long-term effect of the collapse was that Scotland came close to a state from which it could not recover. By 1939 Clydeside had shed over 100,000 shipworkers, permanently.[10] Tom Johnston, MP for Kirkintilloch and an outstanding Secretary of State for Scotland during the War, recalled: "We had seen the rearmament factories being started in England; all we got in Scotland was storage capacity. We saw our girls, 500 per week of them in the spring of 1942, being drafted away to work in the new factories of the south."[11]

Although the service sector was increasing dramatically (by 30% between 1924 and 1935) it was able to absorb little of the heavy industrial labour surplus, and the social consequences were disastrous:

> . . . half these ragged fellows, these slouching dole-men, these pot-bellied deformities, had once stood rigid and magnificent on parade, and marched behind the pipes with kilts swinging, and eaten their food under the storm clouds of death . . . here, with foul shirts and fouler breath, were Mars's heroes. Kings had fallen and nations perished, armies had withered and cities been ruined for this and this alone: that poor men in stinking pubs might have a great wealth of memory.[12]

In 1929 a new system of poor relief was introduced, along with the Means Test, which gave rise to a bitter Glasgow street song:

> Ah'm no' the factor nor the gas man
> Napoleon nor Ronald Coleman;
> But, if ye hear me rattattie at the door
> Hae ye money in the bank or money in the store?
> Ye'd better watch out, or else'll get ye
> Don't try to dodge me if ye can
> For I'm neither Jesus Christ nor Douglas Fairbanks
> I am the Means Test Man

Transitional state benefit (that subject to the Means Test, applying particularly to women and the long-term unemployed) became widespread despite its unpopularity, and by 1932 50% of unemployment benefit in Scotland was means-tested.[13] Edwin Muir observed the psychological consequences of unemployment in *Scottish Journey*.

> The effect of one, or two, or five or ten years of waiting for work can be seen in their attitudes as they stand at the street corners; the very air seems empty around them, as if it had been drained of some essential property; they scarcely talk, what they say seems hardly to break the silence: the strongest impression I received of Glasgow was one of silence. When one goes down to the Clyde,

[6] Tom Johnston: *Memories* (Collins 1952) p.151.

[7] A G Macdonell: *My Scotland* (Jarrolds 1937) p.273.

[8] John Gibson: *Thistle and the Crown* (HMSO 1985) p.73.

[9] Christopher Harvie: *No Gods and Precious Few Heroes* (Arnold 1981) p.77.

[10] *Scotland's Record* (1946) p.33.

[11] Johnston op. cit. p.151.

[12] Eric Linklater: *Magnus Merriman* (1934).

[13] Harvie op. cit. p.76.

Hillington Industrial Garden City.

RIAS Collection

to what used to be the busy shipbuilding quarter, there is hardly anything but this silence, which one would take to be the silence of a dead town if it were not for the numberless empty-looking groups of unemployed men standing about the pavements.[14]

Government attempts to revive the Scots economy accelerated after 1934, with the Secretary of State's appointment of a Commissioner for Special (i.e. Distressed) Areas, Sir Arthur Rose. Rose, his successors and his team spent £4 million in the next three years in promoting Scottish industry. In 1936, he appointed Sir Stephen Bilsland Chairman of a new Scottish Economic Committee, responsible for the creation of the innovative Scottish Industrial Estates Company, the Scottish Special Area Housing Association and the 1938 Empire Exhibition.[15] Housing subsidies were also resumed in 1934, but to many Scots the key symbol of revival was the resumption of work on the giant No 534 in John Brown's shipyard, whose gaunt ribs had towered silently over Clydebank for several years. Subsidised by the government, probably to ease the merger between Cunard and White Star, No 534 was launched as the *Queen Mary* in 1936.

Despite an upturn in the private sector during 1936, mainly in food, dairy and light engineering, it was worsening international politics which finally provided the economy with the momentum it required. Huge armaments and grenade factories were begun in Bishopton and Irvine in 1937, and many of the Glaswegian consumer buildings (e.g. shops and pubs) date from after this time. For the second time, war or the threat of war was to prolong artificially the life of the heavy engineering industries of central Scotland. Despite the rain and the Munich crisis, the 1938 Empire Exhibition represented an £11 million investment in the future of Scotland, and the boom conditions seemed to justify the Scottish Economic Committee's activities. Yet shipbuilding was to slump again later that year, unemployment shot up again and in autumn 1939 the construction industry came close to total seizure following strict Government rationing of building materials—particularly timber. All but licensed construction ceased, leaving, just as No 534 had been left, the carcasses of many half-built projects exposed to the elements. Even the licensing was erratic: Kirkcaldy Town Hall and schools at Tullos, Pilton and Hyndland left half finished, whereas the Ascot Cinema in Anniesland was allowed to proceed.

For non-military projects, the fear of war proved to be a major disincentive.

[14] Edwin Muir: *Scottish Journey* (1935).

[15] In 1937 amending legislation was passed which extended the boundaries of the Depressed Areas, and gave the Commissioner powers to build industrial estates, to subsidise industries, to extend public utilities and to use imagination, such as subsidise film making (Gibson op. cit. p.78).

SCOTLAND'S EMPIRE EXHIBITION

Transgraphics

Thomas Tait and his exhibition.

Although many major projects were announced and designed in 1937–9, few not already on site by May 1938 were built. When considering the architecture of the Thirties, therefore, it should be remembered the majority of the projects date from the short period of 1935–8; a period, when compared with the longer spans of architectural history, as shortlived as a dandelion puff ball. Yet its seeds, like those of the dandelions, were to prove vigorous and widespread.

HOUSING AND HEALTH

Four-fifths of all Scots lived in towns or cities, squeezed into a narrow, heavily industrialised belt running north–west from Ayr to Dundee. The preponderance of building in those areas had been cheaply and grimly built between 1870 and 1910, the scenic characteristics dominated by spoil, soot and heavy air pollution.

Overcrowding was a peculiarly Scots phenomenon. The worst overcrowding in England occurred in Sunderland with a rate of c. 18%: the least overcrowding in Scotland, in Edinburgh, was 17%. The Clyde valley towns had an average overcrowding rate of 40%. National comparisons revealed an English rate of overcrowded homes of 3.8% as compared with a Scottish rate six times worse.[16]

Those conditions underlay the ambitious housing programmes of the period. Mass housing formed the predominant construction, some 300,000 houses being built between 1919 and 1939, the scale of which created immense

[16] Harvie op. cit. p.70. Overcrowding was officially defined on the normal scale, as more than two people per room. In 1921 12% of all Scots houses were one roomed. *The housing of the working classes of Scotland* (1930).

[17] *Planning Our New Homes.* (Scottish Housing Advisory Committee 1943).

[18] Cicely Hamilton: *Modern Scotland* (J M Dent 1937) p.18.

problems of decentralisation and social isolation. The built results were really only visible on the city outskirts as the new estates gulped down cheap farming land. Little change was visible in the inner cities themselves, although the pressure on existing flats began to drop. The preoccupation with solving homelessness, overcrowding and slums took priority over the maintenance of existing stock, so that, by 1941, despite those 300,000 new houses, the shortfall of decent homes was thought to have *risen* to a new high of 500,000.[17]

Before the First War, the declining stature of the average Scot compelled a reduction of 4 inches (to 5 feet 2 inches) of the minimum height requirement for entry to the Scots regiments,[18] attributed to malnutrition, poverty, disease and environmental factors such as overcrowding. Scotland's infant mortality rate was still double that of Holland in 1937 and, in 1938, incapacitating illness affected the highest proportion of insured Scots since records began. Yet remarkable improvements in the nation's health between 1919 and 1939 could be recorded. The average height of 13-year-old Glasgow schoolchildren, for example, increased by 3 inches (T C Smout: *A Century of the Scottish People*), surely attributable to the official health and nutrition programmes.

The dominant Scottish administrative Department became that of Health, and new housing layouts, subsidies and planning had a health bias. Schools were designed with sun-kissed playing fields and bracing ventilation through classrooms. Free school milk was introduced in 1930 in response to pressure from the Rowett Research Institute in Aberdeen (although it helped that Scots dairy farmers were having a rough time as well). There were to be no more than 12 houses per acre, with plentiful drying greens, gardens and children's play areas. Some of the new estates

Below. Infectious Diseases Hospital, Paisley in 1936, in its crisp, white heyday, its clean lines symbolising new attitudes to health. The drawing is of the administration building.

RIAS Collection/Swan

had their own health centres and playschools. Open-air swimming pools and playing fields received official encouragement and subsidy, and infectious diseases (symbolised by the Fever Van and its brown-suited attendants) were tackled by isolation hospitals which, influenced by the tuberculosis wards, had separate wings for each disease, balconies and folding glass walls. Health became a national preoccupation. The Women's League of Health and Beauty performed crippling calisthenics in public, and organised National Fitness Year. Muscle-bound hikers (so cruelly satirised by Compton Mackenzie[19]) would stride out to some of the fifty Youth Hostels which had opened throughout Scotland by 1936.

By the time the four Scottish Departments—Health, Agriculture, Home and Education moved into St Andrew's House in 1939, the size of the Health Department was equal to the aggregate of the other three.[20] Only in 1962, engorged with economic planning as well, did it change its name to its current title of the Scottish Development Department.

NATIONALISM

"We are in danger very soon of reaching the point where Scotland will have nothing distinctive to show the world." John Buchan M.P to the House of Commons. 1932.

"At about this period, several books written in a somewhat self applauding tone by Scotchmen on the subject of Scotland (or condescendingly humorous about the rest of Great Britain) had been published." Thus said the author Anthony Powell of 1934; a situation which he considered called for a counter-satire in the eighteenth-century mode called *Caledonia*. Such patronage, doubtless welcomed north of the border, was possibly just a little too late.

The burst of publishing in Scotland had begun in the late 1920s, with what contemporaries described as the Scottish Renaissance—a vigorous artistic movement involving (eventually) Hugh MacDiarmid, Lewis Spence, Eric Linklater, Robert Bontine Cunninghame Graham, Compton Mackenzie (whose election in 1932 as Rector of Glasgow University led to a House of Commons debate on the state of Scotland), Neil Gunn, George Blake, Edwin Muir, Colin Walkinshaw, George Scott-Moncrieff and William Power. Following bitter experience as Chairman of the Scottish Arts Council, the playwright James Bridie (Dr Osborne H Mavor) plotted with Dr Tom Honeyman and Tom Johnston to lure up to 20 prominent Anglo-Scots back north of the Tweed where they were most needed.[21]

The stir among the Scottish writers was positively exhilarating. It started with the poets, scores of them, led by Hugh MacDiarmid. It spread to the historians ... It infected the controversialists, and their discourses on the general theme of "What's wrong with Scotland" are now two-a-penny on the book-barrows. Then came the realistic novels of Clydeside ... There was, in short, what we were pleased to call a Scottish Renaissance" (William Power: *Scotland 1938*).

Poems, plays, novels, and books of commentary and analysis poured forth, considerably aided by the survival in Edinburgh, and the participation, of the remnants of independent Scottish publishing. Many of the most important contributions bore the imprint of the Porpoise Press and the Moray Press.

A G Macdonell hoped the cultural revival would be the catalyst of political change:

... the essential beginning of all national uprisings is that poets should believe. The young men and women, the writers, painters, dramatists, actors, sculptors, architects, they are the key to freedom ... the Scottish Nationalist Movement

19 *Monarch of the Glen*. But Sir Robert Grieve considers the establishment of these hostels to have been one of the best developments of the Thirties. During 9 months' unemployment in 1933, he spent most of the time walking by Loch Lomond. Each Friday he would return to the lochside, borrow one of three rowing boats left there for the purpose (called Red Klara, Joe Stalin and the Oktober Revolution) row to Balmaha, walk 18 miles into the Employment Exchange in Glasgow, collect his dole, leave some with his mother, buy oatmeal, sugar and flour for flapjacks, walk back out to Balmaha, pick up the boat and row back again.

20 Gibson op. cit. Chapter 3.

21 Johnston op. cit. p.243.

22 William Power: *My Scotland* (Porpoise 1934) p.300.

has begun at the right end. It has not begun as a political dodge or a commercial ramp, but as the spontaneous outburst of the young creators of art and beauty.[23]

Possibly somewhat naïve in his enthusiasm, Macdonell presupposed a common nationalist aim. But the literary heroes were divided amongst themselves. Bridie attacked Macdonell for his English education and domicile.[24] Some, like MacDiarmid, were communist (or had leanings that way), at odds with the more establishment Scott-Moncrieff, Linklater or Mackenzie. Others— in thrawn Scots fashion—were unwilling to commit themselves to overt politics preferring to comment from the sidelines.

The quest for Scottish self-respect was dangerously undermined by a gaggle of Quisling MPs, who informed the Commons (as though it were not already convinced of it) that all the best Scots had already emigrated. Robert Boothby perverted history to demonstrate to eager MPs that the Scots had been savages until the Union, and would revert if independent.[25]

Whilst William Power was celebrating the possibility of a Gaelic University in Inverness, in the presence of Neil Gunn, Sir Alexander MacEwen and Doctor G J MacLeod (who introduced modern Scots Gaelic to Europe),[26] Sir Murdoch McDonald was enlightening the Commons: teaching Gaelic was, he considered, *fantastic* and *undesirable*, because English was "a new lever to help in the amelioration of life—to permit some to wander forth from their native glens—and take their place in the world";[27] as indeed 700,000 had done in the previous 30 years.[28]

POLITICS

The First War was scarcely over before the first of nine nationalist Bills or Motions to be placed before the Commons within the next eight years was presented. Inspired by the notion of national independence within a wider British Empire, such as was being discussed for Ireland and India, the proposal reflected the status of Scotland at the time which, with its own partial administration and legal system, was that of a Crown Colony. Of the early Bills, all but one of the Scots MPs voting were in favour,[29] and the concept of "Scottish national self-determination" was supported by Lords Alness and Shelbourne, Austen Chamberlain and the Duke of Montrose. One by one, however, the Bills were talked out at their second reading; that in 1924 by George Buchanan, being given less than one-third of the Parliamentary time allotted to the London Traffic Bill which followed closely on its heels.[30]

The final attempt at a Bill, in 1927, was supported by a Convention of many of the Scottish Local Authorities, MPs and a broad collection of influential Scots. Its "talking-out" at its second reading was the 21st such rejection since 1889.

Not even the elevation of the Secretary of State for Scotland to one of His Majesty's *Principal* Secretaries could stave off Scots anger. The Scottish Home Rule Association, founded in 1918, had 69 local branches by 1924. Following the 1927 failure, the National Party of Scotland was founded in 1928 by R B Cunninghame Graham, Roland Muirhead and others. The Duke of Montrose and Sir Alexander MacEwen promptly founded a rival called the Scottish Party perpetuating the Scottish habit of disunity.

Even those who were not nationalist found the current system indefensible. John Buchan recommended that Parliament should get rid, once and for all, of the system of "tacking Scotland onto English measures, in one or two interpretation clauses, which are usually obscure and sometimes quite impossible to construe. We want a Scottish policy." Nationalist sentiment would be appeased by an "outward and visible sign of Scottish nationhood" through the erection of a Scottish administration building in Edinburgh. Buchan's notion was plopped, with a neat sense of political timing, into a

[23] Macdonell op. cit. p.267.

[24] James Bridie: *Tedious and Brief* (Constable 1944) p.103.

[25] George Malcolm Thomson op. cit. p.116.

[26] Power op. cit. p.53.

[27] A M Mackenzie: *Scotland in Modern Times* (Chambers 1942) p.328.

[28] Thomson op. cit. p.106.

[29] Mackenzie op. cit. pp.343–6.

[30] Ibid. op. cit. p.346.

"Scotland must plan, or perish" James
Arnott.

row over a proposal for a vast lump of administrative building on the side
of Calton Hill, Edinburgh. It could have been Buchan's suggestion, combined
with the growing fear of nationalism, that lead the Government to abandon
the administrative block in favour of the symbolism of a new headquarters
for the Scottish administration, designed by the leading Scots architect of
the day, Thomas Tait. It was not, at that time, called the Scottish Office
(as it later became); it was the home of the Secretary of State's Departments.

Buchan was not alone in seeking greater self determination for Scotland.
Tom Johnston, "always put Scottish Home Rule on my election programmes"
he wrote, "believing that the Imperial Parliament was so increasingly being
choked with world affairs that it had little time for attention to Scots domestic problems".[31]

The nationalists' strength in the cultural revival was also their weakness.
It was perceived to have an insufficient economic programme:

> The intellectual foundations of the Scottish Nationalist Party would evidently be
> strengthened if it could be shown that its appeal was based not solely on national
> culture and traditions, but can equip itself with political weapons from the arsenal
> of economic interest . . . the task is not to rouse a nation, but to make one, not
> to expose economic and social evils, but to relate such evils to a re-awakened
> national consciousness.[32]

That was written in 1933, and by 1935 Scottish nationalism was thought
to have peaked. One possible cause of the decline was the evil reputation

31 Johnston op. cit. p.66.

32 Thomson op. cit. p.103.

33 Gibson op. cit. p.84.

34 Presidential Address to Edinburgh Architectural Association, 1933.

35 *Quarterly* no 58 (1935) pp.5–11.

the idea of nationalism was beginning to attract, following the activities of the National Socialists in Germany.

Yet it is probable that the nationalist surge had some lasting results. The Scottish administration was moving up to Scotland. The Government had accepted the need for a Scottish policy independent from that of the United Kingdom, and a political climate now existed which permitted Secretary of State Walter Elliot not only to establish the revolutionary Scottish Economic Committee, but also to offer more generous housing subsidies than obtained elsewhere in the United Kingdom.[33]

Throughout the period, nationalism was viewed with caution by the professions as though it did not have the credibility of professional objectivity. Among the overt exceptions was the architect Robert Hurd, who was delighted to be identified as a nationalist. There were undoubtedly many others, but their nationalism was subsumed into their creations, and the preoccupation with expressing something about Scottish identity through their architecture.

CONTROLLING THE OCTOPUS

The loss of identity that so concerned the nationalists was most palpable in the physical changes wrought upon the face of Scotland after the First War (as, indeed, upon the face of most communities in the developed world). A new means of mass transport—the car—combined with cheap land and cheap mortgages led to an eruption of untamed and largely unplanned construction on the outskirts of most settlements. At first, it was seen as a good thing that a greater slice of society was being offered a greater freedom of choice than before. People were tempted to luxuriate in greater privacy and personal space than they had known before, and the trend was exploited by clever house-builder advertising which extolled the virtues of rural living as compared with the evil and illnesses of big cities (see Chapter 10). The resulting tentacles of ribbon development, which gulped such historic communities as lay in their reach, were christened "the Octopus" by Clough Williams Ellis. Roads were widened to carry cars; houses built because cars made the new sites accessible; cars bought to reach the new houses—an endless, circular progress. Sir Frederick Osborne, the Garden City pioneer, came north to warn Scotland of the dreadful example of London: "generations of the more prosperous Londoners, as the speed of transport increased, sought the country beauty, built upon it and largely destroyed it . . . They are still doing it—still killing the thing they love with ever increasing technical efficiency and thoroughness."[34]

He was too late. By 1935, the *Quarterly* editor could describe the "giant, unfettered tentacles of the speculative building octopus making the gateways to our cities hideous, and crushing the very life out of our countryside".[35]

Facing the formidable enemy of the speculative builder who could rejoice in selling a house every ten minutes, was the embryonic planning profession whose institute dated back only to 1914, and whose origins lay in the Garden Cities Movement. Qualification was through a correspondence course with London, but in Scotland, at least, was not a common achievement before the War. The planners, qualified or otherwise, had to effect a change in public attitude; a change which led people to accept some State controls on the freedom of choice. State intervention began in earnest after 1918, with advice on housing layouts and densities which most authorities, perhaps shamed by the 1917 Royal Commission's findings (see Chapter 8) were disposed to accept; and most physical planning of the inter-War period was based more upon trying to channel development pressures than trying to tackle the broader issues of socio-economic planning. Indeed, wild ideas such as the construction of "satellite towns",

RH & P

Robert Hurd, sketched by Betty Bartholomew in 1931.

What the planners considered a threat, the builders greeted as an opportunity.

Mactaggart and Mickel

EVER=GROWING GLASGOW

Closely linked with the growth of Glasgow is the growth of Mactaggart & Mickel—builders of fine houses. The model housing estates at King's Park, Kelvinside and Linn Park bear testimony to their skill in designing and building. Here are houses as modern as the minute—soundly constructed—equipped with the latest labour saving devices and yet obtainable on a scheme that makes purchase easier than paying rent

MACTAGGART & MICKEL LTD
65 BATH STREET GLASGOW
TELEPHONE DOUGLAS ONE

A MODERN HOME BUILT by GEEKIE

HAS ALL THE FACTORS that make for attractiveness, durability and comfort. This firm offers you the maximum value for your money, and a choice of seven building sites in pleasant and healthy surroundings.

UP-TO-DATE Planning and all the Practical Aids for simplified Housekeeping are embodied, including: Large Kitchenette; Modern Bathroom, with Square Panelled Bath, also Chromium Fittings; Outside Walls lathed for Plaster; Tiled Fireplaces in all rooms; Ample Cupboard Accommodation.

The GATEWAY to HAPPINESS

IF YOU WILL CALL we will gladly show you Plans and Specifications, and give you details of our EASY PAYMENT TERMS. The GEEKIE MODERN HOME is of Durable Construction, Beautifully Finished—just the very Home that will give you everlasting joy. DEPOSIT—Only £25.

restoring the heritage and encouraging industrial revival could usually be left to architect planners, patrons and quangos, rather than the Local Authorities (T Warnett Kennedy, the Marquess of Bute and the Scottish Economic Committee respectively).

The authorities had some statutory powers, particularly after 1932, but many chose not to exercise them. Glasgow is a case in point.

Between 1925 and 1938 Glasgow more than doubled its territory, but took little of the comprehensive action as was envisaged by the 1932 Town and Country Planning Act. The Corporation, instead, saw fit to boast that "a considerable amount of latitude is permitted to the landowner in the matter of zoning, and the initiative in the development is left to the proprietor in the first instance".[36] The City's sole contribution to town planning was the employment of four unqualified assistants in the Master of Works' office scheduling roads and open space.[37] By contrast, Lord Provost Henry

[36] Glasgow Corporation: *A Short Account of Municipal Undertakings* (1938) p.51.

[37] Sir Robert Grieve: interview.

Alexander of Aberdeen began work on an overall plan, in association with the Aberdeen Society of Architects, which was so highly regarded that an exhibition of the plan was staged in the Empire Exhibition as an example to others. Yet implementation was erratic. Until 1938 it stubbornly refused to relax its maximum limit of 12' houses per acre which in itself was the cause of huge new greenfield estates at Middlefield, Woodside and Powis instead of rebuilding flats in the City Centre. Architect and house builder Tom Scott Sutherland, when elected Housing Convenor of the Council in 1935 proposed successive schemes of four-storey flats which, at one election meeting, led him to be barracked: "what about the coalmen?"[38]

Above. "Mr T Scott Sutherland, architect, one of the Ruthrieston Ward candidates for Aberdeen Town Council, advocating four-storey tenement houses, was asked by a woman heckler – 'What about the coalmen?'"

Renfrew made an instructive comparison to Glasgow, as the unwilling host of Glasgow's western and south-western expansion. Development was occurring so rapidly that all the maps were out of date and it was impossible for the authority to consider implementing the Planning Acts on defective data. A young Robert Grieve paced the streets with a pieman's board sticking out the front, updating the ordnance survey with tracing paper and measuring tape.

The area beyond the Highland Line was suffering a different kind of disaster. In 1935, Rev T M Murchison wrote to the Prime Minister expressing his concern at the frightening rate of depopulation: "many Highland parishes are becoming inhabited almost entirely by the aged. School rolls are dwindling, churches becoming derelict because so few are left to worship, and ministers officiate at ten funerals for every one marriage or baptism." G M Thomson considered the Scottish Highlands were "an example of a Distressed Area in its final stage".[39] Perhaps an extreme example of population decline was the Applecross peninsula: whilst the population in the nine Applecross communities declined by over 50% in the 50 years up to 1931, it dropped by the same proportion in the 13 years following. By 1944, of the nine communities, five had populations of less than twenty.[40] The Highlands seemed to be without a purpose; and being available for the delectation of tourists was insufficient: "Highland people, so agreeable, even so decorative, do not live where they do just that the visitor may be catered for and amused. They cannot all live as hotel keepers, picturesque fishermen, ghillies and postmasters. They are not there to run a holiday camp."[41] The nationalists waxed indignant. It is "a place of Highland flunkeys, and Anglo-Saxon Lords. It is a sports ground in which the poor . . . can get no sport, but only some toil for the alien."[42]

In 1936, contemporary with the establishment of the Scottish Industrial Estates for the Lowlands, the Highlands Development League began to prepare long-term policies for the Highlands, which were presented by the Scottish Economic Committee to the public in 1939. Perhaps over-reacting to the quip about picturesque ghillies, the League recommended the development of fishery, forestry, hydro-electric power, overhead electricity wires, and road widening, and a Development Commission was advanced to carry out the proposals. The Secretary of State placed the recommendations before Parliament in summer 1939; when, despite Government backing, they were talked-out by English MPs. It took the War, the establishment of the National Government, and the arrival of Tom Johnston, as Secretary of State to compel the Commons to give the Highlands a fair hearing; and when the establishment of hydro-electricity was presented to Parliament in 1943 (this time passed without division), it was founded more upon Highland depopulation and the lack of work, than upon the need for electricity.

INSTITUTIONALISED AMENITY

The task of holding the cultural line against the philistine was early seen as an activity in which the fledgling planners could do with establishment

[38] T S Sutherland. Scrap book. Sutherland was also responsible for Aberdeen's promotion of a housing scheme competition for Kincorth, won in 1938 by R Gardner Medwin and others.

[39] Thomson op. cit. p.98.

[40] *Quarterly* no 67 (1941) p.15. Survey by Rendel Govan.

[41] George Blake: *The Heart of Scotland* (Batsford 1934) p.19.

[42] Macdonell op. cit. p.95.

Approved APRS design for semi-detached rural cottages.
Below. Proposal to rebuild Princes Street in glass, 1938, by R Furneaux Jordan.

support: particularly since some of the establishment's own amenity was under threat by the spread of the plebs. Perhaps that is unfair. Both lay and professional Scots supported state planning controls as the only way to safeguard the country's inherent character and qualities, in addition to ensuring that whatever was built, was built well. Planning controls were therefore seen as positive ways of producing a truly modern, but Scottish Scotland.

The running, in Scotland at least, was made by the professional establishment, greatly aided by George McNiven, depute Chief Architect at the Department of Health. In 1926 Frank (later Sir Frank) Mears[43] persuaded the RIAS to act as a sponsor to a new organisation—the *Association for the Preservation of Rural Scotland*. Mears, and a fellow architect Leslie Graham Thomson were established as joint Honorary Secretaries, and the APRS identified its task: the planning of rural areas, the safety of historic buildings and sites, and the "appalling quality" of design in new rural houses. That poor quality the APRS attributed to the failure by many councils to employ qualified architects. It approached the RIAS, as the professional body for architects, for standard house plans to offer such Councils. The RIAS proving difficult,[44] Mears and Thomson produced their own, APRS approved standard plans, adopted sporadically, mostly in the Borders.

In 1930, the owner of 9000 acres of historic landscape near Newton Stewart wished to leave the estate to an appropriate public body to protect it from the octopus. The Scottish Departments being unwilling, and the APRS being unable, the latter repeated the method of its own foundation by gathering support from a wide range of Scottish organisations to found, in 1931, *The National Trust for Scotland* (NTS) which could own and manage historic properties and landscapes.

In 1936, the foundation of the *Saltire Society* completed the pattern begun by the other two organisations. The APRS dealt with rural Scotland, buildings, sites and planning; the NTS would own historic buildings and outstanding landscapes: whereas the Saltire intended to tackle the wider "encouragement of Scottish culture", in every kind of artistic activity. "It envisages a new Scotland with a vigorous intellectual life, drawing on the past for inspiration to new advances in art, learning and the graces of life. All who care for the preservation of what is best in Scotland's legacy from the past", declaimed its recruiting poster "all who want to see Scotland develop a distinctive culture of her own . . . are invited to become mem-

43 Sir Frank Mears, known as "Daddy" by his students, was an unlikely radical. Son-in-law of Sir Patrick Geddes, the father of town planning of whom it was said "he used to light a lamp in your land and run off", Mears lectured at Edinburgh College of Art, and practised with the aloof Carus-Wilson. A tall, military figure, reserved of manner yet intense, Mears introduced Scotland's first town and county planning course to the College of Art in 1935. To Mears and Carus-Wilson may be attributed the restoration of Gladstone's Land, Edinburgh, the exquisite Lucy Sanderson Homes in Galashiels, and the rebuilding of Kirk Wynd and Baker Street, Stirling in a skilful re-creation of old Scots.

44 Whatever qualms there may have been had vanished by 1943 when the profession eagerly accepted a comparable invitation from Tom Johnston.

45 See *To Foster and Enrich* by George Bruce (1985) for a detailed description of the Saltire's foundation; one which attracted to a common purpose such unlikely bed fellows as Tom Johnston, Walter Elliott, D Y Cameron, William Power, Hugh MacDiarmid, Kurt Hahn, Stanley Cursiter and Compton Mackenzie.

bers". And, amidst its preoccupation with music, poetry and restaurants, it was resolved to encourage good new architecture by introducing an annual award in 1937 for "a high standard of architectural design and layout . . . with due regard for traditions of Scottish architecture".[45]

In 1940 the Saltire commissioned Alan Reiach and Robert Hurd[46] to analyse current trends in Scots architecture in an influential, illustrated squib *Building Scotland* in 1940 (reprinted 1944). Apart from sharing the contemporary distaste for Victorian architecture, the book conveyed three messages: that native Scots architecture had a sturdy simplicity highly appropriate to modern times; that Scandinavia had developed a modern approach to architecture of simple functionalism appropriate to a location well worthy of emulation; and that different building types required different approaches to architecture. Photographs outweighed text by 4:1 (well seen that the authors were architects!) and anything purely fashionable was excoriated. Its reprinting in less than four years tends to indicate a Scots population far more seriously interested in its built culture than its successor 45 years later.

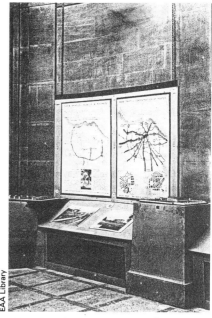

EAA Library

Above. Inside the 1937 planning exhibition in the RSA.
Left. Replanning old towns into sensible towns was the rage. Thomas Adams' 1937 proposals for central Dundee. Note the ovoid tower of *Green's Playhouse* on the right.

RIAS

In 1931 the RIAS, a strong advocate of planning, lobbied the Department of Health on the urgent necessity for a National Plan, and the battle was continued at local level by its Chapters. The Glasgow Chapter campaigned vigorously for a development plan for the city, and for the consideration of a new overspill satellite town. Its leading advocate, T Warnett Kennedy,[47] stood for election in the Sandyford Ward solely on the grounds of the necessity for "rational town planning". Whilst the Dundee Chapter confined itself to an ineffectual squawk at the 90 feet advertising tower of Green's Playhouse in the Nethergate, the Edinburgh architects had grander ambitions. In 1937, three Andrew Grant Fellows—Messrs Sutherland, Galloway and Carnegie from the Edinburgh College of Art, under the leadership of Robert Matthew, staged an exhibition in the Royal Scottish Academy in the place of the Society of Scottish Artists, comprising a detailed illustrated analysis of the growth of Edinburgh, with plans, photographs and models. It savaged what had happened to Edinburgh's approaches and to the

[46] Robert Hurd was English, and arrived in Scotland principally to write about architecture. He stayed, and by 1933 had formed a partnership with Norman Neil. Hurd was well connected (two relatives being MPs) and in 1934 was commissioned by the Marquess of Bute to restore Acheson House, Canongate, from its condition as the abode of 14 separate families back into a single house, as a statement of faith in the future revival of old Edinburgh. In 1939 Hurd ran the risk of expulsion from the RIAS for refusing to submit himself to the Fellowship until the RIAS joined his injunction on Edinburgh Corporation to prevent the demolition of the Tailor's Hall in the Cowgate.

[47] T Warnett Kennedy. A Glasgow architect and polemicist, editor of the School of Art's magazine *Vista*, and founder-editor of the *Scottish Architect and Builder's Journal*, a magazine of exceptional use founded in 1938. Kennedy was a partner of Jack Coia, and is credited with the distinctive *St Peter's in Chains*, Ardrossan.

RIAS

RIAS

Top. Acheson House, as restored in 1937.
Above. The kind of architecture approved by the new amenity movement: *Lucy Sanderson Homes*, Galashiels, by Frank Mears and Carus-Wilson.

[48] Williamson and Hubbard drawings. Bute also asked Hurd to restore Loudoun Hall, Ayr on his behalf.

[49] Ebenezer J MacRae, Edinburgh's City Architect, was an outstanding man. His achievements spanned the design of Tardis (Edinburgh City Police Boxes) to a careful recording and appreciation of Edinburgh's ancient heritage. He was one of the team sent by the Department of Health on its fact finding tour round Continental housing estates in 1935, producing much of the analysis that subsequently appeared in the report.

shore. The exhibition made a considerable impression upon Edinburgh and contributed to a growing acceptance of the need for a more determined approach to planning and control. Yet it was only the War, and the arrival of Tom Johnston as the Secretary of State that brought action.

In 1943, Johnston established two (later three) Regional Planning Advisory Committees, one of which began work on the celebrated Clyde Valley Regional Plan, with Professor Patrick Abercrombie as Consultant, and the active participation of Alan Reiach and Robert (later Professor Sir Robert) Grieve. Sir Frank Mears (as he had become) was consultant to Central and South-Eastern Scotland, and Geoffrey Payne consultant to Central Scotland.

THE RESTORERS

Restoration of the grander of historic Scots buildings became increasingly frequent from the late 19th century (Earlshall, Balmanno, Kellie, etc). What was new between the Wars was the restoration of historic properties in city centres which—almost without exception—had become transformed into multi-occupied slums. (Fourteen families were living in Acheson House which Hurd converted back into a single desirable residence.)

It is possible that the 1933 publication of the final selection from the National Art Survey, which celebrated in immense drawn detail the 15th–17th century skills of Scots masons and architects, may have helped to mould public opinion towards restoration.

A notable leader in this campaign, and considerable patron, was the Marquess of Bute, whose speech "A Plea for Scotland's Architectural Heritage" to the National Trust for Scotland (published in 1936) argued for "an armistice for all old houses, and that the Office of Works be directed to use full powers to schedule buildings, and this without the necessity of immediate reconstruction". He also suggested that the National Trust for Scotland should be granted £500,000 towards purchase and reconditioning of such buildings. Putting his money, as it were, behind his oratory he privily invited Robert Hurd to restore for him Acheson House, Canongate (now the Scottish Craft Centre) in 1935; and three years later, asked Hurd to buy Andro Lamb's House, Leith on his behalf and to secure it against weather for an eventual Maritime Museum. Bute was also the *de facto* founder of "Listing" historic buildings, by his commission to Ian Lindsay to prepare a list of all significant pre-1800 houses for the National Trust. He may also have been instrumental in the request by the National Trust, in 1938, to Williamson and Hubbard to prepare plans for the restoration of the old building in Sailor's Walk, Kirkcaldy, facing the harbour.[48]

E J MacRae,[49] City Architect of Edinburgh, reconstructed ancient houses in both the Canongate and the Grassmarket, invited James Shearer to convert Roman Eagle Hall and Riddle's Court in the Lawnmarket for adult education, and employed a newly qualified town planner, William Dey, to produce a detailed survey of all the buildings on the north side of the Canongate from the Abbey to St Mary's Street. The respect which he felt for older buildings can be seen in his new tenements in the Pleasance, Piershill and Morrison Street, in which the quality of detail and craftsmanship is excellent.

SUMMARY

Thus the Scotland within which architects worked, and to which they responded was one of economic seizure with a brief three-year boost between 1935 and 1938; of great intellectual vigour stimulated by nationalism; of a grim industrial inheritance and Highland depopulation; of the uncontrolled expansion of Lowland communities into the countryside; and of the growth of organised amenity societies, with a greater appreciation of the heritage.

2 ∎ THE ARCHITECTURAL PROFESSION

> Far too long in the past has our profession been regarded as a haven of refuge for those who sought a career where qualification by examination was not necessary. The accomplishment, "a taste for drawing", will now require to be accompanied by others, before even the outer barrier can be passed. The profession means business and the gates are being closed.
>
> James Arnott, 1933

When Sir Robert Lorimer, immediately prior to his death in 1929, had steered a supplementary Charter through the Privy Council to give the RIAS its current title "Royal", it was the final step in the revival begun by Sir Robert Rowand Anderson of the Architectural Institute of Scotland originally founded in 1840.[50] So, located in Sir Rowand's town house in Rutland Square, the RIAS was vigorous in its search for status and growth. It expanded his library and archive with the donation of several important collections of books and archives, the most notable being those of David MacGibbon and Dr Thomas Ross, and began a collection of busts and drawings on the suggestion of Sir John Burnet. The celebrated "Wee Troot", James Salmon, had been first editor of its Journal, the *Quarterly*.

Much of the current state of the RIAS can be attributed to the presidency of John Begg. Begg had been the Government's chief architect in Bombay, but had quit that post after the commission for the new Viceroy's Building in New Delhi was awarded to Sir Edwin Lutyens. He had retired to Edinburgh, carrying on a desultory practice with few buildings—a housing estate in the Grassmarket, and the Westfield Autocar showroom (1936) in Stirling. His primary interest was engaged as Head of the Edinburgh School of Architecture, located in the College of Art. A civilised, urbane man with great insight, Begg failed to communicate with students *en masse*; and the teaching staff were still locked into the craft traditions, as a result of which "the College of Art was going to Hell as quickly as it could go".[51] Begg was possibly unaware of how adventurous he was being in 1929, with his appointment of the radical Eric Anthony Ambrose Rowse, and the young John Summerson as Senior and Junior lecturers. His preference for equilibrium was expressed after Summerson caused to be published an article on the Leader Page of *The Scotsman* in February 1930 appealing for "the New Style". Slightly shocked, Begg suggested to this brash new junior lecturer that it would be best if future articles, had they to be written at all, should be published anonymously.[52]

Begg's influence on the RIAS can be seen in practical matters—the design of the President's chair (cost £24), the beautiful beaten-copper nameplate, and in the organisation of a student award to commemorate Sir Robert Lorimer. Indeed it was one of Begg's sketches of Lorimer that was sent up to the Aberdeen artist John Aitken which now forms the basis of Lorimer's posthumous portrait now in the RIAS.

CONFLICTS OF INTEREST

Between the Wars, the RIAS was preoccupied with the organisational matters of building which still predominate: the need to standardise building

50 The Architectural Institute was founded by the leading architects of the time: William Burn, William Playfair, David Bryce, Robert Reid and James Gillespie Graham. It lasted until c.1870, when the growth of local architectural societies in Glasgow and Edinburgh rendered it redundant.

51 Interview: Esme Gordon RSA, a pupil at the time.

52 Sir John Summerson: paper to RIAS Thirties seminar 1984.

contracts and methods of measurement; the need to achieve proper planning and architectural input thereto; and, above all, the need to preserve the independence of the architect. When Fife County Council proposed to appoint four architects to design houses at the fee of £5 per house (which included the architect's fees, the quantity surveyor's fees, and all expenses), the RIAS promptly banned all of its members from accepting the appointment.

The introduction of Codes of Conduct, following the two Architects Registration Acts of 1931 and 1938, brought an examination (possibly for the first time) of the possibilities of inherent conflicts of interest. How such conflicts were defined is unclear. There were repeated attempts by the Edinburgh Architectural Association to report the Edinburgh architect and house builder James (later Sir James) Miller[53] to the new Registration Council for conduct which they thought unbecoming, because Miller made no attempt to conceal that his predominant activity and income was in the construction and selling of houses.

The profession in Glasgow seems to have tolerated the continued membership of W Beresford Inglis, who was owner and the architect of several cinemas including the Boulevard (Knightswood) and the Toledo, (Muirend). He was the Managing Director of Glasgow Hotels Ltd, and also the architect of their flagship—the Beresford Hotel, Sauchiehall Street, named after him. The one-legged architect, Tom Scott Sutherland of Aberdeen, a founder director of Caledonian Associated Cinemas and Modern Homes (Aberdeen) Ltd, advertised and sold his houses and bungalows from his architectural office address. He was a director of almost 40 companies, and when work was short, his architectural staff were employed packing and posting mail-order boxes of pills.[54] He was a prominent figure in Aberdonian commercial life, and was elected Housing Convenor of the Corporation in 1935. Yet despite those extensive and highly publicised business interests (he held a T Scott Sutherland Annual Dinner for friends and acquaintances) he retained Fellowships of both the RIAS and RIBA.

Among the few trapped in the new moral ambiguity was the Edinburgh firm of Patterson & Broom, designers of a notable garage in East London Street and the Maybury Roadhouse. They tripped the system by applying, in 1938, for election to Fellowship of the Royal Incorporation, an application supported by eminent architects including a future President of the RIAS. A question was raised that they made an income by designing and building

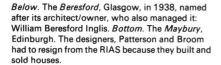

Below. The *Beresford*, Glasgow, in 1938, named after its architect/owner, who also managed it: William Beresford Inglis. *Bottom*. The *Maybury*, Edinburgh. The designers, Patterson and Broom had to resign from the RIAS because they built and sold houses.

Strathclyde Archives

RIAS

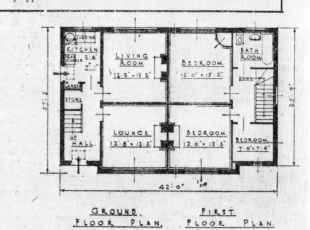

NEW ULTRA MODERN DESIGN.

BROOMHILL "ESTATE" DEVELOPMENT.

FRONT ELEVATION.

Messrs Modern Homes (Abdn.) Ltd.

present something entirely new in houses on a very central site at Broomhill Estate, representing the finest value ever offered in Aberdeen. The average price of a good-class four-apartment bungalow in Aberdeen is £650.

We offer this five-roomed two-storey house (with no lie-in ceilings) at the all-in price of **£620 each**, including the cost of tar macadamising roads and fully stamped Title Deeds.

The houses are beautifully decorated and lavishly equipped.

SHOW-HOUSE.

A permanent show-house fully furnished at 1 BROOMHILL AVENUE will be open for inspection every afternoon and evening. Hours — 2.30 p.m. to 5 p.m. and 7 p.m. to 8.30 p.m.

```
FEU DUTY ............................... £5  6/-
  (With Garage Space) ................. £5 16/-
LOW ASSESSED RENTAL ........ £32 10/-
MINIMUM CASH DEPOSIT ........ £65
All-in Weekly Charge including repayment of
  bond, interest, rates, taxes, feu duty and
  insurance.  From £1 4/-.
```

MODERN HOMES (ABERDEEN) LTD.,
Architect: T. SCOTT SUTHERLAND, 10 ALBYN PLACE.

GROUND FLOOR PLAN. FIRST FLOOR PLAN.

Selling his own designed houses from his architect's office, Tom Scott Sutherland *(below)* was as much a swashbuckling entrepreneur as architect.

"What's all this talk about depression? If you live in a Modern Home, you won't know the meaning of the word". T Scott Sutherland

"Live, love and laugh with life in a beautiful Modern Home".

53 The Edinburgh house building architect Sir James Miller needs to be differentiated from the Glasgow architect James Miller. In this book, the differentiation is through the title "Sir" although it was awarded after the War. Sir James inherited a small house building firm from his father, and trained as an architect. Although his office continued to produce designs for one-off houses (two modern ones in Cramond and Corstorphine being notable) he moved into the mass construction of bungalows (1929) and flats (1935). He was also director of a cinema company for whom he designed the *State* in Leith.

54 Mrs Isobel Adams interview.

houses for sale, and thereby had an interest. Patterson resigned quietly; Broom did not, his defence being that since they used an agent, they had no direct involvement in home sales. At length, RIAS Council concluded that it could not countenance James Broom's elevation to the Fellowship in such circumstances, thinking it wise to invite him to consider resigning from the Incorporation entirely.[55]

ARCHITECTURAL COMPETITIONS

Few significant public buildings of the Thirties escaped the forceps delivery of an architectural competition (and there were complaints about those, such as St Andrew's House, which did). Thus sufficient numbers of competitions were held to justify most architectural journals maintaining a regular column of announcements of new ones and results of old. Competitions provided one of the few ways that new, younger architectural practices could penetrate established patterns of patronage; they were also held to promote innovation—sometimes by trade promoters such as the Cement Marketing Co or the *Daily Mail*, and sometimes by organisations seeking to change attitudes. Such were the EAA's competition for a £1000 bungalow, Glasgow Corporation's competition for four and five apartment houses, and the Department of Health's 1938 competition for rural housing.

One architectural firm which owed its existence to the competitions system was Carr and Howard, which entered with success more competitions than any other in Scotland. Carr had met Howard in Sir Herbert Baker's office in London where they "kept sane" by doing competitions in the evening. Once the threat of redundancy forced Carr to move to the office of Michael Rosenauer (to take charge of building Arlington House), communication with Howard became difficult. "We would get the competition conditions and visit the site at night. We then met once per week. Each of us had to bring a sketch on the back of an envelope drawn to scale. At each meeting we would amend each other's drawing until we ended up with a satisfactory scheme which would then proceed to finished drawings." He recalled working up to 2am finishing the drawings for the Parliamentary Buildings of Southern Rhodesia, whilst the queue of people

Above. Glasgow Health exhibition competition for a five-room cottage. Winning scheme by M Cormie.
Right. The Bexhill Seaside Pavilion.

55 EAA Correspondence and minute books.

Swan

outside shuffled along streets carpeted with rubber paviors to see King George V lying in state.

From 1934 onwards, Carr entered 17 competitions with Howard. They won two—Kirkcaldy Town Hall and a school in Tanfield, Edinburgh (not built because of the War); were placed second four times—Tunbridge Wells Civic Centre, Birmingham Technical College, St George's Hospital, London, and the Waverley Market Sports hall; won fourth place in the Southern Rhodesia Parliament Building, and were commended in Scunthorpe Municipal Buildings and Duncan of Jordanstone College of Art.

The unpopularity of the winning design for Dundee by James Wallace, which attracted general opprobrium, was attributed to the fact that the assessor Julian Leathart, was best known as a somewhat *démodé* cinema designer of the 1920s. In fact the design, as built after the War, was not as was originally; and it was said that the client, Principal Francis Cooper, dominated the assessor to the extent that the winning design was chosen on the basis of strict adherence to the functional brief and correct relationship of lavatories.[56]

RIAS involvement in vetting competitions began in earnest after 1930 and the debacle of the competition for Dumfries Town Hall, which the assessor Sir George Washington Browne awarded to James A Carruthers. For reasons not entirely clear[57] some of the competitors issued law suits against the client. The RIAS Council was horrified. It declared the action of the aggrieved architects to be most irregular, "not only disloyal, but hurtful to the future interests of the profession" and instructed the architects to desist. However, in order to prevent a repetition, it required as a matter of professional conduct any member of the Incorporation to inform the RIAS without delay of the receipt of an invitation from any party either to assess, or to take part in a competition. It further required assessors to submit their proposed competition brief for scrutiny.

The proposed terms of a housing competition in 1934 for a miners' village at Westquarter, by Falkirk, were judged irregular, the County Clerk of Stirling being proffered RIAS assistance. He must have declined, for the RIAS banned the competition. Much the same happened both for proposed competition for Blairgowrie Golf Club (which was abandoned) and for new housing in King Street, Kirkcaldy (which was not). The RIBA, lending its distant support from London, instructed members throughout the UK to refuse to enter: but they did, and King Street was built as designed by Messrs Deas and Bertram; whilst the assessor George MacNiven awarded Westquarter to John A W Grant who constructed it to general plaudits and a Saltire Society housing commendation in 1938.

In 1936, something evil had been detected in Kirkcaldy: a possible competition whose Assessor had neither confirmed his appointment as As-

Swan

Above. Kirkcaldy Town Hall: winning elevation by Carr and Howard. *Top.* Ilkeston Baths: winning competition entry by Alan Reiach and Robert Matthew.

56 David Walker.

57 RIAS Council minutes are peculiarly gnomic on this affair. The reasons for the law suit are not recorded. What may be inferred is that either there was a mistake in the brief; or an ambiguity in the judging; or—as seems most likely—that the winning scheme did not comply in some way with the original brief, rendering the award invalid.

The only placed entry from Scotland in the RIBA building competition: the highly commended entry by Ian Carnegie with T Jeffryes and E A A Rowse.

sessor to the RIAS, nor had submitted the conditions for scrutiny. It was further alleged that the Assessor himself had been invited to design the proposed building himself, and had prepared plans thereto. Most irregular. He was summoned to account; and in February 1937, perhaps Scotland's most eminent architect, Thomas Tait appeared at the RIAS offices for a meeting with the President. "Mr Tait made it quite clear", reported President to Council afterwards, "he never intended, and did not wish in any way, to be involved with any actions which might savour of unprofessional practice. He assured the President that although he had more than once been offered the appointment of architect, he had declined to accept this, and had recommended that the work be put out for public competition."[58] The competition under question was for Kirkcaldy Town Hall, later won by Carr and Howard. When, in the following year, Falkirk Royal Infirmary proposed a competition for a nurses home, the RIAS instructed the President to intervene, and to "act as Assessor": otherwise there would be no competition. He did, there was, Kininmonth and Spence won,[59] but War prevented its construction.

What were the results of all these competitions? Few competition conditions prescribed or implied any architectural style: the important problem to be solved being the plan and accommodation within the cost. The architectural results were rather mixed. Sir William Kininmonth recollects that "entrants probably leaned towards Scandinavia and local planning", such certainly being the case in Mervyn Noad's Prestwick Town Hall and subsequent entry for the Falkirk Nurses Home. Poor old Scandinavia was blamed for a very blank form of architecture, a "stripped-down" classical approach wholly at variance with the exciting new world of the Stockholm Exhibition of 1930.

Kininmonth clearly believed that a war was fought to be won. In 1935, that is to say two years after the completion of his Modern-Movement house at 46a Dick Place, his competition entry for the extension to Falkirk Town Hall was a baroque building with a Swedish campanile.[59] Was this a cynical response to the likely preference of the competition assessor, comparable to the celebrated classical competition entry by modernists Connell Ward and Lucas for Newport Town Hall in Wales? Mervyn Noad, (he who boasted that when he travelled throughout the Baltic countries in 1934 he had refused to enter "an old church, castle or similar architectural monument: my only interest being modern architecture"[60]) entered Falkirk with a neo-Scots, crowstep-gabled scheme influenced (by osmosis) by the adjacent Victorian Scots baronial building. Such pieces of adventurism proved hollow: the palm went to J Inch Morrison with a dull, craft-based design.

Some competition results, pre-eminently James Carrick's two pavilions

[58] RIAS Council Minutes.

[59] It is quite clear from the presentation technique and colouring that the winning submission is Kininmonth and not Spence.

[60] Interview.

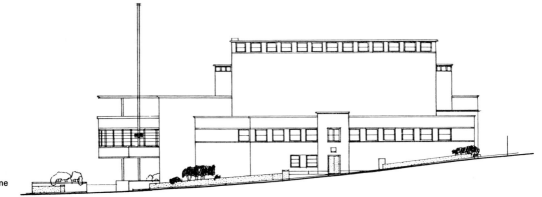

Rothesay Pavilion, 1936 – winning scheme by James Carrick.

in Rothesay and Gourock were excellent. But the preference of many competition entrants for a vague Scandinavian classical as being the style likely to appeal to competition assessors led Jack Coia, before the Glasgow Institute of Architects in 1936, to condemn competitions with a

> perfectly damning criticism of the pernicious and stultifying effect competitions have on imaginative design, creating stereotypes known as the "competition elevation", a flat, anaemic thing showing, at the moment, a slight recall of Stockholm Town Hall.[61]

Yet they kept the architectural profession alive. According to Alan Reiach: "competitions were the life blood: and the aim was to enter one or two every year. It kept you going".[62]

FROM APPRENTICE TO ACADEMIC

During the Thirties, the profession moved from the largely apprentice-based architectural education to full-time learning: a shift accompanied or caused by the changes in architecture, construction and client demand. Predictably, the change emanated from London: equally predictably, the craft-based architects of Scotland were disinclined to acknowledge any value in it. (It is a curious irony that, 50 years later, those debates are being re-opened and re-examined.)

Apprenticeship had meant attending courses in the School of Art (Edinburgh, Aberdeen or Glasgow) between 8am and 10am in the morning; and further courses after a full day's work in the office at the local Technical College between 6pm and 9pm for structures and materials. A student from Kirkcaldy, for example, would have to leave home for Edinburgh at 6am, unlikely to return home much before 11pm. Survival rate was not high. To the radicals, this system offered an ill-defined, narrow and unco-ordinated education,[63] a view shared by some of the older lecturers as well. In the early Twenties, Robert (later Sir Robert) Matthew and David Carr were advised by their history lecturer Carus-Wilson to leave the college, since they would be better off going to Italy. They went: and it was only on their *return* that Carr learnt how to make architectural drawings (in the office of Collcutt and Hamp, London).[64]

Not all practitioners regarded the gradual move to full-time training an undoubted benefit. Ninian Johnston (the son of an unemployed shipyard worker) had started his career as an office boy with Alfred Lochhead before moving up to become the only member of staff Lochhead ever employed. Lochhead had begun to train his office boy as soon as he showed a faint aptitude for drawing, by having him

> draw out all the Orders, cast shadows, learning perspective, and drawing a bay of a Cathedral. He then produced some sketch books from his travels in Italy, in which he had detailed measured notes of windows, doorways, ironwork etc. From these sized notes, I drew out the pieces. I must have drawn about 60 or 70 of these measured notes, all in sepia ink, with shadows projected, on Imperial paper.

With that training, he was rather ahead of his fellow students. "I was obliged to show all my designs to Alfred before handing them in, as he had a poor opinion of the teaching. I recollect his opinion on one of my designs: "The rendering and drawing are very good, but the architecture is so bad it might be the work of Sir Reginald Blomfield.' Johnston's progress led to him being given a scholarship to attend full-time day classes, which he accepted, against the wishes of his benefactor:

> Alfred was against my taking up the scholarship, which was munificent, because he had a poor opinion of the teachers. However, as I had completed five years in his office, he agreed on condition I should continue to show him all my work. On reflection, I think the standard of teaching in the day school was terrible. The professor was rarely seen—he was often attending his busy practice.[65]

R Scott Morton

Alan Reiach, drawn in 1948.

61 *Quarterly* no 54 (1937) p.40.

62 Interview. Competitions also provided a "gung-ho" element for architects. Alan Reiach and Robert Matthew never expected to win Ilkeston. Reiach received a call from the Town Clerk informing him of their success and the client's intention to come to Edinburgh to visit their offices. Matthew was a Civil Servant in the Department of Health. Reiach, squeezed into a garrett in Darnaway Street, persuaded the Town Clerk that it would be better if he went south to Ilkeston instead, visited a nearby engineer on an emergency basis to bone up on structure, and popped in to purchase a brolly on the way without which his credentials might have been suspect. (Interview with author.)

63 Ian Carnegie who joined the College of Art as a lecturer in 1934: paper, RIAS Thirties seminar.

64 Interview with David Carr.

65 Letter to author from Ninian Johnston.

The Aberdeen School, revivified by the arrival of Professor T Harold Hughes, was located in a corrugated iron annexe to Grays School of Art (the "tin shack"), its exams receiving full professional recognition in 1914. Glasgow students (who received Professor Hughes in 1920) studied in the School of Art whose exams, like those of Edinburgh, were also accepted by the profession. Only in 1938, with the arrival of a new Head, John Needham, did the Dundee exams receive such recognition.

The design side of education exuded from the Art Colleges, of which Edinburgh—which achieved an unparalleled record for producing prize-winners in the premier Scots and United Kingdom awards and prizes—saw itself the paragon. The change from a School drifting towards Hades to one on Mount Olympus began with the arrival of the two lecturers from London, John Summerson and Eric Anthony Ambrose Rowse, in 1929. Summerson, rather too refined a man to cope with brawling Scots students (and part-time scout for the *Architect and Building News*) was a fervent advocate of the new architecture emerging from the Continent whilst Rowse, famous for his "broad approach", advocated planning, the primacy of the architect, and a commitment to social building. The entire day school worked in "atelier" conditions, in a single studio with the senior students helping the younger, being helped in turn by the younger in their presentation drawings for awards; all dominated by huge plaster casts of the classical orders. The momentum grew after 1933, when Rowse departed for the Architectural Association (where he had a comparable effect).

TRAVEL

A reason for Edinburgh's success must have been the international outlook of its students. Many went to train in London offices (Lutyens, Baker, Maufe, Collcutt and Hamp) and it was useful that Burnet Tait and Lorne had offices both in London and Edinburgh. Furthermore, the RIAS offered several well-endowed new prizes which encouraged travel to Northern Europe—the Rutland prize specifically encouraging the study of structural techniques; and it was through some of the Rutland reports in the *Quarterly* that the profession in Scotland first had detailed information on the substance of what was happening in the Continent.

But the munificence of Andrew Grant far outshone the profession's prizes. In 1930 he bequeathed £20,000 to fund a two-year, travelling scholarship, and a Fellowship for any student in the Edinburgh College of Art. One Andrew Grant Fellow was Alan Reiach: "As an Andrew Grant Fellow, I had to return monthly sheets: and travelled around America with my typewriter, suitcase and T-Square. You can't underestimate the value of an International Student Pass. Famous architects would almost always give you up to half an hour, or occasionally delegate somebody to show you around their buildings." Ian Carnegie, another Andrew Grant Fellow, visited 35 Rue de Sèvres in 1933: "We were ushered into Monsieur Le Corbusier's office, where for the next twenty minutes we listened to Corb talk about some of his projects, then were shown round the Drawing Office by himself, finally given a list, in his own handwriting, of his recently completed works."

What impact did modern ideas have on the schools? The younger element in the Edinburgh College of Art was enthused, but the older element rather remote: at most benevolently neutral. It was different in Glasgow, under Professor Hughes. Whereas all those who knew Hughes speak of his great skill and sensitivity, as late as 1937 the first task given to his new students was to draw Trajan's Roman Alphabet; which may serve as a hint of his predilections.[66]

66 Archie Doak interview. During his pre-War years of training Doak received no information on the modern movement.

In 1933, an anonymous student contributor to the *Quarterly* from Glasgow complained that:

> In pre-War times, students had a definite objective. The work of the Beaux Arts School was the star to which they all strove to hitch their wagon. They knew what was expected of them, and browsed over the plates of the French School, like sheep in a lush meadow. But what of the present day student? They look for a lead from the prominent members of the profession. They are told by their instructors to keep close to the essentials, to read Belcher on the *Essentials of Architecture*. Then they get hold of Corbusier and wonder what is essential. It would be less of a wonder if they had fallen into a hopelessness engendered by the vacillating view of practising architects.

Another student, John Graham, wrote in a succeeding issue:

> What impression does the modernist make on this young mind? Why should the so-called architect be permitted to erect façades that are grimly and unrelievedly hideous? Why should schools look like barracks, and colleges of architecture like factories? Perhaps some modernist who really knows the excuse for his apparently lacking sense of beauty will take the trouble to alleviate the sufferings of one who still shivers on the brink of his career.

Ninian Johnston, then Deputy Editor of the Glasgow School of Architecture Magazine *Vista* responded:

> Poor Mr Graham! He shivers on the brink, despite his heavy clothing of caps and cornices. Does he not envy me swimming and plunging about in the pool like a veritable sandboy? Does he not envy me my naked body glistening in the water and the sunlight, clean, fresh, invigorating, rhythmic, alive, gloriously white and shining silver?[67]

If, on this subject, Hughes was ever in the closet, he took the opportunity of a keynote speech at the RIBA Conference in Glasgow in 1935 to come out of it. His paper was entitled "The Modern Movement—A False Start" (in place of his original title "This Bunkum of Modernity"). Whilst he had agreed that modern architecture had to rid itself of the excrescences and bad practice of previous generations, modernists were perpetuating equal faults. He questioned the morality of imitating Continental concrete forms in whitewashed brick, the weathering properties of flat façades, the problems of heat gain and heat loss through the enormous new windows, and the lack of thought given to the long-term life of these buildings:

> We have been moving too quickly—perhaps the natural result of the Great War. Photographs replace serious study, and give us the opportunity to copy the latest tricks. It is novelty of features—the outer fashion in dress, and not the true spirit of the building progress that we seem to catch. Modern architecture bears to real architecture the same relation as "hot Jazz" to Weber.[68]

Up spoke one of his own students, John Hird, impertinently. Hird claimed that all modernism was being dismissed, without making an attempt to distinguish between the good and the bad: "A little more thought should be given to modernism in schools. The good in modern architecture should be pointed out, and pointed out very forcibly; so should whatever is bad and rotten." The rare spectacle of a student challenging his professor in the RIBA Conference caused amusement as well as outrage. Sir John Stirling-Maxwell found it "a very pleasant feature to hear Professor Hughes taken to task by one of his own students. That shows, if I may say so, that the right spirit is to be found in the Glasgow School." The correspondence that appeared subsequently in the *RIBA Journal* was decidedly less urbane. Raymond McGrath waded into Hughes, claiming that his speech made "melancholy, almost mediaeval reading", supporting the voice of the "impertinent student".

[67] *Quarterly* no 47 (1934) p.52.

[68] *Quarterly* no 50 (1935).

Henry Elwig, an irate Fellow (unbelievably from Tunbridge Wells) condemned the student's impertinence, believing that modern architecture was "merely a passing phase and will not survive". The impertinent student returned with "if all the Messrs Elwigs of the past had had their way as Mr Elwig of Tunbridge Wells now wishes to enforce his, we should, in all probability be living in baked-mud huts". The correspondence was topped out by T Warnett Kennedy, who dismissed the debate started by Hughes as a schoolboy one. "The controversy on tradition verses modernism at the Glasgow Conference is of the greatest moment to the profession. Its entertainment value cannot be under-rated. This is great fun . . . after I have earned my living, I think I will design a traditional building and become famous."

THE RIAS *QUARTERLY* AND OTHER MAGAZINES

The influence of magazines upon fashion during the Thirties was marked—witness, for example, Hughes' attack. The glossy image and stark photograph was so dominant that one enterprising publisher, realising the extent to which architects disliked reading anything, produced a magazine consisting entirely of glossy photographs, captions and advertisements: even plans were rare in *Architecture Illustrated*. The fashion leader was the *Architectural Review* (although *Ideal Home* and *Country Life* were both more interested in contemporary houses than they are now), its stablemate, the *Architects Journal*, being the principal weekly architectural newspaper. None of these gave more than scant coverage to Scots architecture. Both the *Architect and Building News* and the *Builder* gave a more balanced and exhaustive coverage, but usually without the delectable illustrations.[69]

The small Scottish profession had therefore to rely upon the *Quarterly*, *Building Industries* and the *Scottish Architect and Builder's Journal*. The *Quarterly* developed early a tradition of young, vigorous Honorary Editors: John Summerson in 1929, John Watson in 1931 and R Mervyn (Dick) Noad in 1933. When Noad handed over to the tam o'shantered Ian Lindsay in 1935, he recorded with satisfaction that "with articles on modern continental work and architectural theory, the Journal has . . . been brought abreast of the time". In January 1939 Lindsay gave way to Frank Connell, thus maintaining the tradition of radical young editors. What is quite clear from the *Quarterly* is that however much, or little, Scots architects decided to import from abroad, their decision was based upon neither ignorance nor upon reaction. They knew, and were interested; but did not necessarily *adopt*.

The *Quarterly's* policy of publishing essays by prizewinners who were at the younger end of the profession displayed to Scottish architects, possibly in greater detail than was currently available in England, an examination of current French, Dutch and Scandinavian architecture.

The Scottish Architect and Builder's Journal was founded in 1938 by T Warnett Kennedy, "one of the liveliest of the many live wires in the Glasgow Institute", as a monthly magazine aimed at a readership wider than just architects. It thus included details of contracts let, and a series of articles on building research; but its real value lies in the publication of buildings unknown anywhere else, illuminated by gossip in the column "Entasis". It closed with paper rationing in September 1939.

THE ARCHITECTURAL WORLD

One advantage of recent history is that some of the protagonists are alive, whilst others are yet well remembered; and it is often the incidental details that brings an otherwise dry picture to life. It may not add to scholarship, but it is surely fascinating, to know that George Boswell (an ex-chief-

[69] David Carr's recollection of how he used journals was typically incisive: "I was influenced little by the *Architects Journal* which always seemed to be searching for something new, not necessarily good or better. *The Builder* gave cost information and good new fittings and fitments. I read the *Review* for pleasure."

assistant of James Miller) had, as a client, the eccentric E A Pickard who once stood for election as the Millionaire Candidate for Maryhill, Glasgow, and discharged his accounts with threepenny bits in canvas bags.[70] Mrs Isobel Adams remembers no apprentices in Marshall Mackenzie's office in Aberdeen. Duties relating to the coal fire were exercised by an excellent Clerk of Works. If the staff had to work late John Marr (in charge of the office) would order up for each scrambled eggs on a silver service from the restaurant below.[71]

Architectural practices were fundamentally parochial and "local", having to apply their hand to all types of building. Many were successors to, or had absorbed, offices with origins in the mid-Victorian period, and had their roots firmly based in the pre First War craft approach to building. In consequence, we are rarely looking at the coherent, modern output of certain trail blazing firms as we can in the Home Counties. A modern building could surge out of a practice wholly preoccupied with bungalows given the right client impetus and happenchance. The more traditional Arts and Crafts firms did indeed attempt to modernise themselves, with rather more sleek (sometimes Tudor) country houses or the occasional horizontal window. Those who did not change, and those who were not slightly more aggressive about getting work or entering competitions became relegated to country house repairs, lodges and churches.

Above. Cluny House, Inverness. *Left. Sunningdale*, West Ferry, by Donald Ross in the office of Thoms and Wilkie.

Those who specialised, by contrast, in churches and country houses formed the principal exception to the pattern of local architects working locally. Dr Reginald Fairlie, for example, designed over 23 Catholic churches during the Thirties, in addition to his schools and the National Library, in location from Mallaig to Tayport. The majority were sub-Byzantine in style, derivative from Westminster Cathedral and built of brick. Fairlie had little enthusiasm for many of them, observing "it seems to be what they want".[72]

The production of a "modern" or innovative building can sometimes be attributed to new or youthful blood in an established practice. The modern houses in Culduthel and Old Edinburgh Roads, Inverness have been attributed to the young Donald Fowler and William Allen, working in the

70 Ninian Johnston.

71 Interview with Mrs Adams.

72 D Walker.

office of Carruthers Ballantyne, Cox and Taylor. The increasingly stream-lined schools emanating from Aberdeen's School Board architect J Ogg Allen are attributed to his younger partner David Ross; just as Dr Marshall Mackenzie's office in the same city was transformed by the arrival of David Stokes as design partner in in 1933, and the return of his son Alexander from London in 1936. Neither Patrick Thoms, of the celebrated Dundee Arts and Crafts firm Thoms and Wilkie, nor his nephew Tommy, liked modern architecture; and they left the adventurous Sunningdale in West Ferry to the assistant Donald Ross. The adventurousness of T C Marwick's office in Edinburgh has been attributed to Philip McManus and to David (Speedy) Harvey[73] who, between them, produced designs at the forefront of mid Thirties Scots architecture. McManus had been a Rutland Prize winner (explaining the buildings of Duiker and Dudok of Holland in the *Quarterly*), but left Scotland in 1937 to become a planner in Cape Town.

There was a dearth of architects reaching maturity. Those whose careers we now study for awareness of the new architecture in the Thirties were still training in the 1920's. By the time they had qualified, the slump was at its deepest, with clients to feed new practices as scarce as a badger in sunlight. Yet there is limited record of mass unemployment within the small band of 430 architect members of the Royal Incorporation of Architects in Scotland. Some architects left offices for shop counters, some sold shoes and paint, builders offered crazy discounts simply to win tenders, and some professionals worked purely for the experience.[74] Few, if any, architectural firms expanded. The depth of the slump was, for the most part, tided over by a continuation and completion of jobs already in hand. In 1931, the Royal Institute of British Architects established an Architects Unemployment Fund, recommending all those earning over £250 per annum to donate a minimum of 1/7d per week to the Unemployment Fund. The RIAS, by contrast, encouraged all members to subscribe to the Benevolent Fund with their annual subscription, and requested supplementary capital from London to deal with hardship. The RIAS *Quarterly* held that the unemployed architects were all public sector former employees and was thereby stridently opposed to the RIBA proposals (the editor subsequently being reprimanded by the Council).[75] In the event, only three hardship cases reached the Council, in mid 1932, and they were offered a *loan*.

An interesting illustration of the growth of a new practice can be seen in the early careers of William (later Sir William) Kininmonth and Basil (later Sir Basil) Spence.

William Kininmonth set up on his own after college in 1931–2 in loose association with Basil Spence[76] (still a student and earning pin-money by drawing perspectives for architects such as W J Walker Todd, Reginald Fairlie and Leslie Graham Thomson) with a few house commissions. On qualifying, Spence became a lecturer in the Art College, whilst continuing with Kininmonth. In 1933, Kininmonth was glad to accept a partnership from the skilful but erratic A F Balfour Paul, inheritor of Rowand Anderson's office, but on condition that Spence could come too. Balfour Paul agreed providing they both used the same drawing board[77] in rotation. The office was really a conglomeration of three separate offices, which kept their individualities[78]: Balfour Paul working on Pollok House; Kininmonth on his own house, and the Deaconess Hospital; and Spence on Dr King's house, Broughton, and other projects. Kininmonth and Spence continued in its own right; as indeed did Spence on his own, designing the extraordinary EAA Stand in the Scottish National Housing and Building Exhibition in the Waverley Market, March 1935: a giant fibreboard hollow cube entered between a pair of evidently fake, gigantic, gilt Ionic columns: "post-modern" before even modern had been invented. Three years later he designed Gribloch,

73 Harvey was a notable perspectivist, responsible for the best colour perspectives of the Empire Exhibition done for Thomas Tait. After the War, he established with Alex Scott the firm of Harvey and Scott.

74 R Mervyn Noad. Interview. Also letter from James Shiell. Shiell worked as a young engineer on the Portobello Swimming Pool, being paid in tram travel tokens only.

75 RIAS Council Minutes.

76 Interview with Sir W Kininmonth.

77 R Ewing information.

78 Interview with William Dey.

Ewing

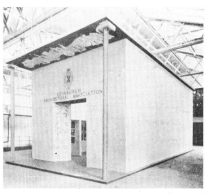

Left. Basil Spence and William Kininmonth in 1938.
Above. The EAA stand in the Waverley Market exhibition, 1935. Basil Spence going post-modern in fibreboard. *Below left.* Kininmonth's own house in Dick Place, 1933, the brick skin not yet rendered.

The Hollywood-regency interior of *Gribloch*.

RIBA Library

RIAS/Baxter

THE SCOTTISH THIRTIES

by Kippen, in association with the New York architect Perry Duncan, which may account for its air of Hollywood regency; and was deeply involved with the Empire Exhibition.

Spence, regarded by his contemporaries as brilliant, had an unmatched facility in architectural analysis and speed of composition. Two 1933 buildings—the house for Dr King in Easter Belmont, and the garage in Causewayside—led contemporaries to believe that here could be Scotland's leading modernist.[79] Yet since those buildings were amongst the last "modern" buildings carried out by that practice, the idea has taken root of an unfulfilled modern genius suffocated between the slump and the Second World War.

But there may have been other reasons. Of the many houses designed by Spence in the Thirties, only the first had a flat roof, and it failed ("King was decent about it").[80] Another reason is one suggested by Kininmonth: "I suppose we rather prided ourselves on being able to work in any style". What anathema to the purist! No Howard Roark here.[81] The moral commitment to modern architecture as a means of changing society, worn on the sleeves of the London pioneers, was absent in Scotland. The possibility of a third reason may be inferred from other Spence houses—4 Easter Belmont and the Scottish Council house in the Empire Exhibition. Modern in the sense of planning and detail, these houses are nonetheless very Scots: great pitched roofs, white harling, and horizontal glazing. From these—as much as from his more overtly historical buildings such as Broughton Place (1937), and from a speech given in defence of the Empire Exhibition, one can see that Spence, too, shared some of that seeking after native roots for modernism that was motivating Hurd, Reiach, Mears, Lindsay, Mansfield Forbes, Sir John Stirling-Maxwell et al:

> Our tradition is really a sensitive reaction to existing conditions, and the production of a building that is fitted for its purpose, direct and simple in its conception, with an eye for proportion, and the understanding use of materials ... the judicious selection of forms during the Renaissance and Regency periods prove that old forms adapted to conditions that are suitable for their use is a sound policy.[88]

A comparable pattern of younger men reinvigorating older practices existed in Glasgow. George Shanks joined E G Wylie, Ninian Johnston George Boswell, the young James Carrick his father and, pre-eminently, Jack Antonia Coia who had joined James Gillespie and Kidd during the First War. Coia, like Spence, is somebody around whom legends have grown: the absent-mindedness of arriving to lecture at the Art School in his pyjama trousers (so extreme as to suggest a certain artifice) and painting with his tongue when unable to grasp the desired effect with brush or fingers.[83] He struck contemporaries as being more intuitive than intellectual[84]—a bird-like creature with glinting spectacles and a perpetual scarf wound round his throat against the chill. His principal output in the Thirties was Roman Catholic churches, but it also included a house or two, (unbuilt) schools, a super cinema and an ice rink (neither built), the latter two about the time Warnett Kennedy had become his partner. In the Empire Exhibition, Coia was supervising architect for the Palace of Industry (North) and designer of the Roman Catholic pavilion which Thomas Tait, controlling designer, considered one of the best. Tait thought Coia "very brilliant", but observed dryly: "It used to worry him a great deal that when he arrived on the job with the working drawings, he found that the contractor had finished the building."[85]

Robert Matthew, with his brother Stuart, were the sons of J F Matthew, Lorimer's long-time chief assistant and later partner, who became, on the latter's death, principal of Lorimer and Matthew. The firm was busy during the slump, with churches and church halls, and an identifiable Robert hand

[79] For a clearer definition of modern, see next chapter.

[80] Interview Sir W Kininmonth.

[81] Architect hero of Ayn Rand's *Fountainhead*, allegedly based on the career of Frank Lloyd Wright.

[82] *Building Industries* (April 1939).

[83] Interview Robert Rogerson: see also Jack Coia (1986) by R W K C Rogerson for further information.

[84] Interview George Lawrence.

[85] *Quarterly* no 60 (April 1939) p.6.

36

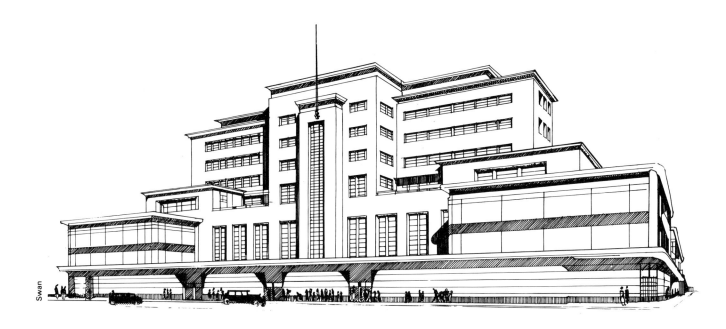

Swan

can be seen on the heavy-shouldered Wheatsheaf Inn, Saughton (1934); but the firm's massively elegant design, like London's John Barnes' store in Finchley Road, for huge new offices on the site of the Union Canal Basin in Lothian Road was supplanted by a less elegant one by Stewart Kaye.[86] In 1936, Matthew joined the Department of Health, causing a stir by designing (in his private capacity) an elegant house for Professor Kemp Smith in Kilgraston Road, Grange. The following year, he was the leader of the four Andrew Grant scholars who staged the town planning exhibition in the Royal Scottish Academy. His surplus leisure time was spent entering architecture competitions alone or with Alan Reiach.[87]

Of the older generation, James Miller (born 1860) and Thomas Tait (born 1882) stand out as giants. Miller, a reserved, quick-tempered man, who died in 1947, was at the end of a highly successful career dating back to 1890, including the wonderful railway stations at Wemyss Bay and Stirling, the 1901 Exhibition (which he won in competition) the SS *Lusitania*, the London headquarters of the Institution of Civil Engineers, and numerous houses and churches. By the 1920s he was living in Stirling and his office, possibly under the influence of Richard Gunn, had shed its Scottishness, moving to a fine series of American-inspired banks, followed by a number of Portland stone and brick commissions (e.g. Stirling County Council 1936). The later hospitals in Canniesburn, Greenock and Larbert all showed a considerable grip of modern architecture. It was said of him that his success was due to his felicity in producing designs to any style that suited the client. Only up to a limited degree did Miller's office act as a training ground for other architects. In 1943 the RIAS encouraged Miller to retire, so that they could do him the signal honour of electing him as an Honorary Fellow of the RIAS in recognition of his contributions to architecture in Scotland.

Thomas Smith Tait (1882–1952) became partner of Sir John Burnet in 1920 having worked in the office before the War but quit after a row in 1914, visiting America in 1914–15. Burnet's Beaux-Arts trained office attracted attention for the pioneering way it tackled large, framed buildings—a diaphanous and insubstantial dress for Kodak House (1910–11), and beautifully modulated imperial uniform for Adelaide House (1921–4) both in London. Tait's personal style can first be seen in Silver End Village, Essex,

Proposal for offices and shops at Port Hopetoun, where Lothian House now stands, by Lorimer and Matthew.

[86] It was said of Stewart Kaye that if you spotted a fire engine roaring along Princes Street, he would be in the car immediately behind, sketch plans already prepared. (Interview Dey, Carnegie, Reiach.)

[87] In 1936 they entered a competition for a £1000 bungalow agreeing that Reiach should submit a flat roof and Matthew a pitched. Matthew won. They subsequently entered for Watford Fire Station, Waverley Market, Tanfield School (3rd prize) and Ilkeston Baths (first prize). It was a sign of the times that Ilkeston had to include air raid shelters.

88 Sir John Summerson interview.

89 Royal Masonic Hospital, for example.

90 Mackintosh is recognised as a pioneer of note in the *Quarterly* from the outset of the decade. His reputation swelled quickly and came to a head at the 1935 RIBA Conference in Glasgow which made a special visit to the School of Art. At the dinner thereafter, President Percy Thomas exhorted his listeners to make a detailed record of the buildings of "that genius Charles Mackintosh" before it was too late.

designed as a factory village for Crittal window workers from 1926. He attracted to him younger designers, such as Franz Stengelhofen, Frederick MacManus and Clifford Strange: the proportions of their architecture are chunky, the roofs flattened, the walls whitened, and the projecting triangular window, first designed by Peter Behrens in Northampton, spread liberally. The austerity of these buildings, and the way they were plonked down on the landscape, seemed very Scottish—and a similar Scottishness shows through the house Crowsteps, Newbury, Berkshire a few years later. The office was also used as a finishing school by many Scots students wanting wider experience.

In 1930, the firm was joined by Francis Lorne, Falkirk born and Glasgow trained, who had just returned to Britain from spending time in the office of Bertram Goodhue in America (a link which could well explain some similarities between St Andrew's House, Edinburgh and some of Goodhue's buildings).[88] It was probably Lorne, a vocal polemicist, who influenced Burnet Tait and Lorne toward their subsequent preoccupation with streamlining—particularly visible in buildings in London and on the south coast.[89] For Tait's buildings show a preoccupation with the interplay of geometric shapes, the vertical interlocking with horizontal: always dominated—as for example, in the Empire Exhibition—by the vertical.

In 1932, Tait won (courtesy the assessor James Miller) the competition for the Paisley Infectious Diseases Hospital, Hawkhead, possibly the finest hospital of its type in Scotland during the Wars, and in 1934 he was the obvious choice as the architect for the proposed St Andrew's House. After 1934—amidst several appointments as competition assessor (including that for the Bexhill Pavilion whose architecture clearly influenced the Empire Exhibition)—he designed a housing scheme in Johnstone and the following year was invited to design a similar scheme in Elgin, followed shortly by yet another at Lincluden (neither transpired). In 1936, he was appointed controlling designer for the 1938 Empire Exhibition, for the execution of which he assembled a team of young Scots architects including Jack Coia, Basil Spence, Esme Gordon and Margaret Brodie. At the onset of War, his office was turned over to the design of evacuation camps. Clearly influenced by Dudok, Tait's buildings are logical, and clearly and precisely designed. They are perhaps simply not quite risky enough.

A dominant firm in Glasgow was John Keppie and Henderson—possibly by virtue of its close links with the Art School. It seems to have had no clear design philosophy during the Thirties (perhaps reflecting the established dominance of Graham Henderson), and Cloberhill School, which won the RIBA Scottish Bronze Medal in 1937, displays unusual uncertainty in its mixture of modern and traditional features. Despite a steadily growing interest in Charles Rennie Mackintosh, the firm steadfastly disowned him.[90] Much more prominent in the quality of its buildings was the office of Edward Grigg Wylie (later Wylie Shanks and Wylie). Already noted for its grand Scottish Legal Life building in Bothwell Street, Glasgow, the Dental Hospital and Lennox Castle Hospital, it specialised later in the decade and into the 1950s, in industrial buildings: the pioneering SIEC estates at Hillington, Carfin and Larkhall, and the amenity building for Weir's of Cathcart.

The cinema architects seemed to have formed a grouping slightly outside the centre of normal professional life. C J McNair and Elder, John McKissack and Son and John Fairweather and Son (the older Fairweather had been one of the Glasgow City Improvement Trust architects) all of Glasgow, designed upwards of twenty cinemas each. T Bowhill Gibson of Edinburgh had a like record, whilst Col Alec Cattanach of Kingussie produced considerably more, scattered throughout the whole of the north of Scotland, for Caledonian Associated Cinemas. A lesser, but nonetheless interesting

Early Mackintosh adulation: 1935 sketch by Hugh Casson of *Cooper's Cafe*, Ingram Street.

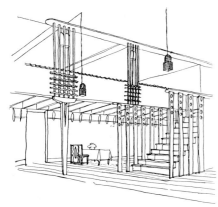

RIAS

Scottish Architect and Builder's Journal: Edinburgh District Libraries

The Empire Exhibition Team: Thomas Tait (in circle): taken from top left, clockwise – T. Waller Marwick, Margaret Brodie, Launcelot Ross, Esmé Gordon, Gordon Tait, Jack Coia, J Taylor Thomson, A D Bryce and Basil Spence (with puppies and pipe).

contribution to cinema output, was received from Lennox and McMath (Glasgow), Gardner and Glen (Glasgow), James Houston (Kilbirnie), Alister MacDonald (son of Prime Minister Ramsay), Sir James Miller (Edinburgh) and A D Haxton (Leven). These latter architects were more general-purpose architects, who happened to design a few cinemas as well. Apart from the odd roadhouse, hotel, dance hall or hostel, the former seem to have designed very little else.[91]

Professor T Harold Hughes, a refined scholar who contributed an excellent pioneering series of historical architectural biographies to the *Quarterly*, had made an uneasy marriage to Edith, beloved niece of the kindly Sir John Burnet, who had been one of his first two students. (Edith was refused employment in London, on the grounds that lavatory accommodation for ladies was inadequate.) Modern architecture seemed to offend Hughes'

[91] Charles McNair got the work—almost exclusively cinemas, and Robert Elder "chain-smoked, sat in the back office and just drew" with five architects and an apprentice. The principal client was an old-fashioned entrepreneur, George Urie Scott. He would come into the office, look at a map of Glasgow, count the number of houses, and circle a location on the map most suitable for a new cinema. It would be built to a nine-month programme, and the aim was to cram as many seats in as possible. Air conditioning to remove cigarette smoke was critical. On the opening of a new cinema, the entire staff would be given the afternoon off to attend. (Ex. info Robert Forsyth: the apprentice.)

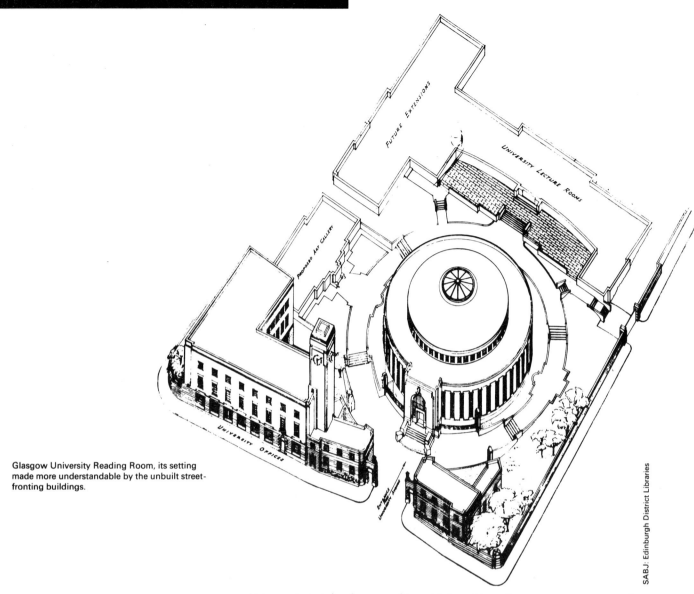

Glasgow University Reading Room, its setting made more understandable by the unbuilt street-fronting buildings.

patrician, scholarly instincts, and he withdrew himself to a remoteness—well remembered by his students in the Glasgow School of Art, who tended therefore to listen more to the radical young lecturers. He may possibly be considered as the Scottish equivalent of Sir Albert Richardson although his Glasgow University Chemistry Building, with its concrete frame and huge stair windows of the Erich Mendelsohn type indicates that he was less of a reactionary than his 1935 RIBA Conference speech implied.

The age gap caused by the First World War could be said to have made the Thirties a young man's decade—in Scotland at least. Tony Cox, Editor of the AA Magazine *Focus*, and under the influence of E A A Rowse, wrote in 1938: "we were born in the War. We were born into a civilization whose leaders, whose ideals, whose culture had failed. They are still in power today. . . .". [92] Less so in Scotland. By the end of the decade, new regimes had taken over at most Scottish architectural schools with Joe Gleave in Edinburgh, John Needham in Dundee, and young lecturers like Jack Coia and Ninian Johnston in Glasgow. Kininmonth, Spence, Hurd, Lindsay and Carnegie now held senior posts within the EAA and RIAS. The *Quarterly* had been in the hands of the young through the decade. By

92 Tony Cox's editorial in *Focus* was exaggerated. Maxwell Fry told the author that about 1936–7 he had visited RIBA Secretary Sir Ian MacAlister to proffer the services of the young radicals. MacAlister replied to the effect that whilst he watched the radicals with the keenest interest, he, MacAlister, thought that involvement in the RIBA might stultify them. They should carry on trail-blazing in the knowledge that they had friends at court.

current (1986) standards, the opportunities open to young architects under the age of 35 in the 1935–8 period were extraordinary.

ECHOES OF WAR

Politically conscious people, like Sir Robert Grieve, regarded the League of Nations as the only bastion against the next War. When it failed to tackle the Japanese invasion of Manchuria in 1931, "it was the beginning of the end". David Carr, like a number of others, felt apprehension at Hitler becoming Chancellor of Germany in 1933.

Most architects, however, seem to have shared William Kininmonth's disinterest in politics, so preoccupied were they with the post 1935 upturn. In mid 1937 the RIAS Council was invited by the CBI to debate air-raid precautions, in which it showed fair interest. Barely a year later, the Munich Crisis brought the profession up with a jolt: entrants to the Falkirk Nurses Home competition were given a month's extension once the crisis was over; many architects had enrolled in the TA, and during the crisis, were given tasks (like David Stokes) of reinforcing underground arches. Spence, Carnegie and Joe Gleave were invited to form the 94th Heavy Ack-Ack manned by students from the Edinburgh College of Art. Large developments, Rosemount Square (Aberdeen) and Kelvin Court (Glasgow) for example, were designed with air-raid shelters in the basement. The Empire Exhibition, and its vision of a glorious colourful future, coincided with an Air Raid Precaution Conference.

All Alan Reiach noticed was the nuisance caused by the blackout tests; the international situation preyed on the mind of David Carr: "It was hellish. Really hellish. You stood at your desk, telephone in hand listening to know whether the War was on or off." From early 1939 the "emergency"

McKean

Tullos School, Aberdeen (1939). The classroom walls could fold back to allow the children the full enjoyment of the temperate Aberdonian climate.

looms increasingly large, and the provision of evacuation camps became more prominent. Hindsight helps us appreciate the irony of the Waverley Market competiton, whose submissions were due to be lodged on 31 August 1939.

"We return to this", as the *Quarterly* noted sourly that autumn. The decade had begun with collections for destitute architects suffering from the slump. It ended with a further collection for architects suffering as a result of the War, for rationing of timber had brought construction work to a total stop. Kirkcaldy Town Hall was stopped at first floor level as was Tullos School; Ainslie Park School at the stage of cleared site: the Kincorth Housing Scheme in Aberdeen at road layout only. Some dispensations were available: work continued on the Ascot Cinema, Anniesland, and the Cameron Infectious Diseases Hospital near Kirkcaldy.[93]

The *Quarterly*'s advice to architects as to what to do during the emergency was simple: 1. If you have a job, stick to it unless you have good reasons for not doing so. 2. If you have no job, you can do one of two things: 2.1 Enrol in the armed forces or in a full time branch of a National Service. 2.2 Find a job. 3. If you wish to join the armed forces, consult your Local Territorial Association.

The War made a dent into the small Scots architectural profession as into everything else. It called up many, killed some, changed some and diverted others. Jack Coia was interned; Basil Spence used the opportunity to split from Kininmonth; Howard left for London with the Tanfield winning scheme, whilst Carr remained in Edinburgh with Kirkcaldy; Pat Ronaldson, the Rowand Anderson Medal winner sent by. John Summerson to sketch, clandestinely, the proposed Scottish Office building in 1929, and Colin Fraser (a prizewinner), were both killed; Alex Wylie (whom his tutor thought quite the most brilliant designer in Scotland) was diverted to planning; George Lawrence to Government Office; and T Warnett Kennedy, after a brief flash of fame from designing a spaceship in the *Britain Can Make It Exhibition* in 1946 departed for Vancouver, Canada where he became Mayor.

The client patterns the young chaps had been building up were severed; and those who returned to architecture after the War were faced with seven years of building licensing and few clients. A large number chose the burgeoning new discipline of town and regional planning.[94] The architectural priorities in the small amount of new building permissible had changed to reconstruction and large-scale rehousing at maximum speed using prefabrication wherever possible.

[93] Robert Hurd carried out a survey to the value of work stopped in Edinburgh: hospitals etc £800,000; commercial work £2 million; housing £2 million; private houses £98,000; church building £62,500.

[94] Hubert Fenwick has said that the principal reason Ian G Lindsay turned to specialise in historic buildings after the War was the near-impossibility of building anything new in this period (source: Ian Gow) yet Lindsay's detailed interest in historic buildings pre-War tends to belie this.

3 ■ THE NEW ARCHITECTURES

Nothing is planted on my building. All the units in it are interwoven. They are the parts – stilled in mid-air – of an orchestral suite which you don't hear but which you see instead. I am the conductor. I conduct my own music, my own design. My musicians are all craftsmen who follow my baton. And the music they play! New chords, new forms; new forms, new harmonies; modern architecture! Ninian Johnston

"ARCHITECTURE OR REVOLUTION"
(slogan of Le Corbusier)

Trying to define Thirties architecture is like chasing a chimera: the closer you get, the further out of reach it seems. Its sheer variety is typical of a period of transition, for this period was the knuckle between two different worlds—the Edwardian pre 1914, and the Elizabethan, post 1952.

To the outsider, the period seems to contain three main strands: traditional (a continuation of development of Scottish craft-based, stone or harled buildings); modern (usually best recognised by brilliant white, flat roofed structures); and Art Deco (the popular decorative version of modern). But the reality is considerably more complicated. This chapter hopes to simplify and explain the varying philosophies and architectural approaches; identify key features to recognise; and to examine the reaction of Scots to the new movements in the light of the nationalist cultural revival.

The architecture of the late 19th century was, in the main, florid, richly decorated and dependent upon historical motifs. To the young, it represented an over-blown civilisation ripe for otherthrow. They preferred an architecture that went back to basics for inspiration—to primary geometric forms, to nature or to cultural roots. Broadly similar feelings spread throughout Europe,[95] and manifested themselves in Scotland in Art Nouveau and the buildings of Charles Rennie Mackintosh, whose obsessive attitude to design encompassed details right down to clocks, lamps and window snibs. In 1908 the Austrian architect Adolph Loos published a polemical squib *Ornament and Crime* in which he linked moral decadence in architecture to that in society. Although his attack seemed to be directed at the ice-cream baroque trimmings of the Austro-Hungarian imperial architecture, it may also have been a sideswipe at the increasingly mystic productions of the Art Nouveau adherents.[96]

The future lay elsewhere. A number of art and architectural movements were at the forefront of a violent reaction against the establishment: hence Cubism, Vorticism (whose journal was titled *Blast*), Dada and Surrealism,[97] later joined by Futurism (mainly from Italy) and de Stijl, based in Holland. They also explored newly understood relationships between the perceived and the unperceived, preoccupied with patterns, planes and exploding reality.

Although each generation seeks to overthrow its predecessor, the savagery of the First World War seemed to give the radical young artists and architects objective reasons for overthrowing the trappings of a civilisation that had caused such carnage. Architects added to these artistic movements

[95] In Austria, the Sezession; in Germany the Jugendstijl; in England Arts and Crafts, in Scotland Art Nouveau, in Italy Futurism.

[96] C F A Voysey, the English Arts and Crafts architect, characterised Art Nouveau as the "Spook School".

[97] Edward James, patron of surrealist painters, defined surrealists as "people who are close to their subconscious".

Entrance front of administration building, Werkbund Exhibition, Cologne, 1914, by Walter Gropius. Note the projecting glass staircase towers.

RIAS: Wylie Collection

98 Bruno Taut's book *Alpine Architecture* of 1919 purveyed mystical images of now a new, crystalline, glass architecture could, in itself, improve man's condition. The secret of this and other "expressionist" designs of the period lay in the intention to accentuate the essence or spirit of a given project in physical form.

99 Kenneth Campbell, former Housing Architect to the Greater London Council, recalled being instructed to design a hospital with a symmetrical, pedimented, classical façade. The only place for the operating theatre was behind the pediment; and the only light into it was through the round bull's eye window which, for reasons of the façade's proportions, was at floor level. (Interview, author.)

100 "Bakelite, chromium alloys, artificial silk, oil products, reinforced concrete, glass wool, asbestos, plywood, cork and rubber; the modern architect tries to discover the language of their form, and so a new aesthetic develops." C T Warnett Kennedy, 1937.

101 Maxwell Fry claimed that it was the sight of stone cherubs being fixed to steel-framed Devonshire House in London that drove him modernist.

102 Walter Gropius: *The New Architecture and the Bauhaus.*

a practical dimension: they proposed to develop new structures and materials to aid the social programmes required by the new order, in such a way as to provide spiritual uplift.[98]

One of the many reasons why young architects rejected the past was the belief that predetermined historical styles, and the notion of symmetry in particular, were in conflict with the use of the building.[99] That lead to a *first principle* of the new architecture: that the function of the building as expressed through its plan should be the starting point of architecture. A second reason for rejecting the past was its failure to exploit materials to either their full technical capacity, or to their full aesthetic value.[100] Many great metal-framed buildings were constructed in Scotland after the 1880s, and the first mass concrete houses were built in 1870–1 in the West Highlands. But it had always been thought necessary to elaborate, by clothing the frame with stone trimmings[101] or adding classical details to the concrete houses to disguise the fact that they were built of concrete.

Thus the *second principle* of the new architecture is without stylistic implications: "a modern building should derive its architectural significance solely from the vigour and the consequence of its own proportions. It must be true to itself, logically transparent and virginal of lies and trivialities. . . ."[102]

A *third principle* deriving from the Arts and Crafts movements in England and Germany, was the involvement of artists in production. The new architects endorsed the necessity of mass production—particularly if the new social targets of housing the people cheaply were to be met—and believed that it could be turned to creative ends. Walter Gropius (in 1910) and Le Corbusier (in 1917) both experimented with pre-fabricated mass-produced house prototypes. Thus the new architects were enjoined to favour rationalised constructional principles, and details which could be mass produced and assembled on site.

Any difficulties inherent in these new principles only became manifest when it came to the time to design a building. The new architects, many of whom were messianically puritan, disliked the thought of "style". If the three principles were followed, each building would be unique—so there could be no "style". Berthold Lubetkin fell out with Wells Coates and the proposed MARS group for this very reason.[103] Gropius attacked those who had made "modern" architecture fashionable with "formalistic imitation and snobbery".[104] Yet style there undoubtedly was, perceptible to any onlooker who had not decided, *a priori*, that there could not be any.

A good illustration of the move from precept to aesthetic can be seen in Le Corbusier's *Five Points of a new architecture*, enunciated c.1928 in relation to houses. These points were thus:

> 1. The house to be constructed on columns (stilts or pilotis) to free the ground floor for other uses. 2. A roof garden or solarium permitted by the flat roofed structure. 3. A free internal plan, created by a framed structure. 4. A free facade—carrying no structural load and thereby able to express whatever the function required of it. 5. A continuous ribbon window.[105]

The most influential exemplar of these points is the Villa Savoie, Poissy, near Paris. What is clear from that building is how far from being universal those points are. The solarium, flat roof, and the long holes in the skin of the building are more appropriate to a warm climate than to a Scots one.[106] Furthermore, the fulfilment of all Five Points in a house presupposed a fairly large house on a substantial budget—a house of a scale rarely built in Scotland.[107] The specification, however, of a continuous ribbon window is logically inconsistent with the demand that the façade should reflect only what the interior required: it might not require such a window. However much the new architects wriggled, a new aesthetic was beginning to emerge. That point was well spotted by the unlikely figure of Sir Giles Scott at the RIBA Conference in 1935: "Though the modernist may claim

[103] Wells Coates invited Lubetkin to join the Modern Architecture Research Group (MARS). Coates himself had evolved a style of architecture which included fashionable streamlining motifs such as tubular rails, portholes, curves and long sweeping balconies. Lubetkin rejected the invitation on the grounds that the new Group's aim to demonstrate publicly a common approach to architecture would, of necessity, lead to a style, i.e. formalism.

[104] Gropius Ibid. p. 18.

[105] Le Corbusier. *Complete Works*: vol. 1 p. 128.

[106] Aberdeen's climate is 300% more severe than that of Buckinghamshire. Its relationship to that of Poissy has not been calculated. (Source: Scottish Development Department.)

[107] Villa Savoie had living-in servants' quarters. Few of the "modern" houses in Scotland provided that.

"Modern developments have undoubtedly brought a breath of fresh air into what had become a stagnant architecture atmosphere, and now that the modern expression has affected most architects, it is to be hoped that it will, by trial and error, and by elimination of mere stunts, gradually develop into a tradition, and bring all architects to work in the same style" Sir Giles Gilbert Scott

Villa Savoie, Poissy, drawn by Rendel Govan.

RIAS Quarterly

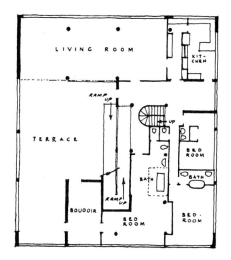

Above. Rosenberg, 1930 Christmas Card: from ocean-liner to streamlining as a style. *Right.* Humber Snipe Imperial: establishment streamlining with running boards. *Below right.* Architecture sympathetic to machines: Central Scotland airport at Grangemouth.

[108] *Quarterly* no 50 (1935) pp. 8–9.

[109] Of course many theorists tried to defend both on functional grounds. Gropius justified the flat roof as being more functionally useful, in allowing a full useable floor where previously an atticked or mansarded space had to suffice. Furthermore Gropius and Le Corbusier (later echoed by John R H MacDonald) held that a flat roof permitted a free plan in the floor below to a greater degree than a pitched one. Where money was no object, that might have been the case. In poor Scotland, however, a flat roof was not used to provide a third full floor in place of the pitched roof: it was usually used to cap the first floor, thus depriving fairly small houses of useable loft space.

[110] Raymond McGrath was a pioneering modernist architect in England whose first major commission was a house interior for Cambridge don Mansfield Forbes, Finella. He subsequently designed some houses and BBC studios in London. In 1934 he published *Twentieth Century Houses* from which this point is taken.

his effects arise naturally from a logical working out of the problem and not from design, it is quite clear that by using the grouping and massing of parts, and the pattern of window opening, he does design".[108]

The use of a concrete frame and a flat roof to liberate the house interior from constraining load-bearing walls followed the new dictates; but the commandment regarding strip windows trespassed into aesthetics,[109] since it was an *a priori* command irrespective of internal function.

Windows, long, horizontal, streamlined and curving round corners, played a key role in the horizontality that was the dominant factor of most Thirties designs. Where glazing bars were needed, they were usually metal and emphasised that horizontality. Raymond McGrath[110] argued that less money for construction predicated lower ceiling heights, and that horizontal strip windows provided the only means of restoring adequate light to house interiors: thus developing Corbusier's fourth point. Yet taking a window round a corner was also the most dramatic physical manifestation of how the walls were now relieved by the new framed structures of carrying loads. They were making a point intelligible to those who understood structures, that the corner and its previously critical role in stabilising a building's structure could be dematerialised.[111]

The purist aesthetics of the Thirties can mostly be traced to these new imperatives, and to the metaphors which Corbusier, Gropius *et al.* used to propagate their case. First comes the demand for rationalisation and mass production—the metaphor being machinery. It was only a slight step to advocating a machine aesthetic, that of the smooth, unclutter lined lines of objects stripped to their bare essentials which, by 1940, was being promoted avidly.[112] That theme was further developed in comparisons with machines of travel—cars, ocean liners and aeroplanes.[113] These embodied the combined virtues of being utterly functional, stripped to their bare essentials, and shaped according to necessity: or so it was said. Speed being the ethos of the Thirties,[114] it was only a short step for the actual motifs of these travel vessels to transfer to buildings. They became, in short, *streamlined.*[115] The "nautical style" as it has been called, sported white walls, tubular railings, portholes, balconies and flat roofs for recreation. Fashionable clients could have their very own sundeck in Scotland. Gropius had written: "We want an architecture adapted to our world of machines, radios and motor cars". Thus it comes as no surprise to hear Thomas Tait explain the design rationale of the Empire Exhibition thus: "The tendency throughout the world today (as architecture, like politics, is international) is to produce that simple streamline treatment which is seen on ocean liners and aeroplanes".[116]

The demand that the plan of the building should determine its architecture also had stylistic consequences: this time, with what is now christened *White Architecture*. The new morality predicated that different functions within a building could announce their presence to the onlooker outside; and that idea coincided with the artistic aims of Cubism and de Stijl, namely, the

McKean

Above. Burlington School, London. Burnet Tait and Lorne. Influential brick horizontality: note the staircase tower.

McKean

111 The point was easily traduced. Traditional builders quickly found a method of boxing out a concrete frame for a corner window to transfer the thrust sideways, which worked very well, and permitted even the dullest building to sport the insignia of the new liberation.

112 J M Richards: *An Introduction to Modern Architecture.*

113 Le Corbusier: Walter Gropius.

114 See Chapter 4.

115 As a young man Sir Robert Grieve had occasion to hear Thomas Tait advocate streamlining in buildings, in emulation of ships, cars, aeroplanes etc. The following impertinence took place: "Why are cars and aeroplanes streamlined, Mr Tait?" "To make them go faster." "Why do you want your buildings to go faster, Mr Tait?"

116 *Quarterly* no 60 (1939) p. 6.

Left. Highpoint 2, Highgate, London, by Tecton. It has all the classical attributes of grace, rhythm, proportion and "movement" without any superfluity.

Le Château, Silver End, Essex. The Manager's house in Crittal's factory village, by Thomas Tait.

RIBA Library

ROOF EXERCISES

' HIGH TEA.'

SPRING DAYS.

RIBA Library

Some of John R H MacDonald's ghastly cartoons proselytising the advantages of a flat-roofed house.

intention to revert to primary geometric forms which would be recognisable by all peoples regardless of creed or language: cubes, rectangles, squares, cylinders, circles and triangles. The new architecture would be created by marrying the uses within the building with these geometric forms, and creating architecture therefrom. Thus Le Corbusier[117]: "Architecture is the masterly, correct and magnificent play of masses brought together in light".

The commonest interplay of forms was the juxtaposition of the rectangle and the cylinder: the cylinder, often glass-enclosed, containing the staircase (in offices or factories); the drawing room (in houses) or the café-restaurant (in entertainment buildings). A refinement of that idea was the exploded rectangle, whereby its innate shape was obscured or gingered up by projecting balconies or roofs, recessed windows and porches, and stepped sun terraces. An alternative refinement, latterly christened the "International Style" after the construction of a complete estate of houses in the Weissenhof Siedlung (White House estate) in Stuttgart[118] developed the idea of the wall, which need no longer carry any weight, being treated as a two-dimensional curtain (hence the term curtain-wall) stretched tight over the frame. That idea utterly contradicted that of "white architecture", and latterly became tagged with the notion of functionalism.

Functionalism represents the puritan arm of modern architecture, implying that the satisfaction of a functional brief is an end in itself. The celebrated sculptor, Eric Gill, understood both the attractions and dangers of the puritan wing:

> Man has always been liable to fall into puritanism; for man is a bit of a rabbit and is frightened of his own lusts . . . What puritanism did not destroy has been made absurd by industrialism. Machine-made ornament is absurd . . . There is beauty in useful things, but it is not the beauty which is done for love, it is the beauty of functionalism. You can only sell things on account of their *utility*.[119]

Frank Lloyd Wright had the same reaction when asked by the young Alan Reiach for his reaction to modern European architecture: "What modern architecture needs today, young man, is more love".[120] When Sir Giles Scott presented Willem Dudok of Holland with the RIBA's Royal Gold Medal for architecture in 1935, it was clear that the British establishment regarded

The *Lorne* Cinema, Glasgow (demolished).

Art Deco pediment from the *Broadway*, Dundee.

Scottish Film Council

Davies

Singleton Holdings

Original perspective of the *Cosmo*, Glasgow.

Troxy, Leven, by A D Haxton. Night architecture with neon, and interior.

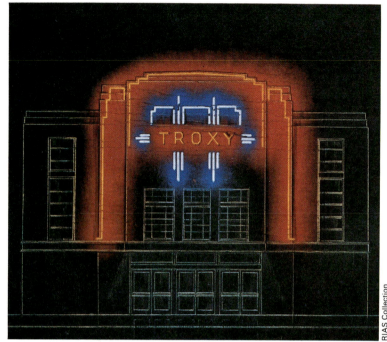

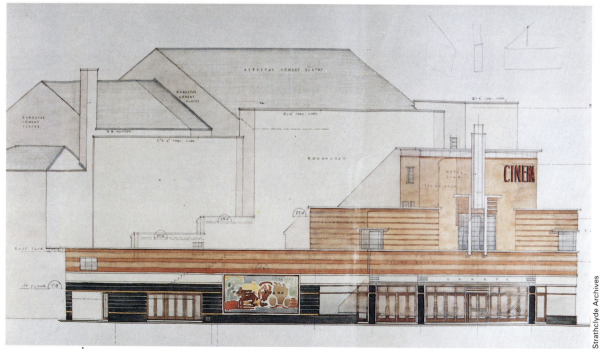

Proposed cinema, Govan, by C J McNair and Elder, 1936.

RIAS Collection/James Houston

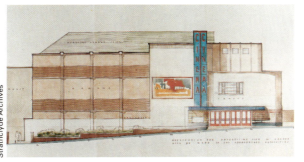

Strathclyde Archives

Far left. Light from the *Viking*, Largs: note the dragon motif. *Left.* King's Park cinema by McNair and Elder, 1937. *Centre.* Interior of *La Scala*, Sauchiehall Street.

Scottish Film Council

The *Maybury Roadhouse*, Edinburgh.

Ayr Ice Rink, designed by James Carrick in 1938. One of two neon proposals.

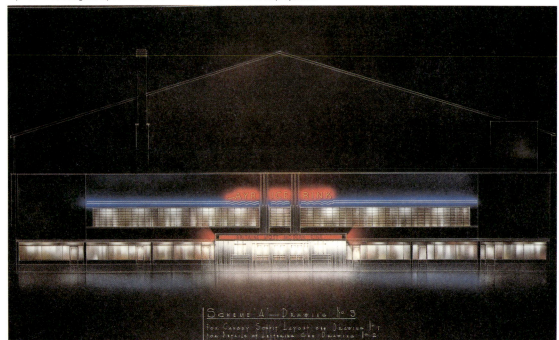

Cragburn Pavilion, Gourock. Competition-winning design by James Carrick (1935).

Dudok's brick, geometric architecture as the human face of modernism in contrast to unspecified "harsh robots, cruel and terrifying in functional expression".[121]

So whatever else functionalism represented, it was loveless, harsh and inhuman. "A functionalist is a man who writes to the architectural papers that several foreign architects with unpronounceable names were sent by God to show us how architecture should be done. They weren't of course".[122] So functionalism became associated with a mimimalist approach. Yet there is some doubt that it ever existed, or could exist, other than as a pejorative catchword. Lubetkin, at the point of design, produced high art. F R S Yorke, despite advocating "honest" use of materials in true functional manner, nonetheless advocated rendering or plastering brickwork in certain circumstances to produce "an over-all smooth image".[123] It is clear, as Sir Giles Scott had said, that the modernist *did* indeed design.

People were perhaps too afraid of the polemicists to investigate such inherent contradictions. Gropius warned that solving function was not enough: "Building is merely a matter of methods and materials. Architecture implies the mastery of space."[124] Le Corbusier, whose artistic achievements have so often been obscured by the mis-use of his idea of a house as *une machine à habiter*, was even more specific: "Architecture is lowered to the level of its utilitarian purposes: boudoirs, WCs, radiators, ferro-concrete, vaults or pointed arches etc etc. This is construction, this is not architecture. Architecture only exists where there is poetic emotion."[125]

The extent to which people *did* miss the point is exemplified by the recantation of Sir John Summerson in 1984: he who, as a young lecturer, had published his plea for the new architecture in *The Scotsman* in 1930. Where he had gone wrong was to present Le Corbusier as a pioneer of new structures and a new, objective architecture, whereas his true greatness was as an artist in the Cubist mould.[126]

Thus the principal streams of new architectural thought included the following: *White architecture*: Cubist inspired, geometric interrelationships. *Expressionist architecture*: the essence of the building symbolised and glorified. *Functionalist architecture*: minimalist, probably curtain-walled, stripped to its bare essentials: possibly prefabricated. *Dutch geometric/Dudok*: usually brick, fewer cylinders, more rectangles, greater humanity in the use of colour (tiled mullions and door surrounds) and gardens; usually massing up to a tower. *Streamlining*: the nautical image; portholes, railings etc.

Whilst architects were occupying various ivory towers of varying height and colour, the more popular world was moving also. There were two main streams: *Moderne* and *Art Deco*.

Moderne can be defined as a style in which the visual characteristics of *White* or streamlined architecture are applied to an otherwise wholly conventional building: a half-hearted horizontality with some jazz decoration about

Dutch institutional architecture of the English improved model: Hornsey Town Hall, by Slater and Uren.

117   *Vers Une Architecture* translated 1927 by F Etchells.

118   The Weissenhof: a demonstration housing estate organised by German architect Mies van der Rohe, to which he invited some of Europe's leading *avant-garde* architects to design a part. They included Le Corbusier, Walter Gropius, and J J P Oud and Mart Stam from Holland. The common visual characteristics of the buildings—flat roofs, white walls, strip windows etc led Henry Russell Hitchcock and Philip Johnson to coin the phrase the "International Style".

119   *Quarterly* no 49 (1935).

120   *Prospect*. He also advised Reiach to buy a second-hand Ford and "keep away from the Schools". Almost 20 years later, in 1953, he was asked for his opinion of le Corbusier, when addressing the Architectural Association: "A journalist and a great painter" was the reply.

121   *RIBA Journal* (27 April 1935).

122   Ninian Johnston: *Quarterly* (1934) no 47 p. 52

123   F R S Yorke: *The Modern House in England*, (1944 edition) p. 20 (insert).

124   Gropius op. cit. p. 20.

125   *Vers Une Architecture* page 000

126   Sir John Summerson: paper to RIAS Thirties seminar 1984.

Architecture as advertisement. The emperor of Art Deco in Britain – the Hoover Factory, London, by Wallis, Gilbert.

the doors and windows. The probable distinction between a *moderne* and truly modern house is that the latter would be designed from the inside out, and the former from the outside in.

Art Deco is wholly different from moderne. Far from being a pallid imitation of something else, it is a subculture entire unto itself. It is usually very colourful—either through paint or the use of glazed tiles and, as is proper, all the parts of a building contribute towards its visual climax—balconies, ironwork, lamps, lettering, windows, doors and parapets. There is a fondness for a many-layered recessing of doors, giving a "jazz" imagery appropriate to the time. Customarily, Deco buildings will be symmetrical, and will emphasise the principal entrance with a flat-topped pediment, frequently enhanced by flagpoles. Popular Deco buildings such as cafés and pubs made considerable use of etched glass, brightly coloured vitrolite and chrome. The term Art Deco derives from the 1925 Paris *Exposition des Arts Decoratifs*, although, as a style, it predated and outlived that exhibition. As against an increasingly abstract architecture, Art Deco provided those who hankered after symbolism with a richer vocabulary.[127]

Quite separate from the broad cultural streams outlined above, a number of individual architects commanded a following simply by virtue of the quality of their architecture. Three were pre-eminent: Frank Lloyd Wright of America, whose influence was thought to be replacing that of "white architecture" by 1939;[128] Mies van der Rohe of Germany (latterly America) whose approach to design and the shaping of spaces had attracted world-wide publicity in his Barcelona Pavilion (1930); and Alvar Aalto, a Finnish architect who seemed to the Scots to fuse together a truly modern architecture with a truly nationalist (or Finnish) sense of place.

THE REACTION IN SCOTLAND

Scots were informed early of the stirrings on the Continent—the architectural profession particulary through the *Quarterly* and the reports of its Rutland Prize winners. In the year the RIAS President A N Paterson chose to attack the "misleading precepts" of the modernists, F O Templeton, the then Rutland winner, published a series of detailed articles enthusiastically advocating those very precepts.[129] The first public debate—and a limited one—was created by Summerson's article in *The Scotsman* in 1930, one response to which, from sculptor C d'O Pilkington Jackson, was to dismiss the new European movements as "steamboat architecture".

The Scottish context was one of traditional craft-based architecture except for large offices and factories for which the customary approach was a steel-framed building with a façade in American classical style. Robert Lorimer had died only in 1929 and the influence of his office, Lorimer and Matthew, and of his students and pupils such as Leslie Graham Thomson continued strong into the decade. Yet Thomson, as Lorimer's obituarist (and skilful polemicist) claimed that Lorimer had quit historic styles at the point of his death, and was veering toward "that Scandinavian modernism which finds its happiest expression in Sweden . . . for in modern Swedish architecture is to be found a certain traditional feeling combined with modernity of outlook which is almost entirely free of the crudities of archaism on the one hand, and ultra-modernism on the other".[130] Scotland lacked any substantial neo-Georgian into which so many English architects retreated.

There was surprisingly little defence of pre-War architecture. The First World War had discredited pre-War attitudes and changing social requirements and diminishing amounts of money people were prepared to spend on buildings made change inevitable. On the other hand, there was no clear direction in which to go. Thus during this transition from old to new, architects often chose the easy option of exchanging the baroque or free

[127] One might compare the Chrysler building, New York, by William Van Allen (1930), whose top 12 storeys comprised superimposed sunburst motifs, with Howe and Lescaze's Philadelphia Savings Fund skyscraper (1934) whose rectangular serenity is only really modified by the way the building steps back to culminate in a slender tower: massing is adequate for the latter; style essential for the former.

[128] Goodhart-Rendel, President RIBA, addressing the RIAS in 1939.

[129] *Quarterly* (1927).

[130] *Quarterly* no 31 (1929) pp. 63–76.

Renaissance trimmings of their commercial buildings, libraries and the like for American classicism or ponderous Art Deco. Town halls and magistrates courts, classical in the early 19th century and romantic Scots in the late 19th century, reverted to a bare classicism of a Scandinavian sort. Moderne streamlining and Art Deco found their most appropriate outlet in the the novel building types of the architecture of pleasure; the cinemas, roadhouses, garages and travel buildings.[131]

The connotations of health and fresh air conveyed by the nautical imagery encouraged its use for hospitals and schools. The sturdy, functional brick geometrics of Dudok had their best expression in Scotland in pithead baths and factories (as compared to the Dudok-influenced town halls in England, particularly London).[132]. Such buildings were not particularly far removed from the pre-War great brick warehouses and sheds: they were simply better serviced, more economical, horizontal in proportion, and massing up to a tower.

The architecture of housing, the largest construction category between the Wars, showed the greatest departure from pre-War patterns. Before 1934, most housing was built at low density on garden-city lines with vaguely picturesque imagery. After 1934, there was a move to higher density in tenement flats, the designs influenced by Continental, mainly Austrian, examples. Bungalows and speculative houses were stylistically various although *moderne* motifs, and tile hanging from England both won many supporters (see Chapter 10).

Historically, however, signs of cultural change have been most perceptible in the design of the private house—and thus it was in the Thirties. With rare exceptions like the Rothesay Pavilion, "white architecture" in-so-far as it exists in Scotland, is to be found in private house design.

John Summerson, in his *Scotsman* article had tried to promote the cause of architectural modernism by persuading his readers that the Scots were somehow lagging behind an *avant-garde* Europe. He could not have chosen a worse way of attempting to influence Scotsmen. They could (and did) shrug off yet another young man's views on the grounds that what was suitable for Europe was by no means necessarily suitable for Scotland—particularly in the overheated nationalistic climate of the Scottish Renaissance. Those who followed with similar aspirations were rather more canny, and tried to draw a continuing thread from historic to modern, via Mackintosh:

> Buildings from the earliest to the latest, especially when they were faced with rough stone, harled and whitewashed, have a certain monolithic character; they are definitely cubic, if not cubist . . . The tall tenements which still rise like cliffs along the ridge of the old town of Edinburgh . . . show the direct line of descent which passed through the work of Mackintosh to such buildings as Adelaide House and so much of the adventurous architecture of today.[133]

Robert Hurd identified the time around 1600 as Scotland's "most national period", suggesting that if such period details as towers, crowsteps and ornamental dormer windows were removed, one would be left with a simple stone structure with exciting projections.[134] Ian G Lindsay, editor of the *Quarterly* considered that the simple L-shaped Lairds' houses of that period, exemplified by Barscobe in Kirkcudbrightshire, demonstrated that architectural simplicity and functionalism was characteristic of historic Scots architecture.[135] He claimed to his support the *avant-garde* Cambridge don Mansfield Forbes: "his interest in the Scots baronial style was by no means antiquarian; and in the fluid use of small rubble and harling, he saw a good foundation for a more plastic modern Scots architecture carried out in concrete". Small wonder that Sir John Stirling-Maxwell was amused at the notion of clients wanting Craigievar Castle with Corbusian windows thrown in.

So the radical nationalists hijacked "white architecture" and emphasised the

John Begg reacted against nationalism of any kind, writing to Indian architects in 1934 as follows: "I find myself with the rooted conviction that nationality of any sort is perhaps the most formidable enemy to any species of art development. The creative faculty is a feature in human consciousness of such delicacy and poise that it can hardly but be utterly upset by any manifestation of self-consciousness—national or international".

[131] See Chapter 4.

[132] Hornsey, Brent and Greenwich.

[133] Frank Mears: *RIBA Journal* (January 1938).

[134] Hurd: *Scotland 1938*. p. 121.

[135] *Quarterly* no 52 (1936).

singular similarity between Scots 17th-century architecture and the Cubist ideal of geometric shapes interacting in light; and sold it to the Scots as a rediscovery and a reinterpretation of their roots. Judging by the results—over 150 flat roofed, white houses in Scotland, they were not only successful, but also successful to a greater degree than was the case south of the border.[136]

These houses do not represent a Weissenhof Siedlung: they are almost all fairly small—only two or three as large as Maxwell Fry's Sun House in Hampstead. They break almost every one of Le Corbusier's Five Points: no framed structure, few roof gardens, no solaria, no piloti (or stilts) and little internal open plan. There is some evidence that climatic factors may have militated against open plan. All these houses are vertical in general proportion, and firmly plonked on the ground. There is little interpenetration of the outdoor and indoors, and the flat roof—far from being a functional opportunity, is an aesthetic determinant—it oversails, is usually thick, and is not infrequently painted black. Balconies and patios are kept to a minimum: in short, as few openings for the weather to exploit as possible.

Yet it is wrong to dismiss these creations. They were built in the teeth of both conservatism and practical experience. Flat roofs in Scotland had a notable record of failure.[137] The builders Sunlight Homes and Mactaggart and Mickel both advertised advanced, purpose-designed flat-roofed houses, and either found no takers or withdrew the offer. The *Quarterly* enthusiastically published research on flat roof failures. Thus those choosing a "white architecture" house in Scotland were knowingly entering a high risk area[138]: but an area which combined a public statement about the modern world and about the progressive nature of Scottish nationalism. It thus found expression in locations as dispersed as Stranraer, Alness, Gullane, Dunoon, Inverness, Bearsden, Elgin, Gattonside, Carmunnock, Ballater and Helensburgh.

It is known that several of the clients were either foreign, or had been abroad and required a "modern" house, sometimes against considerable reluctance from the architect. Dr King had visited Weissenhof: the Haggards held a competition for Hethersett; the client of Ingle Neuk wanted a house in the "modern English" style; Gysels in Cupar was Belgian; the client for Bella Vista, Dunfermline was Swiss; and John R H MacDonald had been to Weissenhof; nationalism was thus blended with produce of more than one country.

It has sometimes been said that the War prevented the full development and flowering of "white architecture". Whilst it is true that the exigencies of war led to the development of certain strands of modernism (e.g. prefabrication) at the expense of others (e.g. poetic emotion) there are signs that "white architecture" was already on the wane by 1939, both in Scotland and England. The change in England is signalled by the enthusiastic review of a small, pitched roof, brick house with canted balcony, designed by the Architects Co-operative Partnership in 1940. The reviewer, a young Leonard Manasseh, considered that with this little house, England seemed to be achieving a truly native modern architecture. What price Cubism then?

Much the same is apparent in Scotland. The battle of function versus formalism had been won; but the heady days of white Cubism were being replaced by brickitecture. Instead of holes punched through white solids, windows were being given thin concrete reveals. The obsessive horizontality of much Thirties building was changing and the vertical mullions in the Empire Exhibition presage a motif of the Fifties. Yet the memory lingered; flat roofed, white "cubist" houses, dating from the early Fifties can be found in Elgin, Dunfermline, Dunoon, Stranraer and St Andrews—and doubtless elsewhere besides. Early post-War factories, such as the Timex and National Cash Register factories (1946–7) by Beard and Bennett in Dundee; the 1948 Creamery in Perth or the new Scottish Industrial Estate

136 *Modern Houses in Britain 1919–1939* by Jeremy Gould lists six modern houses (defined as having the common characteristic of a flat roof) in Scotland, as against some 780 for the rest of the United Kingdom. The number in Scotland so far discovered is approximately 150, excluding comparable local authority housing schemes. Since one normally multiplies the Scottish factor by ten to obtain a UK comparison (population, number of architects, construction industry etc) that would imply that there is a higher proportion of such houses in Scotland than is the norm for the United Kingdom. These figures for Scotland exclude flat roofed "modern" mass housing estates as in Pilton, Tillicoultry, Denny, Kilmarnock and Aberdeen. Furthermore, flat roofs were an acknowledged liability in Scotland. If one therefore considers Thirties houses with a pitched roof (as the climate suggested) but with other Thirties attributes—whiteness, cut-away corners, first floor balconies, curious windows to indicate the location of the stair, concrete porch canopies etc, the number would be much higher.

137 As, unfortunately, they continued to do. Thirties houses in Kirkcaldy, Cupar, Carntyne and Stonehaven have all had their flat roofs capped with the pitched, pantiled variety. Many of the original roofs still give trouble.

138 Alan Reiach, David Carr and George Lawrence were all wary of using a flat roof on a house in the Thirties, only Lawrence succumbing to the temptation on his second house, once he had learnt a bit more about the technology. Reiach was concerned at architects designing beyond their knowledge, whereas Carr regarded the flat roof as an inescapable source of trouble to be avoided wherever possible.

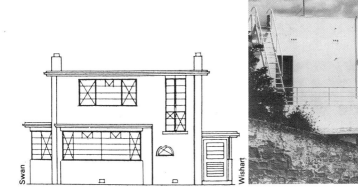

Far left. 1937 house in Garthdee Road, Aberdeen, by Roy Meldrum. The stair window is self evident. *Left.* On to the sun deck, chaps! Top two storeys of *Ingle Neuk*, which faces across a chill North Sea from Arbroath. *Below.* Staff houses, Paisley Infectious Diseases Hospital. *Bottom.* Section of *Lishmor*, Easter Belmont, Edinburgh. Bedroom balcony above drawing room bay clearly visible.

"The architects who have thrown up the sponge and turned into engineers seem to some of us to have made a bad mistake. They have emancipated themselves from tradition. But have they not paid too dearly for their freedom? A design stripped of association of the past may have the evanescent charm of novelty, but it is a cold, lifeless thing". Sir John Stirling-Maxwell.

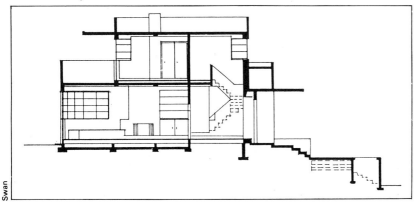

Top. The triangular window – to say nothing of the porthole. *Balnagarrow*, Cramond, by Sir James Miller. *Below.* Even the bellhop was streamlined at the *Beresford Hotel* in Glasgow (1938). *Right.* The storm prow, or fin, James McKissack's *Riddrie*.

Shona Adam

[139] The RIAS Thirties Study achieved an inadvertent result. Its instruction to its lay photographers to photograph any buildings, in addition to those already identified and listed, that they thought might be of the Thirties period, brought in a crop of 1960s and 1970s buildings. Looking at these afresh, it is easy to see how they could have been mistaken for the real article. Conversely, it demonstrates the extent to which the architectural aims of the Thirties—those of that short 1935–8 period—lasted for over 40 years thereafter, and may survive yet.

Swan/Weddell and Thomson

Company's estate at Newhouse—retain the geometric massing, and much of the detailing of the Thirties. In general, however, Thirties buildings had an individuality and character in addition to aspiring to logical function; a quick flicker of a character which, blown out by the War, rarely seemed to return.[139]

SOME THIRTIES ARCHITECTURAL MOTIFS

Semi-circular glazed bay, projecting forward from a rectangular block: in *houses*, usually indicating the lounge; in *entertainment building* the café, restaurant or bar; in *factories or offices*, the staircase. Origins for staircase derive from Mackintosh's Scotland Street School (Glasgow) and the Administrative office, Cologne Werkbund Exhibition by Walter Gropius (1914); re-affirmed in the 1930 Stockholm Exhibition by Gunnar Asplund, and the 1933 de la Warr pavilion in Bexhill by Mendelssohn and Chermayeff.

Nautical style—flat roofs, tubular railings, portholes and gangways : deriving from the streamlining imagery of ocean liners and used in private houses, pavilions and some entertainment buildings. In England, much identified with buildings near the sea, and often called seaside architecture.

Fins or prows : tall fins soaring up the façade of buildings into the roofline. Traced by John Summerson in 1938 to the "storm prow" first introduced by "that incurable romantic" Frank Lloyd Wright in an 1896 windmill. Easily adapted to an advertising tower, and thus much used in cinemas, garages etc.

Triangular windows : used mainly to illuminate (and identify) the staircase and occasionally the hall in private houses, sometimes a central motif in an Art Deco façade. Derives from the house for R W Bassett-Lowke in Northampton designed in 1921 by the German architect Peter Behrens; and later in Silver End village (1926 onwards) by Thomas Tait. Other typical staircase window shapes were a tall strip, L-shaped, or rectangular with a lower rim stepped up in sympathy with the stairs.

Square headed pediment : above the main entrance, usually symmetrically placed in the middle, in Art Deco buildings. Much in evidence in garages, cinemas and the like: but also in cafés, hotels etc. Often visibly paper-thin with no roof behind it. Thought possibly to be a distant descendant of the amazing skyscraper fantasies of the American Hugh Ferris.

Corner windows : no better way of indicating the use of a new type of structure than to put a hole at the key point of a traditional structure. Crittal windows provided factory-made metal corner windows in their thousands. In Scotland, the motif was usually a trick: a traditional structure with a concrete box taking the load around the weightless new window.

Singleton Holdings

McKean

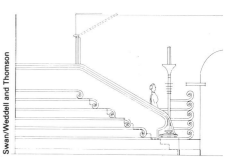

Swan/Weddell and Thomson

Above. The projecting bay: conjunction of cylinder and rectangle. Barnton villa, by W Innes Thompson. *Top right.* A guest flowing down the staircase in the *Beresford. Upper right.* Provincial Art Deco. Panelling at Broxburn by A D Haxton.

RIAS Collection.

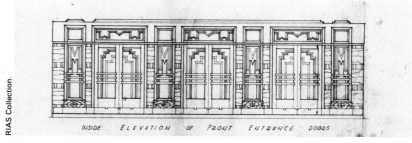

INSIDE ELEVATION OF FRONT ENTRANCE DOORS

Swan/Weddell and Thomson.

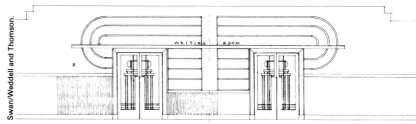

WRITING ROOM

Right. The *moderne* Writing Room of the *Beresford. Below.* The nautical style at full speed ahead. Sun deck, portholes and cut-away prow shape, *The Moorings*, Largs (since altered), by James Houston. *Below right.* Art Deco pediment, East London Street, by Patterson and Broom.

RIAS Collection/James Houston.

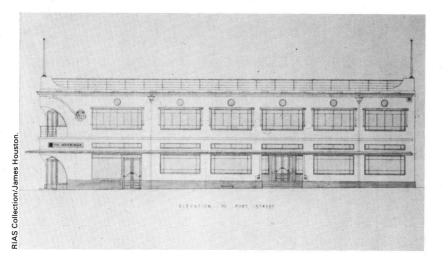

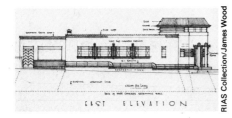

Above. The *Anchor*, Granton. Streamlined railings and Art Deco doors from cinema architect T Bowhill Gibson. *Below.* Weir's amenity building, Cathcart, by Wylie, Wright & Wylie: note tower, clock, flagpole and glazed staircase. *Centre.* Flagpole and cut-away corner tower on former *Binns*, Princes Street (hence the incised "B").

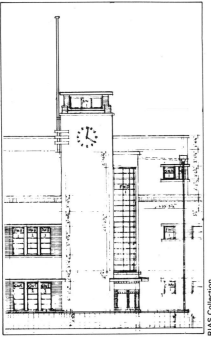

The flagpole: more than a sign of imperialist loyalty, the flagpole was a critical part of the design in many buildings, emphasising verticality and the main entrance.

Coloured mullions: porch columns, or columns within windows of coloured (e.g. usually, green, yellow, blue and black) bricks or tiles.

Towers: squat, flat towers, used usually in Art Deco buildings either to emphasise the entrance, or to frame the flanks. Often carved with historic (e.g. Mayan, Assyrian—or wherever the current archaeological fad was in progress) decoration.

Chamfered corners: the Thirties response to a corner was to reject Edwardian exuberance, and cut it away in a flat chamfer (usually in a different material). The resulting corner would be carried above the parapet as a tower with a flagpole.

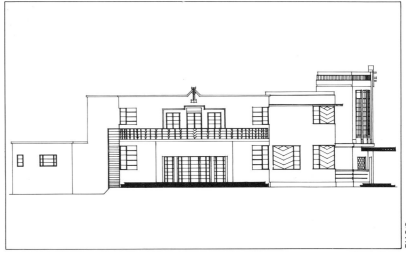

Maybury. Note the zig-zag Art Deco motifs.

4∎ PLEASURE AND LEISURE

The building should give an emotional reaction. Most of us have realised the thrill which comes from boarding an ocean liner or flying to France on one of the big Imperial Airways 'planes, or sitting at the wheel of a high-powered motor car. They are so eminently suitable for use and so attractively presented that they give us an emotional "kick".

Francis Lorne

Shona Adam

Maybury – fireplace and clock..

Possibly the critical impetus came from the technological developments in fabrication, movement and machinery caused by the First World War. These developments made the popular car, the 4000 seat moving picture talkie "kinema" and the enclosed ice rink—barely conceivable in the Edwardian period—a reality by the 1930s. The new technical opportunities served fundamental social change: principally the concept that "pleasure" (stripped of the Victorian implications of self-improvement) and the leisure to enjoy it, should be available to a far greater number than before. That was sometimes rationalised as a need to forget the horrors of the War. The dominance of this aspect of the Thirties has led to the description of the inter-war period as "the long weekend".[140]

The notion of improvement through faster and more refined methods of travel was a metaphor for the progress of society as a whole. When Batsford produced their *Book of Speed* in 1934, the reaction of the reviewer in the *Quarterly* was that "with the present acceleration of life and the efficiency needed to make it possible, this high speed feeling should be in our bones".

Thus the roadster, the aeroplane and the ocean liner generated a sympathetic architecture much dependent on style. Clone-like, the garage, the roadhouse, the country hotel, the airport building, ship and ferry terminals adopted the features of the cars, ocean liners and aeroplanes they were there to serve. It was an architecture that aimed to be as "streamlined" as its clients.

Most of the buildings arising from this leisure industry had no appropriate precedent. Edwardian music halls had neither the image nor the facility to cope with the requirements of a super cinema. Scottish pubs—sawdust floored drinking howffs—presented an image wholly at odds with the needs of the Tourer, his wife and children. Stables were not designed to cope with the spatial needs of cars and lorry repairs; and the motor bus required shelter of entirely new dimensions. Whilst miracles of adaptation were sometimes achieved,[141] new building forms were required: quickly.

Thus it was that many cinemas, garages and ice rinks (like their industrial counterparts) were created the easy way: tacking the "style" on to the front of a huge, beetling barn behind: an approach to architecture aptly characterised by Norman Foster as "Lipstick on the gorilla". Although reprehensible to the moderns, this attitude was well founded in the Scots urban tradition whose cliff-like streets concealed who–knew–what behind. Part of the architectural interest of the Thirties lies in observing architects evolving a new building form appropriate for these uses.

140   Robert Graves and Alan Hodge 1940.

141   The Paragon Cinema, Gorbals: George Singleton recalled: "I was born on 1st January 1900 and in 1920 bought my first cinema, the Paragon, Gorbals, which had been converted from the Church of Scotland. It had been run by a bookie, "Little Titch" before I rebuilt it. My father had been a printer and put me in the business, but after five years I was learning nothing. My father had bought a few halls—Salvation Army and the like— any hall you could tie up a screen or a sheet at one end and crank a projector at the other. The risks that were taken were enormous. A packed hall full of people smoking cigarettes and, despite the presence of highly inflammable liquids, throwing butts anywhere. Even before I left school at 15, I was managing the picture house in Hamilton in the evenings. I rebuilt the Paragon using the architects Gardner and Glen. I never used them again. Gardner was the most awful faker in the world. He used every substitute for the decent thing. They had no taste." (interview with author)

Singleton Holdings

Mr Cosmo (George Singleton) inviting clients to his cosmopolitan cinema in Rose Street, Glasgow *(right)*, clearly influenced by the *Curzon*, London *(bottom)*, by Burnet Tait and Lorne.

McKean Collection

142 Chris Doak: *Klondyke of the Cinema World* (1979).

143 Anna Blair: *Tea at Miss Cranston's*. (Shepherd-Walwyn 1985) p.63.

144 Otherwise known as Mr Cosmo—Mr Cosmo earned his nickname from his cinema. According to his son, he spent his life trying to make the cinema respectable. Continental films were being lost to Britain since the language barrier prevented the larger cinemas being filled. Singleton, impressed by the Curzon and Academy cinemas in London, determined to emulate them in Glasgow, with a cinema outside the pressures of the commercial circuits. It was a purely commercial decision. He liked and enjoyed good films from the Continent, and gambled that sufficient people in the west shared that taste. It hit it off from the beginning. The audience came to depend upon Mr Cosmo's judgement, and to rely upon always finding a high quality film. He adopted the pattern of one major feature supplemented by a number of shorts. (interview with author)

CINEMAS

Cinemas have become the building type most peculiarly identified with the Thirties, and Scotland had a particular affinity to them. Glasgow, with perhaps 120 separate cinemas in 1937,[142] had more per head of population than any other city in the world; and Edinburgh with approximately 65, was not far behind in proportion. It was as a Glasgow solicitor that John Maxwell, founder of the ABC Circuit, first surfaced and flourished, and in Edinburgh that he is reputed to have had his first cinema. The largest cinema in Europe was built by George Green in Renfield Street, Glasgow: for which he dispatched his architects, John Fairweather and Company, to America to imbibe latest trends, the result being, on their return, the creation of the celebrated Playhouse with 4200 seats, and a ballroom upstairs. Indeed, the Ballroom was almost as celebrated as the cinema: "Green's, wi' the different big bands like Joe Loss and Geraldo, was the really classy place".[143]

Edinburgh's Playhouse (a different promoter but also designed by Fairweather two years later) seated 3200 people, and the Green's Playhouse in Dundee (1935) was larger again. Scotland was movie mad: communities throughout the country as small as Newport on Tay (The Rio), Anstruther, Grantown-on-Spey, Dufftown, Turriff and Kilbirnie had their own cinemas, whilst towns of the size of Kirkcaldy had five. Although a number of early cinemas were converted from theatres and music halls, the striking innovation of the new animal was that communities which had never before been able to sustain a theatre or music hall were able to sustain a cinema.

A singular feature of Scottish cinema was the existence of several independent circuits—among them George Singleton (Glasgow),[144] J B Milne (Dundee), George Green of the Playhouses (Glasgow), Harry Frutin (Glasgow), James Donald (Aberdeen) who owned 26 cinemas plus the ice rink, the Poole Family (Edinburgh), Kemps (Ayrshire), Peter Crerar of Dunfermline[145] and Caledonian Associated Cinemas possibly the largest with 51 cinemas—all in addition to the home-grown ABC circuit which, by early 1936, was opening its 43rd Scottish cinema. This multiplicity of endeavour may explain the absence of the dominant house style of, say, Oscar Deutsch's famous Odeon chain. When Deutsch decided to move into Scotland in 1937, he bought existing circuits, mainly the Singleton Circuit, rather than build anew.[146] Hence there is nothing in Scotland quite to compare with the house-style of the English architects George Coles, Harry Weedon and Andrew Mather. The latter did come north with Deutsch in 1938, but his two Odeons—Motherwell and Ayr—are not striking, and are outmatched by the best being produced by the leading Scots cinema architects of the day—John McKissack and Son (Glasgow), C J McNair and Elder (Glasgow), T Bowhill Gibson (Edinburgh), James Houston (Kilbirnie), and Col Alexander Cattanach (Kingussie) who was virtually the house architect of Caledonian.

The cinema had to advertise its presence, had to offer subsidiary facilities like sweetie shops, lounges, bars and—in some cases—restaurants and tearooms; and had to provide a real experience in the auditorium—a fusion of decoration, atmosphere, orchestra and organ to complement the film itself. So it provided an adventure of which the film was only part, in standards of luxury and appointment previously the sole preserve of the wealthy. (Children in many communities (Dundee, Leith, Gateshead) paid for their entry to this Nirvana using jam jars as currency.[147]) Most cinemas had an interior "theme" made up from the combination of lighting, chrome, terrazzo floors, carpets, fibrous plaster details, and auditorium decoration.

Quality cinemas were those which supported a cantilevered balcony—with the additional seats, investment and constructional problems that entailed.[148] The smaller, or "Stadium" cinema consisted of a simple chamber with raked seating. Some of the very small cinemas were poorly provided. It is said

Singleton Holdings

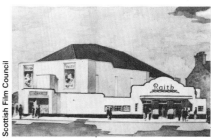

Scottish Film Council

Top. Communities too small to sustain a theatre could easily sustain a local cinema, which became part of local life. The *Regal*, Lanark. *Below.* The *Raith*, Kirkcaldy, by James McKissack.

145 A bus operator who moved over to cinemas as his rival, William Alexander, expanded.

146 See Janet McBain's excellent *Pictures Past* (Moorfoot 1985) for much greater information on cinema operation.

147 Payment by jam jars was as much the reward of thrift for better-off children as the means of paying for the poorer ones.

148 David Walker.

Below. The Spanish fortress of the *Toledo*, Muirend, by Weddell and Inglis. Interior of this "Atmospheric". *Above*. The façade.
Top. Caledonian Associated Cinemas' flagship: the Perth *Playhouse*.

of a cinema in Leith that, in the absence of WCs, young patrons were expected to relieve themselves on the seats in front, being sprayed with disinfectant by ushers· in the aisles.[149] In Tain, patrons were expected to use the walls outside (presenting a problem in the long northern summers). Only a few years ago, an Irish cinema's door marked "toilets" ushered the patrons out to the fields.

One of the principal architectural problems was that of constructing massive, fire proof buildings with easy means of escape, good acoustics, air conditioning, excellent visibility and lighting, within an exceptionally short time scale. The Perth Playhouse, for example, a 1700 seater designed by Alec Cattanach with Bowhill Gibson as consultant, 1933, was completed within 9 weeks from laying the first brick, which *Ideal Kinema* considered a record. The Playhouse, complete with restaurant, became Caledonian's flagship; and is remarkably similar to Cattanach's Regal in Rothesay four years later.

The most elaborate cinemas were called "Atmospherics" and were relatively rare in Scotland. An exact definition of an "Atmospheric" is impossible. The most that can be said is that the chosen theme is wholehearted, and consistent throughout. Only one survives: The Toledo, Muirend (1933) by William Beresford Inglis who also designed the Boulevard, Knightswood (1928). The Toledo attempts a Spanish fortress exterior, complete with cannonmouths, outlined somewhat wildly in neon, the ticket office a tile-capped Spanish window, and the ceiling above as the sky. The auditorium posed as a Spanish courtyard, with imitation stone walls, tower, turrets, a relief landscape viewed through an arch on one side, artificial windows on the other, a summer's sky above, and deep purple curtain adorned with butterflies on flowers.

The alternative to the "Atmospheric" was the "theme" cinema, two of whose most striking examples were designed by James Houston of Kilbirnie. The Radio Cinema in Kilbirnie takes the radio as its theme, elaborated by the motif of Mercury's winged sandals. The miracle of electronic communication was another theme of the period (viz Radio City in New York)

149 Brendan Thomas: *The Last Picture Shows*: Edinburgh, (Moorfoot 1984).

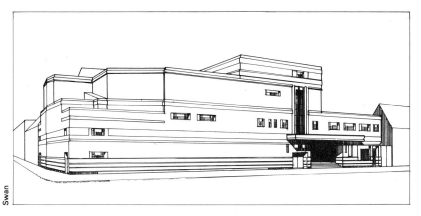

Swan

RIAS Collection/James Houston

RIAS Collection

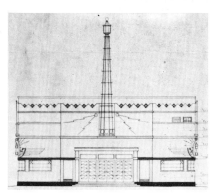

McKean

and Houston was an addict. The Viking, Largs, opened the day before the Germans invaded Danzig in 1939, celebrated the Battle of Largs between the Scots and the Danes. A galley projected from the main entrance, the clients entered between splayed walls and beneath a battlement and advertising portcullis, and the auditorium was decked out in "Viking colours".

Thematic treatment was superseded later in the decade by the innovative use of light. The growth of new lighting techniques, combined with a growing interest in the cinema as an architectural form in its own right, led to auditoria whose character was achieved by simple shapes and massing accentuated by clever lighting. An early example of a plain, subtle, geometric interior is the exceptional but now sadly decayed, Playhouse, Montrose designed by Alister McDonald (son of Ramsay) in 1933. "Holophane" lighting, which first arrived in Edinburgh at Poole's Roxy, Gorgie Road in 1937, allowed architects to provide walls and ceiling of simple shapes and surfaces onto which would be projected constantly changing coloured lights. The State, Leith, designed in 1939 by Sir James Miller for the company he chaired, had an auditorium specifically designed to take advantage of holophane, with plain walls in green, silver and ivory. Not one to miss an opportunity, Miller also provided the cinema with four shops, two billiard saloons and a skittle alley.

So much for the atmosphere. What about the architecture? Most Scots cinemas predate the Thirties: only 11 out of the 65 Edinburgh cinemas were

Top left. The Montrose *Playhouse*, by Alister MacDonald, the Prime Minister's son. *Left.* The *Viking*, Largs: galley prow, portcullis and towers, by James Houston. *Above, top and middle.* The *Radio*, Kilbirnie. Houston's fascination with communications is indicated by the Radio Tower and Mercury's winged sandals. *Above.* The *State*, Leith. Sir James Miller also included two snooker lounges.

Above. Night architecture: the *Rio*, Edinburgh, as most Scots would have seen it. T Bowhill Gibson. *Below*. *Granada*, Parkhead. The perspectivist has deleted the auditorium behind.

150 Letter to the author (1975).

151 *RIBA Journal* (1935).

152 George Green, responsible for the 90' high advertising tower outside his Playhouse in Dundee, began his career in fairground booths in 1896. The Greens came to Glasgow from Preston in a caravan, and lived above the paybox in the Whitevale Cinema. All their cinemas—including the two largest · in Europe—were built by direct labour. The sense of carnival clearly stayed with him for the Playhouse interior was magical: great columns in the restaurant ringed with neon, neon zig zags across the ceiling like lightning flashes, and stairs at the far end formed with stepped, glowing balustrades like a set from a Hollywood movie.

purpose-built within the decade and only the Paramount and the Cosmo in central Glasgow. The rest were suburban: presenting a quite different architectural opportunity whose three principal elements were these: the advertising tower or beacon, the huge bulk of the auditorium, and the grand, welcoming entrance.

Cinemas received a bad press—particularly from contemporaries. They were thought to be vulgar and an intrusion into the street scene. Maxwell Fry, the leading English-born modernist, described them as "really dreadful by-blows of unawakened commerce, which failed to achieve a total form of any consequence, but merely added to the corruption of the High Street".[150] At the RIBA 1935 Conference in Glasgow, Professor Harold Hughes singled out teashops, public houses, cinemas, hotels and other buildings as "spurious modern work, put out purely for effect".[151] He condemned the "craving for novelty and advertisement. The majority of modern buildings are produced merely to be novel, to catch the eye, and to become easily notorious." He, and other purists, reacting against what they regarded as a meretricious phenomenon, failed to realise that a reticent cinema would be a contradiction in terms. Its important advertising beacon, often realised in the form of a fin running from top to bottom, can probably be traced back to the cinema's origins in the fairground. Indeed, much carnival razmatazz clung to the cinema in its move from fair to city and suburb: a vividly uniformed staff, parties, ceremonies and brilliant night time illumination.

"Night architecture"—a term seemingly invented by the Germans—was critical since most Scots would be visiting the cinema after dark. Thus grew the idea that cinemas could advertise themselves by the use of neon: and the exterior of the cinema could be transformed—just like the interiors after · the introduction of the holophane lighting—into largely plain surfaces irradiated by light. Colour formed an important part of the daytime spectacle elementnot simply on the principal surfaces, but also in the lettering, canopies, advertisements and the sides of the brightly tiled entrance doorways.

Most older cinemas, fitting into an existing street front, could hide the bulk of the auditorium behind, leaving it as a vast, undecorated, brick clad, corrugated asbestos-roofed, windowless shed. The front-of-house, thus divorced from the bulk at the back, could be extravagant like a tinsel show. Most Art Deco features in cinemas in Scotland are in those where the effort has been thus expended. As cinemas began to require larger sites—particularly following the introduction of talkies in 1929 they could no longer hide the bulk. In inner locations, corner sites were preferred: in suburban locations, free-standing sites.

The architectural problem faced by large cinemas in central sites was how to integrate the huge bulk of the auditorium in such a way as to be architecturally respectable, and not to present too uninteresting a façade to the street. That problem had only recently been extremely well solved in the New Victoria Cinema, in Victoria, London by E Walmesley Lewis (illegitimate stepsons of which are Bowhill Gibson's cinemas in Perth and Rothesay), who placed a vertically proportioned, ribbed entrance tower at one end of the block, the bulk of the remainder of the building streamlined with horizontal parallel strips in what contemporaries thought was Germanic fashion. An interesting comparable Scots example is the Montrose Playhouse: rather more blank than the New Victoria, but nonetheless a clever attempt to create a coherent street façade to the flank and rear of the auditorium. The Paramount, Renfield Street, 1934 by Verity and Beverley occupies the entire block between Renfield and West Nile Streets. Since the entrance corner is clad in a completely different material from the bulk of the building, which is in plain, well designed, dark red brick, the resolution is not

Scottish Film Council

D. C. Thomson

quite so architecturally respectable. However at night the entire complex was given a semblance of unity by being outlined with strips of neon. The "night architecture" lent the building a unity which eluded it during the day.

The small Cosmo, Rose Street, Glasgow, was the nearest Scotland approached to Thomas Tait's Curzon Cinema in London. George Singleton required his architect James McKissack (assisted by W J Anderson) to design an intimate cinema of only 825 seats for specialist audiences. The intention was to feature the best continental films (symbolised by the globe in the entrance hall). It was in this cinema that the persona of Mr Cosmo was most evident; and the club atmosphere was reinforced by patrons being invited to help select future films by filling out sheets as they attended. Opened in May 1939, its self-conscious brick geometrics were as much a display of its continentalism as its programme.

The George Cinema (later County) by T Bowhill Gibson, Portobello, 1937

Top left. Paramount, Glasgow at night. *Above. Green's Playhouse,* Dundee. The second largest cinema in Europe had the tallest advertising tower – 90 feet. *Below.* Interior of Edinburgh's *Dominion,* by T Bowhill Gibson.

RIAS/James Wood.

153 James McKissack was a distinguished photographer and cameraman, as a result of which he had been used as a film-booker for Cranstons Picture House. A gentlemanly man of taste and refinement he travelled to Germany, other parts of Europe, and to New York, sometimes exhibiting his photographs. The overt continentalism of the Cosmo may derive from these trips although his partner W J Anderson, a quiet, unassuming man, was the actual designer.

Right. Cosmo interior. *Below.* Reconstruction of the *Argyle*, Glasgow, by George Boswell. *Bottom.* The *County*, Portobello as originally designed, and as now truncated.

being surrounded by buildings, only needed a façade. Its entrance, beneath a sweeping canopy, is flanked by two great drum towers rising three storeys, between which there used to soar a tall semi-circular, projecting advertising tower that projected well beyond the height of the central flat topped tower. The original facing block (currently brilliant white) was in two shades of light blue, and the 33' high advertising tower was entirely glazed, and illuminated at night from inside by means of cyclo troughing, giving constantly changing pastel hues. The top of the building was outlined by a thin line of neon tubing, and the remainder of the façade was floodlit by lights hidden behind the canopy.

The concentrated obloquy cinemas attracted at the 1935 Conference was almost three years old before the second generation of suburban super-cinemas were completed, in which great efforts were made toward creating the "total form" required by Max Fry; and that emergent architectural form may be perceived in a small group constructed towards the end of the decade. Each makes no pretence to conceal or ignore the auditorium behind but in some way or other, tries to integrate it into a single design.

Causewayside garage, Edinburgh. Newly discovered alternative scheme by Basil Spence (1933). The drawing shows Spence's facility at free flowing perspectives. Note the scale of the car to that of the people.

RCAHMS/Ewing

Weddell and Thomson

Rogano's Oyster Bar, Glasgow, with the recent conversion scheme by the original architects Weddell and Inglis (now Weddell and Thomson).

The first extension to Templeton's Carpets, Glasgow, by George Boswell, as drawn by Ninian Johnstone (*right*); as built (*above*).

Dunfermline Fire Station, by James Shearer.

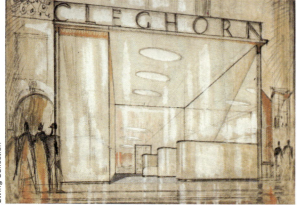

Left. Caledonian Insurance
Company, St Andrew Square – now
GRE (drawn by J N Graham).

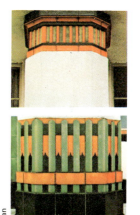

Left. Cleghorns, Edinburgh, by
Kininmonth and Spence (in Spence's
distinctively flamboyant style).
Above. India of Inchinnan – main
door and the base of a column.

Right. Chemistry building staircase, Glasgow University, by T Harold Hughes.

Below. Kelso Academy science block tower, by Reid and Forbes; clearly a prototype for Chirnside School (*bottom*) the following year.

Robotham

McKean

McKean

The Aldwych, Cardonald by James McKissack was a gigantic box, front and back tied tight by a cornice, of a size and proportion to comprehend the auditorium within. McKissack[153] was also responsible for the Vogue cinemas in Govan and Riddrie in the same year. Govan, the promotor's favourite, took its corner entrance façade to full height, screening the entire bulk of the building: whereas Riddrie develops the concept of differing volumes arranged in proportion to each other.

Equally accomplished designs come from the hand of C J McNair and Elder, who designed four super cinemas between 1937 and 1939: the State, Kings Park; the State, Shettleston (now badly robbed of most of its important details); the Lyceum, Govan and the Ascot, Anniesland—which was barely begun in 1939. Each of these buildings, in its own way, glories in the entire building form, playing one mass against another to lead up to the climax of the main entrance. The drum towers of the Ascot have noticeable similarities to buildings of the 1938 Empire Exhibition. The Lyceum, Govan on the site of a burnt-out Musical Hall, is sandwiched between tenements on a very large corner site, completed in 1937. It consists of a huge curved brick screen, originally outlined in black so as to emphasise

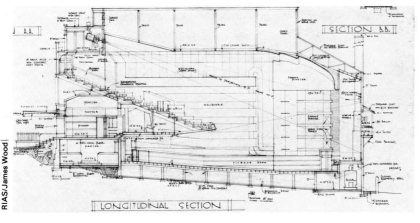

Top. The *Dominion*, Edinburgh, the sectional plan on the left showing projection and sight lines. *Above middle. Vogue*, Govan. *Left*. The *Vogue*, Riddrie, when first completed. *Above. Aldwych*, Paisley Road.

its streamlining, at the apex of which the brick wall is punctured by three, two-storey, glass block windows, with blue tiled mullions. These indicate the location of the entrance, and the light shining out through them at night provided its own advertisement. It seems, therefore, that by the time of the War, the cinema was indeed about to achieve its true architectural form.

It was said at the time, and often since, that the cinema profited from the Depression. A rather more accurate description would be to say that the cinema's popularity was a creation of the Depression. Perhaps, therefore, it was not simply the growth of television in the 1950s, but also the growth of different economic and social conditions which caused the effective closure as a cinema of nine tenths of those which had existed. In particular, the move to the specialist film (notably the X film), killed the large family attendances on which the supers depended.[154]

Right. Lyceum, Govan. *Below*. The former *Ascot*, Anniesland.

White House

W Dick

[154] Interview: Mr Castell, Caledonian Associated Cinemas.

BUILDINGS OF TRAVEL

Steamships, aircraft and limousines seemed to extract from architects buildings sympathetic to the streamlined sleek nature of the machines themselves. There was some demand for ferry terminals and aircraft control towers and clubs, and scattered or mutilated remains of ferry buildings of the period may be seen in places like Kyle, Port Ellen and Stornoway—indicating that the lure of brilliant white geometrics with cut-away windows was predominant.

THE AERODROME

Of the few air buildings constructed before 1940, virtually none survive unaltered. The demolished control tower at the Central Scotland Aerodrome Grangemouth (1939) was a very confident two-storey, semi-circular building with curving bands of windows and a viewing platform above designed by Alex Mair. Norman and Dawbarn's Perth aerodrome was something of a disappointment after their glandular Birmingham circular control tower: simple sheds with a tower in one corner. Noad and Wallace's Renfrew Aerodrome Club House was a precise, two storey building, its horizontals emphasised by the banded brickwork linking the two sweeping lines of windows, a four storey control, symmetrically placed tower with a tall triangular window, indicating the main entrance.[155] Those in charge of Prestwick Airport were more philistine; they smashed a four-storey concrete control tower through the roof of 18th century Orangefield House, the top two storeys being a crude assembly of tubular railings and unexciting structure. The nearby Air Training School by James Munro and Son was a very plain, white, two-storeyed, block with a foreshortened 3rd floor as tower in the corner. The entire neighbourhood was transformed by Mair in 1939 when he supervised the re-erection of the Empire Palace of Engineering as part of the Prestwick complex.

Transgraphics

Above. The opening ceremony at Grangemouth aerodrome in summer 1939.

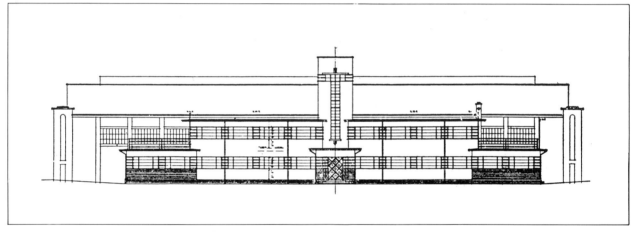

Renfrew Club House.

THE GARAGE

Three separate duties attended motor buildings: the filling station (petrol, water and tyres only); the garage (repairs) and the showroom (sales). Some garages performed all three, a pattern which became more common as the decade progressed and provided the greatest architectural challenge.

Romance had attached itself to the long distance tourer, swapping pioneering yarns as to how quickly he had "eaten up" the Great North Road with his fellows in the smoking room at Scotch Corner. The principal routes gathered nicknames, and trouble spots horror stories.[156]

A sense of adventure was in the air, and the garage was there to serve it. At its humblest, there was but a filling station: a hand-cranked pump, a low screen wall and a little office—often constructed of timber, and full of things to buy. They spread along the main routes like measles. In 1929 a competition was held for a filling station design, the winning Scottish design by Alex Cullen being built in 1930 in Hamilton. How pretty it was:

[155] Wallace, who was interested in flying, was having a drink with a pilot. The pilot agreed that facilities were poor and wondered where he might find an architect. Wallace rose nobly to the occasion. (interview)

[156] In 1935 almost double the number of people were killed on British roads than had been killed in the entire Crimean War (A M Mackenzie—op. cit.)

Right. Causewayside garage: Basil Spence, 1933.
Below. A few pumps, railings and shed would do.

White House

Strathclyde archives

157 Although you could get a car for as little as £100, the middle classes bought better. A Ford V-8 cost £240, and a Humber £330 (rising to £735 for a Pullman saloon). On the same day James Keanie advertised a bungalow to last, for £535, SMT advertised the Buick Regal Coupé for the same price (and a Pullman limousine for £925). There are few cars nowadays advertised for general purchase at twice the price of a 3-bedroomed house and garden.

a front and back screen wall, terminated by little pillars with ball finials. It had a centrally located little pitched roof office, and a stand for pumps. It was the Edwardian country garden approach—with no recognition, as yet, of the need for a canopy to keep off the rain. Town filling stations were often a triumph of image over reality. All that was needed was a gap site between buildings. The gables on either side would be painted white, a low, white screen wall would line the pavement: one or two Técalmit signs; a pump; a white timber cabin—and hey presto! a filling station.

The garage was up a scale. It could (and usually did) offer petrol: but its principal function was to repair vehicles—in those days a middle-class participation sport. What was needed was a large shed, with pits and good height clearance. The roofs were usually corrugated asbestos or metal, with the roof structure frequently used as a scaffold for hanging tools or car parts. The pervasive smell of oil-impregnated concrete was an abiding joy (to those who could choose when to enjoy it). But these great barns needed a front: both for image, and for security; and so they were screened off from view by a façade, often extended with wings on either side. The façade was customarily designed with the fashionable Art-Deco stepped parapet, and might occasionally run to a canopy over the pumps in front. The appropriate colour to accompany the·modernity of the cars themselves was white.

As the office, then the works reception, and then the showroom itself became more important, these were added as elements to garage design, and were turned into an architectural composition. The Sighthill Garage for example, has a narrow three-storey administration tower with Art Deco clock and strip windows, a flanking garage and showroom, and a thin cantilevered canopy. A more rustic version is Ken Cooper's garage at Bannockburn, where the office is a two-storey, flat-roofed, creamy-white cube, with triangular corner buttresses as a sign of keeping up with the times: sales to the left, and repairs to the right. Williamson and Hubbard's Fidelity Garage, Kirkcaldy, 1938 uses an advertising tower as a key component in the design, not only turning a corner, but emphasising the location of the main entrance.

Car showrooms had not quite the novelty of garages. There were many precedents for showrooms, the only innovation of the car showroom being the requirement for the products in the window to be able to drive out of the shop window forwards into the street, or back into the body of the building.[157] A number of car showrooms survive, and most attempt the fusion of the large plate glass windows necessary to sell the vehicle, with the imposition of Art Deco detailing in brightly coloured paintwork, a spectacular survivor being the Alfa Romeo showroom in Angle Park, Edinburgh.

Some garages were self-consciously "architect-designed". Basil Spence designed an infill garage, as a front for a larger garage behind Causewayside in 1933: an elegant structure in cantilevered concrete and plate glass, of—given the genre—remarkable felicity. It clearly influenced Patterson and Broom's 1935 Art Deco version in East London Street. John Begg designed showrooms and offices for Westfield Autocar on the corner of the Craigs, Stirling in 1935; a great brick building with sweeping corners, which is as lacking in superficial style as the Spence building, but lacking in some of the flair as well. A G R Mackenzie's 1937 showrooms for John Jackson

Sighthill Garage. Note flagpole, clock and strip windows.

Art Deco for Alfas in Angle Park, Edinburgh.

Dick

(now SMT), Bon Accord Street, Aberdeen is a formal composition of considerable grace. Its side façade consists of a central, glazed tower with streamlined, curved-window wings; and its entrance is through an Art Deco tower with attached clock, vertical strip windows and curved doorway. The 1937 SMT garage, Salkeld Street, Glasgow, possibly designed by James Miller (and which was ironically transformed into the Horse Mounted Police headquarters for Strathclyde, and losing some of its detail in the process), features a corner stair tower and entrance, flagpole, and strips of window on either side.

Even today, after the destruction of many garages, and the mutilation of many more, it is still possible to spot many traces of Thirties survivors: the flat, white façade to the repair building, often capped with a stepped, horizontal-shaped pediment; the occasional flagpole; the white-painted screen walls; and the concrete canopy.

Above. Built for cars, now used for horse-mounted police: SMT garage. Salkeld Street, Glasgow.
Right. Note the adventurous canopy above the pumps, designed by a youthful George Lawrence.
Below. John Jackson's garage, Bon Accord Street, Aberdeen (1937), by A G R Mackenzie.

Brogden

RIAS Collection

ROADHOUSES

The majority of new Thirties roadhouses and hotels seem to be linked to the growth in car traffic and touring. How else can one explain the growth of hotels with car parks on the new main routes to the north, to the western Highlands, to the the north east, and to the linking roads between? Even were it not so, contemporary hotel design itself tends to confirm a link, since the style usually adopted was one of streamlining, or "moderne".[158] The distinction between hotels and roadhouses is probably that the latter were usually built sufficiently close to larger urban centres as not to require any hotel bedrooms. Those which offered accommodation should be considered as the Thirties equivalents of the old coaching inns. Sometimes, where the roadhouse was large and rural, or the hotel very small, the distinction between them was blurred.

White House

Wheatsheaf, Saughton.

The roadhouse was a new animal. Scotland was short in what might be called the English "inn": there seems to have been a gap between the grand Victorian hotel and the drinking "howff" with sawdust on the floor. One of the new "roadhouses", close to the centre of Edinburgh was the White House, Niddrie Mains Road, 1936, designed by W Innes Thompson. It was built for Mrs G H Gair, with the same explicit purpose according to her daughter, as the Maybury, the Robin's Nest and the Hillend Roadhouse: "the idea was to improve the image of public houses, and to supply meals and games, such as skittles, and other entertainment, in addition to the drink to the patrons".[159] That encapsulates their clientèle very well. They were not catering for those who drove Rolls Royces, Bentleys or Daimlers, Minervas or Packards and went to the stately hotels (if to hotels at all). They catered, rather, for the upwardly mobile, the top echelon of which would drive the new fashionable SS Roadster (regarded as not quite the thing by the upper classes). The style had to be smart, to match. The motorist, in short, created his own ambience.

The Wheatsheaf, Saughton, Edinburgh was designed by Robert Matthew in 1934, and considered by contemporaries to be redolent of the Home Counties. The "pub" influence can be seen in the long sweeping roofs, and general air of cosiness: but a study of the sculpture attached to the chimney stack reveals hitherto unknown Art Deco tendencies in its architect.

McKean

The White House, Craigmillar.

158 An exception to this general pattern is the idiosyncratic Oakwood Motel, by Elgin, whose adoption of a "rustic" imagery is taken to the lengths of the log cabin, with split and unsplit logs and wooden shingles. It was designed in 1932 by Dougal and Andrew Duncan, Dougal having spent some time in Canada. It became quite the place for Sunday afternoon tea.

159 Letter to the author.

Transgraphics

RIAS Collection/James Wood

Top right. The *Hillburn*. The stairs to the bowling alley. T Bowhill Gibson. The exterior shows it in pristine form. *Above*. The *Delmore*, Inverness. *Right*. Newhouse Hotel.

In 1937, Edwin Muir travelled from Kilmarnock to Glasgow: "the petrol stations along the roadside steadily thicken; and beside one of them I found, but did not recognise at first a little country tearoom to which I had often walked out from Glasgow on Sundays fifteen years ago, quite a long walk then. I stopped for old times sake and ordered tea. The little house was quite changed; new rooms had been added; and it was now so obviously a place of call for motorists and not for walkers, I was almost afraid to ask the proprietress about certain of my old acquaintances whom I had once met there. They seldom came now, she told me: one does not walk for miles, over fields and moorlands, to join a rush of motorists"[160].

The architecture of the White House, although excoriated by Reiach and Hurd as "vulgar and trashily smart",[161] was a client choice. Mrs Margaret Hendry explains its origins:

It was one of several designs submitted by the architect. My mother preferred the traditional designs, and I now regret my influencing her towards the "modern" one. I was studying for my Highers at the time, and was full of ideas about buildings displaying the new construction methods in their outward appearance. Applied Art was one of my subjects! Unfortunately, the flat roof gave easy access to those who lived by breaking and entering.[162]

The Hillburn, by T Bowhill Gibson, conceals its modernity beneath a green glazed pantiled roof, and a brown ochre skin: but was clearly flash enough, near to a suburb of Edinburgh that was expanding during the Thirties. That there were other roadhouses throughout Scotland that attracted considerable attention is clear from the comment of visitors to the RIBA Conference in 1935: "the roadhouses are a credit to the country"; and toward the end of the decade they became increasingly flash. Witness the Delmore Roadhouse, Inverness, the 1938 Newhouse Hotel, and the Silver Link Roadhouse at Kincardine Bridge whose speciality was (*O tempora! O mores*) "Dancing every Sunday afternoon and evening".[163]

160   Muir, op. cit.

161   Reiach and Hurd: *Building Scotland* (Saltire 1940).

162   Letter to author.

163   Advertisement in *SMT Magazine*. August 1938.

McKean

Swan

By far the most splendid survivor of this group is the Maybury, situated at what used to be called Edinburgh Turnpike. The Maybury was introduced to the public in 1935 as a "new form of Inn" by the Edinburgh firm of Patterson and Broom, in the shape of a long, white limousine entered through a tower representing a car's radiator grill realised in concrete. Details are Art Deco, particularly the light fittings and the use of walnut veneer, and it is considerably better of its time and type than the North British hotel is of late Victorian railway hotels. The entrance tower is constructed of mass concrete, and contains within it a double-height entrance hall with a double sweeping staircase, like a miniature set for Busby Berkeley movie. Balcony lights are contained within grotesque mask heads. The long projecting wing, including some significant Art Deco fittings, contains a ballroom with an upper balcony running around the top from which people could dine looking down over the dancers below. Double glass doors open from this balcony onto a large semi-circular cantilevered balcony. In their employment of mass concrete, the architects displayed a more wholehearted awareness of modern trends than was the norm in Scotland. The original plans provided for games on the flat roof.[164]

Adam

Adam

The *Maybury*, Edinburgh, probably the finest of all Scottish roadhouses.

McKean

164   Ex info Anne Riches.

Marine Hotel, Oban, 1936, by James Taylor.

Transgraphics

HOTELS

"I think it is rather ominous that the new style should be so very popular with hotel keepers and with cinema companies, neither of whom are very ascetic in their character". Sir John Stirling Maxwell

The Thirties was not a great hotel building age, possibly because Scotland was well stocked with Victorian and Edwardian hotels for main city provision. A number of them were extended, supplemented by the creation of a slightly larger number of new ones, mostly in the countryside on the main routes, taking advantage of the new road traffic.[165] Dunoon, Rothesay, Oban and Fort William experienced considerable hotel activity. The Thirties does not seem to have required any new function from hotels, save possibly the provision of car parks. But the attractions of fresh air and the broad outdoors can be interpreted from the construction of sun rooms with roof terraces above, lounges with a view, roof gardens, dining rooms with projecting semi-circular glazed bays, balconies and separate function suites. Otherwise, the Thirties hotel may be regarded as an existing building form dressed up in more modern clothing, the function rooms re-arranged to cater for the new preoccupations.

The demolished Pantiles, in West Linton, by Leslie Graham Thomson was an elegant, sweeping V-plan building, with semi-circular drum towers at each apex, but rendered domestic by the pitched roof. Drumossie, by Inverness, is a great long, downhill sweep of a buiilding, entered through a 3-storeyed, curved tower protruding from the front. Laird and Napier designed the Bay Hotel, Gourock, opened in May 1938, to attract visitors from the Empire Exhibition, its key features a tall, glazed stair tower and

The formerly green and white Bay Hotel, Gourock.

165 The new Queen's Hotel, Perth, for example, advertised itself specifically as "an ideal centre for tourist at the gateway to the Highlands" (SMT Magazine).

Transgraphics

David Brown

Northern Hotel, Aberdeen.

a roof garden with views over the Clyde to Cowal. The function rooms on the first floor are identified by a brick band, whereas the ground floor street façade was given over to a bank, shops and the hotel garage. The cocktail bar was "strikingly modern". A more wholehearted version of the "nautical" style in hotels is to be found in the unlikely location of the shore in Oban—the former Marine Hotel, 1936, designed by James Taylor. A 4-storey block with flanking ground-floor wings with curved windows, it has roof-terraces with tubular rails, and two tall flanking towers with corner windows oddly reminiscent of those in the Hoover factory, London. The rear façade is modern in a wholly different idiom of brick geometrics. The Cnoc-na-Faire Hotel, Arisaig can be seen for miles: a small square rectangle of brilliant white set against the heather. On closer inspection, it maintains its imagery until the twin chimneys and linking roof peeping behind the front proclaim the fact that this hotel is an extension of an original croft. The Grampian Hotel, Dalwhinnie is a rare survivor, for its spartan interior implies a faithfulness to the original intention. Its various parts have been arranged according to modern expression: the lounge with a semi-circular glazed bay window looking over the hills to the west and the dining room, at the other end of the block, a similar to the east. The space between is occupied by a filled-in sunroom with a terrace on top. A squat stair tower dominates.

The Northern Hotel, Kittybrewster by A G R Mackenzie, 1937, was the most fashionable hotel in the north-east in its day, and presents a round-ended four-storey, flat roofed stump, with long strip windows boxed out in darker masonry, and a continuous balcony along the first floor level to indicate the location of the ballroom. It illustrates how granite block was not a material to which the Thirties' aesthetic lent itself. The proportions seem somehow foreshortened, as though it should really have been either longer or taller, or have some other commanding feature, to realise its own design potential.

Of the humbler sort, the Station Hotel, Grangemouth, is a 3-storey pavilion to end a row of shops, the ground floor of the entire row faced with pleasantly banded stonework. The entrance is on the rounded corner, distinguished by the tall windows with Art Deco details above. It implies the hand of Matthew Steel. A hotel of a different sort is the Transportel behind Tesco's in Perth. Now in a rather sorry state, it was constructed by the Railway Company as overnight lodging rooms for train drivers: and despite its current gloomy colours, the building has a geometric precision in the arrangment of its masses that catches the eye.

The most notable of the Thirties hotels was the Beresford Hotel, Sauchiehall Street, Glasgow (now Strathclyde University's Baird Halls of

Beresford Hotel, Glasgow.

Weddell and Thomson

J G Lindsay Pate

Far left. Grampian Hotel, Dalwhinnie. *Left*. McColl's Hotel, Dunoon. *Bottom*. Drumossie Hotel, Inverness.

Residence): named after its architect W Beresford Inglis, director of the client Glasgow Hotels Ltd. The only new Glasgow hotel to greet the Empire Exhibition, 1938, it opened with only weeks to spare. It is a very large building, constructed against a steep hillside and a tight programme: seven storeys plus entresol. It cost the truly gigantic sum of £180,435.0d.[166] The façade is ten bays wide, plus two prominent, semi-circular projecting bay windows. "I determined to introduce the colours and lines of the cinema", wrote Inglis; "it was easy to arrive at a faience front instead of stone, and then to select a combination of colours that would attract attention".[167] A number of architectural devices have been used to minimize the hotel's bulk, the most important being the fins, originally scarlet and black, which streak up the main front and the east façade. The twin bay windows rise right up beyond the roofline and end in drum towers, originally capped by flagpoles. Faint, etched detailing indicates pilasters at the corner of the building: and there is an indication of a cornice above the seventh floor. The details—particularly the radiator grills, the rainbow arch, and some of the stairway—are somewhere between Art Deco and moderne: whilst the interiors as a whole veer towards streamlining.[168] The decorative intentions are thought through to the tiniest detail. Fashion being what it is, were the Beresford to be restored from its current use as a hall of residence back to a Thirties hotel in central Glasgow, it would probably be a tremendous success.

[166] Plus £13,000 furnishings. An updated total cost would be in the order of just under £4 million. Inglis sold the Boulevard cinema, Knightswood, to George Singleton to raise capital for the Beresford. Singleton found him "curious". He told Singleton that he could no longer stand the pressures of running a cinema, the booking of films etc. Once the hotel was running, Inglis met Singleton again, and complained about the pressures of bookings, the cooks, the management, and running hotels generally. He had thought running cinemas was bad, but this was much, much worse.

[167] Article in *Building Industries* (April 1938). p 21.

[168] Lounge furniture was in bleached oak upholstered in blue, with fawn walls; the Ladies Retiring Room in lavender with a "misty feature" on the walls. The Lounge had walnut woodwork with furnishings of crushed strawberry and blue spot with walls of orange, copper columns, splattered with red, and an apple green ceiling. (*Building Industries*)

J Alexander

PAVILIONS

Pavilions and ice rinks were built by the authorities as commercial ventures. Swimming pools and playing fields, by contrast, had a social purpose since the Government accepted that swimming and games formed an essential part of its health campaign, and made grants available for their provision. Competitions for leisure Pavilions in Rothesay, Prestwick, Dunoon and Gourock represented, by contrast, an attempt by those resorts to stem the drain of their traditional clientèle, liberated in their choice of resort by the

The competition-winning Rothesay Pavilion, 1936, by James Carrick.

RIAS Carrick Collection

arrival of cars. Cragburn, Gourock won by James Carrick in competition in 1935, provided dance halls/function suites and tearooms. Architecturally comparable to some of the later cinemas, it is a chunky composition of white rectangular shapes, massing towards the main entrance, (the brickwork on the outside a post-war accretion). Its sad condition must be evidence that Gourock has continued to lose that type of holidaymaker. The 1936 Rothesay Pavilion was won by Carrick in competition because of the emphasis he placed upon its dance hall. A rectangular dance hall/auditorium formed the main bulk of the building, with a huge, glazed, semi-circular buffet (now cafe) cantilevered out from the first floor, a roof terrace, and covered terraces with a canopy above. Now enclosed in glass on the ground floor, this series of glass cylinders, in contrast to the rectangle behind, seems to be a tribute to the finest of all such seaside pavilions—that at Bexhill, recently completed by the architects Erich Mendelsohn and Serge Chermayeff. Rothesay lacks the Bexhill's long white sweep, and uses its semi-circular glazed tower to house the buffet instead of the stair. The brilliantly coloured stairs are themselves grand. Rothesay Pavilion offered the Glasgow holidaymaker an experience at the forefront of style in Scotland.

McKean

Left. Kirkcaldy Ice Rink, by Williamson and Hubbard, Murrayfield. *Below.* The Murrayfield Ice Rink, by Dunn and Martin.

ICE RINKS

Ice Rinks share with cinemas the need for a prominent, nightlit, welcoming entrance fronting an even larger, single-storey undistinguished shed. Neither promoters nor architects seem to have been worried about the absence of a coherent form for this type of building. Most larger local authorities produced a rink, sometimes with a plain Art Deco pediment front (as in Perth), sometimes in brilliant colour and "moderne" streamlining (as in blue-lined Kirkcaldy by Williamson and Hubbard 1937), and sometimes with vivid neon strips as in James Carrick's Ayr. One infers a sense of civic competition in the fact that the now demolished Ayr ice rink was held out as having both the widest span and the grandest facilities. Dundee, (1937) by William Wilson, is more carefully Art Deco and, thereby, old-fashioned. Wilson and Wilson's rink for Falkirk (1938) was a coherent, self-conscious, two storey rectangle, with a glazed semi-circular bay in the middle: but oddly puts the entrance on one side. In addition to the usual club and changing rooms, facilities at Falkirk included a lounge, restaurant, milk bar and shop. J B Dunn's Edinburgh Ice Rink at Murrayfield (1938), probably the largest of all, has portholes, projecting bows and like tricks; but is fundamentally of the same type, and in urgent need of a new white coat. The Lanarkshire ice-rink near Motherwell, by Jack Coia and Warnett Kennedy, is something of an enigma from its drawings. Such information as survives implies a determined effort by the architects to integrate the façade with the rink behind; but the War caused the project to be put on ice.

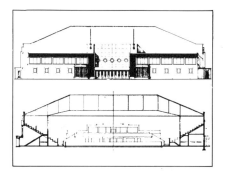

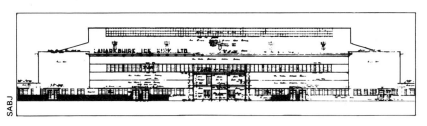

SABJ

The Lanarkshire Ice Rink, by Gillespie Kidd and Coia (unfortunately never built) is an attempt to integrate the skating barn with the façade. Skating and dancing never had invested in them the quantity of money or quality of materials available to cinemas.

Swan

SWIMMING POOLS

The ordinary enclosed Swimming Baths, unconnected with other developments, was something of a rarity in the Thirties. The Edwardian period had stocked the country well with such provision. There were exceptions, a noble one being the great granite box of the Justice Mill Lane Baths in Aberdeen (from 1932); and as late as 1940 Kilmarnock was equipping itself with a new pool with a fancy wave machine, and a brick façade that would have done justice to a new factory. Generally, however, indoor pool developments of the Thirties were tied to grander civic aspiration.

In 1933, Mervyn Noad won the competition for a new civic campus at Prestwick, comprising Municipal Offices, Pavilion and Baths surrounding a public garden and band stand. The only connection between the Concert Hall, the Baths, the Public Library and the Council Offices was the paymaster. The architecture was a blank form of Swedish classicism, with tall vertical windows for the Council Chamber, and more appropriate horizontal windows everywhere else. The scheme was never built. Two years later Coatbridge held a competition for a Baths linked to what we would now call a Health Centre. Won by James Davidson and Son, the winning scheme also used the two buildings to form a courtyard in architecture similar to Noad's: the one building contained Baths, changing and clubrooms and laundry, and the other rooms for opticians, dentists, doctors, Health Visitors, and for treatment. It was the link between swimming and health made manifest.

The principal swimming innovation, inter-war, was the encouragement of·the Open-Air Pool: more bracing times for families inured to the elements by.the open-air schools, recycled into chilly dormitory suburbs at eight houses per acre, and encouraged to go hiking into the brisk north. The fashion caught. Places like North Berwick and Stonehaven used their open-air pools as the principal feature in their holiday marketing, and comparable pools could be found in places as various as Burntisland, Arbroath, Saltcoats and Portobello.

The simplest version of the open-air pool consisted of a pool, enclosed by a screen—solid to land, railings to sea, changing rooms and showers being contained in a pavilion at the entrance. The pool would be surrounded by terraces (their edges painted white) a white diving board, and tubular rails.

The king of them all was the stately Portobello pool, completed in 1936 to the admiration of all. A D Mackie, describing Edinburgh for visitors to the Empire Exhibition, listed the Pool as the fifth wonder of modern Edinburgh, along with Holyrood, the Castle and the Zoo. Designed by Ian Warner in

RIAS/Scott Sutherland Scrapbook

Top. Portobello swimming pool as first built.
Above. The launch of T Scott Sutherland and the Justice Mill baths in Aberdeen. Note the one-legged swimming costume.

the office of W N MacArtney, Edinburgh City Engineer, Portobello was no ordinary pool. It was designed to the then Olympic specifications, with seating accommodation for 6000 spectators, and lockers for 1284 bathers. The pool was 1.13 acres in extent, and the scale of ancillary provision is impressive even by today's standards. There was a snack bar, restaurant, lounge hall, open air tea gardens and rest rooms. The pool was equipped with the first wave-making machinery in Scotland. Two young (but later prominent) engineers cut their teeth on the pool, James Shiell and George Geddes. Their entire remuneration consisted of tram tokens. Emanating as it did from an engineer's office, its most impressive festures were those of engineering—the construction of the pool itself, the method of heating the sea water, the elegant concrete cantilever above the west stand, and the even more splendid five-tier diving platform. Its architecture fell foul of Reiach and Hurd in *Building Scotland*; for the architecture was, for its date, away behind the engineering. The northern spectators entrance block was old-fashioned, symmetrical Art Deco—with a square pediment, Art Deco clock, and green and yellow tilework. The Pool survives yet, magnificent in its dereliction; and an excellent candidate for proper re-use.

Penilee Sports Pavilion, by J Steel Maitland.

PAVILIONS AND CLUBHOUSES

Garscadden Sports Pavilion, by T Harold Hughes as first built.

Vast numbers of pavilions and club houses were constructed, from scout huts to memorial sports pavilions, the majority in timber and some of an ugliness scarcely believable.

Those with aspirations beyond a wooden shack probably faced new playing fields or golf courses, and were usually traditional ("and is there honey still for tea?")—pitched roof, cupola and verandah. Modernism made some rare inroads: chunky white buildings plentifully supplied with balconies and railings (e.g. Lowmoss, by Lenzie, and Musselburgh Golf Club); or buildings in which the cupola was replaced by a squat, clock-bearing, square tower of the Dudok type as, for example, in Robert Gordon's Pavilion, Aberdeen

David Brown

Swan

Top. Aberdeen University Pavilion by
A G R MacKenzie. *Above.* Devonvale Hall,
Tillicoultry, by Arthur Bracewell.

and Pitreavie Pavilion, Dunfermline. Steel Maitland's elegant, curved staired Penilee Pavilion, Paisley, is possibly the best of the former; whilst Garscadden Sports Pavilion, Glasgow, designed by Professor T Harold Hughes in 1936 is an outstanding version of the latter. The sleek modernism of Garscadden is a distinct oddity in the corpus of Hughes' works. It is an excellent little building (whose neglect should make the university blush), two wings of changing rooms radiating from the central pillared, glazed bow (a tearoom and lounge). The plain tower above contains the stair to the caretaker's flat, and the clock above conceals the water tank. The contrast between solid and void, black and white, horizontal and vertical, rectangle and circle are all exemplified.

The Aberdeen University Sports Pavilion by A G R MacKenzie 1939 eschews the more overt stylisms of the earlier building in favour of utterly classical proportions, design and layout. The principal rooms are on a fully glazed first floor, a *piano nobile*, reached up a double flight of steps: the centre of the building emphasized by an oversailing canopy, capped by a slightly projecting cornice. It is not only a sports pavilion, but a sports complex complete with swimming pool and squash courts; and is one of the purest examples of modern architecture in Scotland.

5 ■ EATING, DRINKING AND BUYING

SHOULD ARCHITECTURE BE TAUGHT IN OUR SCHOOLS? It would certainly give laymen an architectural vocabulary and make them conversant with our terminology. Quite recently an architect entered a certain restaurant and asked to be shown the Mackintosh frieze. Great was his surprise when he was handed the cold menu, and was told that the ices were ''off'' to-day.

The Quarterly

RIAS Quarterly

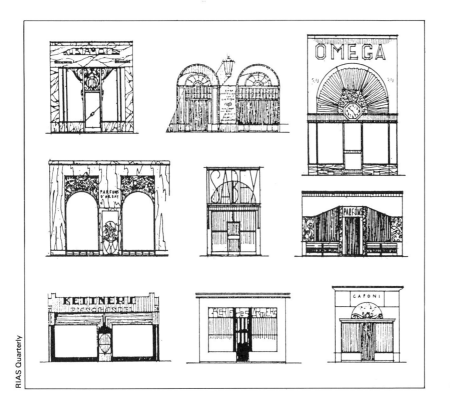

Drawings by Robert Rennie of various shop fronts of 1933 in London and Paris.

The architecture of restaurants, pubs, tearooms, cafes and shops has this in common: the notion of street architecture. What matters—and all that matters—is the street front at pavement level. They could be carved out from older buildings, or contained within purpose-designed brand-new ones as necessary. Visual impact was all: they relied upon the glamour, glitter and seduction of the façade to entice the client to enter and be parted from his pounds. That said, there was a fundamental difference between shops and the rest. Pubs, restaurants, tearooms and cafes (with rare exceptions like Nardini's and the Moorings, Largs) required only a façade: the interior could be concealed by that façade and be of a wholly different character. A shop, by contrast was selling not so much image as the product. Shop design, therefore, concentrated on making that façade as transparent and invisible as possible, putting both the product and the interior on display.

TEAROOMS

There was some re-modelling of tearooms, but not much. Scotland was well supplied with them already (Miss Cranston's in Glasgow for example). Indeed, the dominance of that social habit attracted much amused comment:

> the tearoom is an institution of Edinburgh, a convention through which the middle and upper-middle classes express themselves . . . the effect these places are designed to produce is one of luxury, and the more select of them strive for an impression of adroitly muffled silence . . . into this silence the discreet sounds of the radio may be safely decanted, whereas that is a controlled and deliberate noise . . . the luxury is intended to build up a deception, to lead the hypnotically blissful tea drinker to the mistaken conclusion that here is something as good as the richest and most leisured can enjoy.[169]

A peculiarity of tearooms was that they were often attached to shops, and frequently upstairs—and thus had little architectural personality of their own. So although MacVities produced a major new tearoom in Castle Street, Edinburgh, like others it was upstairs and therefore almost invisible. The Carron Tearoom in Stonehaven, pushed out into the garden as a rear extension to the Co-op, is a rare example in unused but good state of survival: bulbous brick bow, Art Deco glass and metal work, and a terrace.

RESTAURANTS

Few restaurants of the Thirties survived the compulsion to redesign and follow fashion after the War. One of them is Rogano's, Buchanan Street, Glasgow designed by Weddell and Inglis in 1935 (recently rehabilitated with the removal of its shop front by the successor firm Weddell and Thomson). It was, and is, a fish restaurant and celebrated Oyster Bar: hence its image is conveyed by a yellow vitrolite fascia with the name superimposed in green "broadway" lettering, enlivened by a scarlet lobster. The plinth is black with strips of chrome. It is simple, with very little applied style in the sense of Art Deco detail. Yet the sleek skin contains an interior of unexpected richness: bar and open restaurant above, with cubicles below.

The cafés: the *Derby*, Glasgow *(top)* sports geometric ornament. The *Central*, Saltmarket *(above)* retains glass etched in "Broadway" lettering. The *Carron* restaurant, Stonehaven *(right)* has the finest Art Deco patterned glazing surviving (precariously) in Scotland.

"There are also the tea shops, where ladies refresh themselves after an hour of shopping. The consumption of cream buns is enormous; eclairs die in thousands; chocolate biscuits melt away as in thaw. It is perhaps not a wonderful thing that there are so many comfortable ladies in Glasgow when they do themselves so well in the afternoon". J R Allan (*Scotland 1938*)

[169] Muir. op. cit.

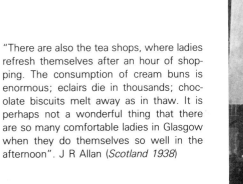

Cafés, ice cream parlours and milk bars provided the restaurants for the people, and were far more widely spread throughout Scotland than purpose-built restaurants. Few Scottish communities were without their "tally-ally", and perhaps because they have continued to provide superlative, pre-artificial flavoured, unwhipped, uncoloured, crunchy Italian ice cream mixed with skimmed milk, many survive almost unaltered. The kit of parts is similar of those used by restaurants. Cafes were generally lodged within existing buildings, identified by long fascias in pastel coloured plastic material (generally yellow, pink or green, which seem to be colours associated with health and freshness) although the smarter cafes in city areas opted for glass etched with Art Deco motifs or lined with chrome strips. The large window displayed arrays of ice cream cones, tubs, sweets or notices. Fashion was satisfied with more chrome used for streamlining particularly on the doors. The interior was generally fresh and usually spartan.

Moorings, Largs.

There were exceptions, three of the most prominent being on the Clyde coast estuary. The Cafe, Main Street, Prestwick, was an entirely new, two-storey construction, whose most prominent feature was not its shop front but the huge cut-away semi-circular window on the first floor. Largs, however, provided two cafes of an altogether different order: not surprisingly perhaps, in a town which aspired to have its cinema represented as a Viking galley.

Nardini's, Largs: an ice-cream roadhouse.

Nardini's, 1935, was designed by C Davidson and Sons as a milk-based roadhouse, with shops, a cafe, a restaurant, and plentiful dairy ice cream, in a vigorous white building which seemed plastered with the stuff. It certainly had style: old-fashioned Art Deco style, with recessing buttresses, entrance doorways and flagpoles not dissimilar to the front of certain contemporary factories along the Great West Road in London. The interior maintains much Thirties atmosphere in its glass, its openness and the atmosphere of a palm court. The Moorings was designed as a super-cafe and restaurant in 1935 by James Houston, and bore the same relationship to cafes as super cinemas did to the picture house. It cost its owner, Mr Castelvecchi the princely sum of £15,000, and was originally designed as

Boundary Bar, Springburn, by W B Inglis.

170 Rudolph Kenna:*Glasgow Art Deco* (Drew 1985).

a two-storey boat, with roof deck and viewing platform. The corner of the building is cut away so as to "read" as a ship's prow to those approaching Largs from Arran by the ferry. A subsequent addition of a ballroom on top has rather spoiled the original concept: and the post-war profusion of signs conceal an inherent quality of design. Long balconies with tubular railings, portholes, sweeping windows outlined in chrome, and other Art Deco details raises the Moorings to one of the best examples of its type in Scotland.

PUBS

Few Thirties pubs survive. After 1936, there seems to have been a considerable expansion in their numbers and, for the first time, some began to provide for wives and indeed for children. Most have now been altered beyond recognition; some (like a few by Sam Bunton in Glasgow)[170] being no loss. However, note might be taken of James Taylor's flashy Thornwood in Partick whose garish yellow and red vitrolite fascia, and chrome is as good of its type as Rogano's.

Right. Thornwood Bar, Partick, by James Taylor.

SHOPS

Shops, like restaurants, are peculiarly vulnerable to the whims of fashion and retailing, and have a short life. So few Thirties examples survive intact; and those that do retain traces of their Thirties design, are usually food shops—small, narrow-fronted greengrocers, dairies, fruiterers, butchers and fish shops. To have survived at all implies that they were, perhaps, neither the most fashionable, nor in the most fashionable location. Most of them wished simply to broadcast how clean and fresh they were with large plate windows, simple fascias and lettering, and a black vitrolite or marble plinth. Perhaps the most complete survivor is Roberts fishmongers in Leith Walk. Clothes shops, by contrast, had to tempt customers within to inspect variety and to try on samples; lured in by the transparency of glittering windows, showcases and clever lighting, enhanced by the use of glass block: and double (or treble) height space inside where appropriate, joined by sweeping curved staircases. A new spare elegance had replaced the rich clutter of Edwardian shops.

Such illustrations as survive of the grander Thirties shops show little use of Art Deco detail but a concentration, instead, upon the effective use of light and glass, in counterpoint to the lettering in the shop's fascia. "Night

RIAS Collection

McKean

RIBA Library

McKean

architecture" seems to have been just as important to shops as it was to cinemas: the difference being that whereas the night architecture of the cinema was usually a neon-lit façade, that of shops was the illuminated interior shining through a transparent façade. (A suspicious number of shops illustrated in the architectural press of the time were illustrated by a night-time view.)

STORES AND WAREHOUSES

Stores and warehouses were usually large buildings, requiring maximum uncluttered space and flexibility. They were thus particularly suited to a wide-span, steel-framed structure. In city centres—particularly in a notable collection of warehouses concentrated in the Merchant City of Glasgow, by Thomson, Sandilands and MacLeod (1927–30)—these buildings were usually very tall, narrow and plain, vertical in emphasis. In smaller communities, they would be lower—usually two storeys, and longer; with the consequent horizontal emphasis. Where they differed one from the other was in how they exploited the elements of the steel framed building to convey whatever image they wished on the exterior. The legacy of the Twenties, almost identical for offices as for stores, was a partially exposed steel frame, the

Left. Jaeger, Glasgow. *Left above. Cockburn's* chemist, Glasgow, by Launcelot Ross. *Top. Findlay's* fishmonger, Brechin, in plain two-tone. *Middle. Roberts*, fishmonger, Leith. *Above. Dobbies'* shop front – when it was in Shandwick Place.

95

Copeland and Lye, 1934 extension, by Launcelot Ross.

RIAS Collection

Arnott's, Paisley.

Carson/Hunter

principle structural members faced with some form or other of decorative stonework. Depending upon the grandeur of the building, that stonework could be classical with columns; it could have Art Deco motifs, or it could be utterly plain. As the decade progressed, the facings became thinner and the metal structure more and more prominent: culminating in the St Cuthbert's Co-operative showroom wherein, between the first scheme and the final result, the facing stonework was dropped altogether in preference for a façade clear of any superimposition whatsoever.

Not all stores used stonework: there was an increasing use of brick and a prevalence of faience particularly in the chain stores. C & A's, Sauchiehall Street, Glasgow (1930) by North Robin and Wildson, before its current recladding, demonstrated the ease to which faience lent itself to Art Deco details, finials, ribs and other jazzy accretions. Buildings on corner sites usually emphasised that corner by a form of tower, the entrance, more often than not, being located beneath. Apart from the lettering on the shop signs, the final element of the architectual vocabulary of such buildings was the treatment of the metal spandrels between the stone cladding. These metal bays were usually recessed, and the spandrels decorated with Art Deco motifs and painted (Binns brown, Burtons blue). Some architects, however, adopted a more aggressive attitude towards these metal bays, and pushed the windows out in 1, 2 or 3 storey metal bays, a motif which some attributed to the projecting library windows of the Glasgow School of Art. These angular glass bay windows can be seen in Watt Brothers, Bath Street (1930) a slightly unadventurous composition by Graham Henderson of Keppie Henderson, in C & A's itself, and in Arnotts, Paisley, by James Steel Maitland.

Burton's, Paisley.

Copeland's interior.

Marks and Spencer, Sauchiehall Street, as it was in 1937.

With the exception of Binns (now Frasers) Princes Street, Edinburgh, few new carriage-trade stores were built between the Wars although some, such as R W Forsyths and Copeland and Lye, were extended significantly. The principal change was the arrival of the chain store, notably Woolworths, Burtons and Marks and Spencer. The two former employed their own architects, those in Woolworths adopting a cautious cinema-style in faience, with fins rising above a standard fascia. Burtons was more experimental, their house architect N Martin using a stone clad metal frame, the metal infil between usually painted blue. The Paisley branch in faience has twin columns with Art Deco capitals, the parapet above decorated with Art Deco motifs and a curling anthemion leaf. Marks and Spencer, who expanded in Scotland after 1936, employed Robert Lutyens (Sir Edwin's son) to design a faintly neo-classical composition of three tall, two-storey windows above the main fascia, with smaller ones on either side. The parapet followed suit. In Scotland, Marks and Spencer's executive architect was James Munro and Son, and possibly the best surviving example of those schemes can be seen in Murraygate, Dundee.

The only Scots-based organisation with a substantial building programme was—if the disparate companies may be lumped together—the Co-operative movement, which only renders their current loss of direction, and contraction that much the sadder. New Co-op shops, stores or warehouses appeared in most Scots communities, many designed by the SCWS architect, Cornelius Armour.

Binns (now Frasers) was designed by J R MacKay in 1934, to terminate the West End of Princes Street: and it was probably the grandest of all Thirties stores. Its classical clothing and proud flagpole have been

Binn's, Edinburgh.

McKean

attributed to the imperial leanings of its expected clientèle.[171] Rather, it is an inappropriate translation of Thomas Tait's Daily Telegraph, Fleet Street, London (1927) to a cramped corner site in Edinburgh, with the result that the building seems rather dumpy than tall, the elements of the tower in the chamfered tower unconvincing, and its main floors squeezed rather than properly horizontal. J G Callander's Falkirk Co-operative (1937), on a similar corner site but two storeys lower, is positively anachronistic for such a late date. It has considerably more horizontal style than Binns, and is entered through a robust tower decorated with Mayan Art Deco details, repeated at the end of each wing by a smaller tower. The flanks have an exposed steel frame, fronted by destylised classical columns, the whole squatting on a granite plinth. Most Co-op buildings had applied Art Deco details, such as a fattened recessing pediment (as in Lawrence Rolland's store in Leven), fluting around the doors, or patterned metal spandrels as in the grand SCWS store (1935) by Cornelius Armour in the Seagate, Dundee.

Stores shared the same need for style with shops: and the more exciting or vivid stores were built when the need to conform was least. On the other hand, the stone quality of Edinburgh's New Town seems to have had an inhibiting effect then as now. Wilkie's, Shandwick Place, Edinburgh (1936) by the successful school architects Reid and Forbes was a symmetrical Art Deco composition of some grace (although it has been altered sadly).

171 R C V Addison. Unpublished thesis (1982).

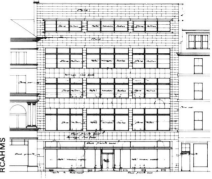

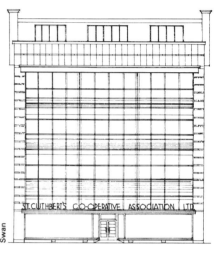

St Cuthbert's, Bread Street, Edinburgh, 1937. *Top.* The originally proposed solid façade, with the revised elevation below. *Left.* As it was completed.

Jay's store, Princes Street.

Shona Adam

Below. Abortive schemes, by Marwick's office for Sun Insurance on George Street. It took 20 years for a scheme to be approved and built.

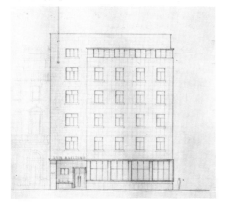

RCAHMS

Even although the façade which remains would greatly benefit from a clean, and the circular staircase survives within, it is a tame composition compared with some of the things which were going up in Glasgow—even shops such as Art Fabrics, Karters and the like in Sauchiehall Street. The timidity is even more evident in Jay's (now Burberry's) Princes Street, Edinburgh by T P Marwick and Son, 1938. The architect has opted for a solid façade of stone, with symmetrically placed windows punched through it, in keeping with the imagined solemnity of the location. The only stylistic motif (apart from the brilliantly coloured awnings which have now been removed) is the division of the façade into golden-section proportions: one third vertically proportioned to indicate the location of the staircase behind, and two-thirds horizontally proportioned to indicate the showroom floors. That division, together with the use of the flagpoles and cornices, are the only concessions to style. In the same year, Marwick used a near identical design for his proposed insurance company offices in George Street which, encountering even greater planning difficulties, was not built for a further twenty years, and even then was severely mauled.

As the inter-war period progressed, there was a clear move towards stripping the frame of its stylistic decoration. That was particularly visible in the taller and plainer warehouse buildings in central Glasgow which have already been mentioned. A slightly earlier example—and possibly the best of its type in Scotland—is the extension to Draffen's Store, Nethergate, Dundee, completed in 1935 by Thoms and Wilkie. There are no overt classical details in the stone façade, and it is so carefully detailed and well-proportioned as to create a style of architecture almost individual to itself. The ultimate development of this approach was the St Cuthbert's Showroom, Bread Street, Edinburgh (1937) designed by David (Speedy) Harvey and Philip McManus within the office of T P Marwick and Son. It was an extension of an existing Co-operative showroom in a north-facing terrace and replaced a church removed to a new housing estate. The first design was for a simple stone-fronted building with long strips of windows on each floor. The design as built was dramatically different: becoming the first building in Scotland to use a curtain-wall of glass for its façade, clear of the structure behind. Not only did this design maximise light in the north-facing street, but it also provided an excellent advertisement by day and night for the goods within, satisfying the 1930s preoccupation with three-dimensionality.

What, exactly, is the Modern Movement? Was it not the movement started only a generation ago by that remarkable Scotsman, the late Charles Rennie Mackintosh of Glasgow? Ask Continentals about this. You will find that they regard Charles Mackintosh as the arch-apostle of the modern school in architecture just as Karl Marx is regarded as the arch-apostle of communism.

John Begg, *Quarterly*, 1936

BANKS AND INSURANCE OFFICES

Branch banks share with shops the necessity to attract customers inside to transact business. But their image was much more tightly circumscribed: it could not be flibberty-jibbet. Banks had to represent the establishment, and convey a sense of security and solidity in a notoriously uncertain world: and, by Jove! did they just do that—with ponderous quantities of dead-pan classicism by such established architects as W J Walker Todd. Many small branches were refurbished or rebuilt and the bank spotter can identify them from the use of polished black marble, often polished grey granite, fluting surrounding the walnut doors, and astylar classical details (columns, antae or pilasters) in a well carved, hard new idiom, framing the windows. Later in the decade, the Savings Bank Movement became more adventurous: witness their 1938 branch in St Clair Street, Kirkcaldy by Williamson and Hubbard—a classical porch surmounted by an Art Deco fanlight, and flanked on all sides by huge metal-framed windows inviting people to look in.

Considerable invention was lavished on some of the free-standing branches, by architects such as Baird and Thomson, and Eric Sutherland. There are examples with domes and towers and one—near the Glasgow Meat Market, with a cow's head carved upon its squat corner tower. A strikingly original example is the Bank of Scotland, Johnstone, a three-storey, stone corner block, the ground floor of polished granite, and the windows of the side flank boxed out in long strips. It turns on a corner emphasised by a tall, elegant chimney. So far, so elegant. What distinguishes this little building in an otherwise undistinguished location, are the projecting first and second floor stone balconies, and the recessing of the windows behind.[172]

Main office banks shared common features with offices and insurance companies: steel-framed structures given shape and proportion by a selective classical clothing. The design would usually be symmetrical, consisting of a base or plinth—one, two or three storeys in height; which would, in turn support a columned principal storey which could rise an indefinite number of storeys up to a strong cornice. Between the columns the metal frame would be indicated by patterned metal panels, concealing each floor slab. Buildings of this kind achieved an immense, frigid grandeur, as exemplified by the competition-winning Scottish Legal Life Building, 95 Bothwell Street, Glasgow by Wylie Wright and Wylie (1927–31). It is a clever design, with a hint of a tower in each corner and, virtually, a double cornice with an attic between. James Miller's earlier Bank of Scotland, St Vincent Street, is more vertical in emphasis, with a taller plinth, and more overtly classical emphasis with its Ionic columns and pilasters. Burnet, Son and

George Wren

Above. Glasgow Savings Bank, High Street, Ayr, 1936, by Eric Sutherland.

172 The 1935 Halifax Building Society, Union Street, Aberdeen designed by David Stokes of A Marshall Mackenzie, Son and George was a rebuke to most Scottish branch banks. Large clear windows, Art Deco doors, and a curving, spacious interior of veneered wood, glass and tubular steel chairs had just the combination of style, faith in the future, and security such buildings should aspire to.

RIAS Collection

RIAS Collection

Left. Commercial Bank, Hope Street, Glasgow, by James Miller. *Above.* Elevation of the Commercial Bank in Bothwell Street.
Below. Bank of Scotland, Sauchiehall Street, by Keppie and Henderson; sculpture by Benno Schotz.

Strathclyde Archives

Dick's offices at 200 St Vincent Street (finished in 1929) has the same underlying discipline. But it is distinctly more Scottish. The entablature is without columns and, far from being curtain-wall, the windows are punched through stone. An elegant cornice surmounts the building, broken only by two corner chimney stacks. There is a distinct echo of Adelaide House in London.

Miller followed his Bank of Scotland with a Commercial Bank on the corner of West Nile and West George Streets, similar to its predecessor, but more of a unity in its carving and decorative treatment. In the same year, 1930, Keppie Henderson began work on the Bank of Scotland, Sauchiehall Street, displaying a more relaxed attitude toward the American discipline. The solid plinth takes up almost two-thirds of the entire façade, the entrance being through a cavernous semi-circular archway surmounted by sculptures by Benno Schotz. Miller followed this with another Commercial Bank, Bothwell Street, 1934–6, in which we can see now that the Scottish architects have now liberated themselves (although strongly influenced by the recently completed headquarters for the RIBA in London). The plinth has been reduced to a half storey in height: or alternatively, it could be

Opposite, top. Scottish Legal Life, Glasgow in American grand style. *Below right.* Commercial Bank, West George Street (1930), by James Miller. *Below left.* Union Bank, St Vincent Street, Glasgow, also by Miller.

"The temporary National Bank in George Street struck a blow for better architecture" Alan Reiach

read as occupying the entire façade. Behind the columns flanking the entrance, the Bank is largely curtain-walled, and liberties are thus taken with the classical discipline impossible a few years earlier.

The temporary Head Office of the National Bank of Scotland, George Street, Edinburgh (now demolished) was produced by the office of T P Marwick in 1936. Incorporating parts of an existing building on the site, this bank had a façade which Robert Hurd considered to be a direct descendant of Mackintosh's Glasgow School of Art Library.[173] The slightness of its projecting triangular windows in the five central bays, and the canopy-capped clerestorey balancing the canopy-capped ground floor produced a precise façade, miniature in comparison with its neighbours. The banking room at the rear of the building was an excellent Thirties interior in walnut curves, the curved motif being reflected in the design of the staircase.

The 1938–9 Caledonian Insurance Company, (now GRE) St Andrew Square, reveals Leslie Graham Thomson and Connell rejecting the curtain-wall, in favour of solid stone and marble. The entrance is through a black marble doorway in a chamfered corner, and the style, such as it is, is conveyed in the windows, balconies, clerestorey and green roof. It was one of three such designs by this firm[174] and reflects Thomson's predilection for Scandinavia. In 1932, he had issued his credo in the Quarterly:

National Bank of Scotland, George Street, Edinburgh (demolished).

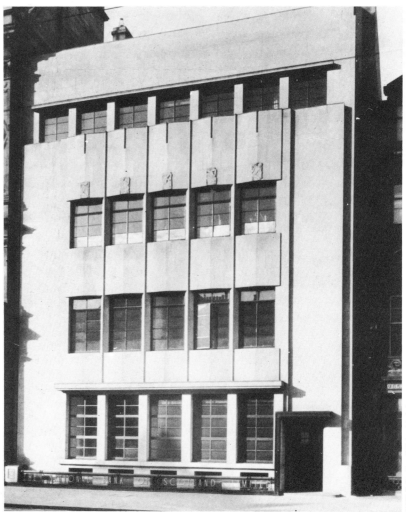

RIAS Collection/Michael Laird

[173] *Scotland 1938.* (Oliver and Boyd)

[174] The office designed very similar buildings for an unbuilt Stock Exchange, and for a YMCA in Castle Street postponed by the War.

I take it that a functional structure is one that severely limits itself to the requirements of the situation . . . but do not mistake me for a hardened anti-modernist. I am as sick as the most ardent of the perpetual use and misuse of the classic styles. I do not think that functionalism as at present practiced, is the solution of the matter. It may be the bones of new architecture, but it is only the bones; it lacks flesh and blood, needs the sweetness, in addition to the light it certainly seems to admit. The mechanistic theory, as propounded by le Corbusier and others, seems to me fallacious: the whole analogy is false, for a building is a static, and not a dynamic structure.[175]

The modernity of the Caledonian's exterior affrighted the Directors of the National Bank on the South St David Street corner, who imported Arthur Davis from London to graft stone classicism upon Thomson's Swedish skeleton.

Swan

Left. Paton and Baldwin's 1936 extension, Alloa. *Below*. Templeton's second extension, 1938: drunk?

Robertson

INDUSTRIAL OFFICES

The easy adaptability of the new framing techniques, and the availability of services, meant that some buildings which could be (and now are) used perfectly easily for offices, were originally built as industrial premises. Templeton's Carpet Factory, Glasgow Green, was extended in 1934 and 1937, to designs by George Boswell. In both cases the façade stands forward from the frame behind, and shows a touch of theatricality. That facing Bridgeton Road is composed of long bands of glass alternating with bands of white faience, tied together by a chamfered corner tower of red brick at the apex. The later extension facing Glasgow Green, which the *Architect's Journal* seems to have thought to have been drunk,[176] has similar characteristics, but with curved windows and a deep fascia patterned in brilliantly coloured tilework in homage to the Doge's Palace next door. The adaptability of these building is shown by their current use as the Templeton Business Centre. The 1936 Daily Express in Glasgow (in an inappropriate setting now that one side of Albion Street has been demolished), by Sir E Owen Williams is a long horizontal design of alternating glass windows and shiny black vitrolite.

The purest of such buildings is William Kerr's extension to Patons and Baldwins in Alloa (1934) whose six-storey building has considerable subtlety. The block is flanked by two vertical elements: the north containing larger rooms and stairs. Between those, the windows themselves diminish in height toward the top creating the impression of a cornice without there being one.

175 Presumably black marble, green tiles and colour banding provided the sweetness Thomson sought. His public did not agree. The Caledonian was generally thought to be an intrusive insult into George Street and St Andrew Square, no matter how much we appreciate it now.

176 It referred to the building as "This Arshetecture"

PUBLIC AND TOWN HALLS

Scotland did not escape, entirely, the craze for Municipal Building which flourished in England during the decade, although its effect was minor. Indeed, two of the most successful architects of English Town Hall competitions won their chance in Scotland. Bradshaw, Gass and Hope surged over Hadrian's Wall with their ponderously classical Leith Town Hall in 1932, and C Cowles-Voysey won Glasgow Corporation's competition for public halls in Bridgeton in 1931. The winning design for Leith provided a semi-circular library linked to two halls behind in bare stone classical style enriched by a rather splendid crush-hall. The Bridgeton Halls, by contrast, present a brick Byzantine façade concealing two public halls catering for cinema, dancing and committee rooms. Edinburgh only followed in 1939, with a competition for a multi-purpose series of halls for films, exhibitions and concerts in the Waverley Market, which the assessor Thomas Tait awarded to Donald Dex Harrison. The distinction of this project was the fact that very little was permitted to be visible: it was a competition for a hole in the ground.

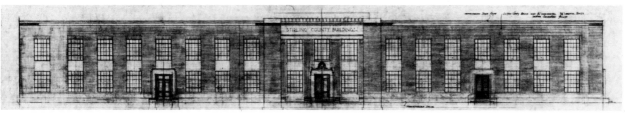

RIAS Collection

Wilson and Wilson

Above. Grangemouth Municipal Buildings by Wilson and Tait, 1935. *Top.* Stirling County Buildings: frigid brick Scandinavian, from James Miller, 1935.

Town Halls tended to be linked to larger complexes. That for Dumfries, awarded by Sir George Washington Browne to James Carruthers in 1930, provided a neo-Classical Town Hall adjacent to a public hall. Then followed Prestwick, the Town Hall and Council Chamber being part of a larger complex including a library and a swimming pool, won in 1933 by Mervyn Noad, but never built. Next to follow was Falkirk, which held a competition for an extension to its Town Hall in 1935. In remarkable contrast to Prestwick, it was won with a scheme of overt Scottish traditionalism, peppered with poorly proportioned crow-stepped gables, by J Inch Morrison and W Carruthers Laidlaw. By contrast, James Miller's substantial 1936 addition to Stirling County Buildings is a severely rational, flat-roofed red brick essay of truly Northern joylessness. Miller also provided comparable offices for Troon, whilst Sir John Burnet's design for a new Civic Centre in Dundee was modified to its detriment and eventually executed by the City engineers's architect 1929–30.[177] The largest of such was probably the competition-winning Kirkcaldy Town Hall awarded by Thomas Tait to Carr and Howard in 1937, a Swedish influenced design which contemporaries considered old-fashioned in the Thirties. It was not completed until the Fifties, by which time it was well beyond the pale; but it can now be appreciated as a building of considerable grace.

INSTITUTIONAL BUILDINGS

The two most important institutional buildings of the decade were the new Scottish Office, St Andrew's House, Regent Road, Edinburgh, designed by Thomas Tait of Sir John Burnet, Tait and Lorne, and Reginald Fairlie's National Library. The former was opened just after war was declared, and the latter almost ten years after peace broke out.

177 McKean and Walker; Dundee: *An Illustrated Introduction* (RIAS 1984).

McKean

St Andrew's House from the south.

The history behind both was fraught with political squabbles. The Government had proposed to construct a large, unlovely administrative complex including a new National Library, the Edinburgh Magistrates' Court and new offices on the side of Calton hill, designed by its own in-house architects. After much adverse publicity, it put a model of the complex on exhibition, but refused to publish any illustrations. A public service was thus done by John Summerson, who instructed College of Art student Pat Ronaldson to produce a perspective drawing of the model.[178] Ronaldson's drawing was published in *The Scotsman* to universal obloquy. The RIAS, supported by the Cockburn Association, campaigned for an open competition, a position eventually supported by Edinburgh Corporation.[179] The Scots were outraged that the designer of the proposed horror would be an English government architect, and the opposition was joined by the Government's new creature, the Royal Fine Art Commission, founded in 1927. Lobbying continued throughout 1930, the RIAS writing to all Scottish MPs on the subject.

Compromising, the Government attempted to break up the monolithic nature of the building proposed for Calton Hill by relocating the Sheriff Court House and the Library elsewhere. It dismissed the Royal Fine Arts Commission of Scotland, as a "much-over-rated body", and took the view that the Scots people would accept no scheme on that particular site. During the 1930 recess the Cockburn Association formed a national committee to fight the proposals. In October, revised plans were put before the Royal Fine Arts Commission, and rejected; and on 1 December 1930, the entire proposal was withdrawn. In 1932, John Buchan made his celebrated speech to the House of Commons, and in mid 1933, the Government held a limited selection of architects (none over the age of 55) for a new building to house "the Secretary of State's Departments". In December of that year the winner was announced as Thomas Tait.

The resulting complex is one of the finest Thirties buildings in Scotland. It consists of a large hollow square of building, with two long wings extending east and west, facing Regent Road and terminated by striking, flat-topped stair towers. Dudok's influence is particularly evident in these stair towers, and in the blue tiled window mullions to the rear; although

178 Interviews Ian Carnegie and Sir John Summerson.

179 *St Andrew's House,* Unpublished thesis by M. K. Young (1975)

Top. St Andrew's House: the principal façade once likened to an Art Deco clock. *Above.* RIBA building, London. Influential competition-winner by Grey Wornum, opened in 1934. *Right.* The National Library of Scotland.

the flat, overhanging roofs may also owe something to Frank Lloyd Wright (whom Tait is thought to have met in America).

The main entrance, and much of the interior, have much in common with the 1934 RIBA Headquarters in Portland Place, London, although different in proportion. One enters St Andrew's House as one does the RIBA, between two piers, up to a pair of superb metal doors. Although the interior plan is wholly different from the RIBA and had been predetermined by the Office of Works, the materials used for the principal corridors and the staircases are very similar, and the suite of conference rooms on the second floor strikingly so, both in their finishes and materials, and in the way partitions between rooms can be sunk into the floor to create a bigger one.

The National Library was the other symbol of Scottish patriotism, and the commission was awarded to the scholarly Dr Reginald Fairlie in 1934, to general plaudits from the profession. It was a considerably more difficult commission than St Andrew's House, and Fairlie did not have Tait's well-oiled office machine to assist him in its execution. People had cultural ambitions for the Library absent from St Andrew's House; and Fairlie endured a three-year period of political side-shuffle, as he tried to accommodate the constantly changing desires of the Scots *illuminati.*[180] His eventual solution seems to be overawed by its location on George IV Bridge; a large plain block, flanked symmetrically by two lower ones. The street façade is largely windowless, shallow, vertically proportioned panels above the plinth enlivened by didactic sculpture. The interior can only be called grand, and, yet again, seems strongly influenced by the RIBA building in its staircase, rear glazing, and door and banister details. It is still a civilised place in which to read books.

[180] Fairlie had been appointed on the recommendation of Sir Giles Scott, and his original brief was to provide a design with dignity and symmetry. That was before he had told to head down the "Greco-Gothic" path, eventually to be directed to consult Sir George Washington-Browne. (Correspondence. RCAHMS).

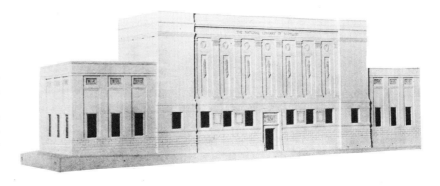

7 ∎ WORKPLACE

Satisfactory modern industrial buildings have an extreme simplicity in elevational treatment with a marked absence of fuss. *Economical building need not be mean, but building solely for cheapness without regard to design would be un-worthy.* The modern trend is towards obtaining effect by line and proportion instead of ornament, towards simplicity of design that makes for inexpensiveness.

J A Dempster, 1936

THE INDUSTRIAL CONTEXT

As was outlined in Chapter 1, the heavy industries of Scotland were in collapse during the 1930s, and the country was finding it particularly difficult to attract new industry. Between 1907 and 1935, the total output of Scotland's traditional industry (i.e. agriculture and heavy engineering) declined by 24% and that of the construction industry by 40%. By contrast, the output of the service sector increased by almost 100%.[181] Between 1932 and 1933, England and Wales experienced a net gain of 563 factories, and Scotland a net loss of 31.[182] Thus Scotland's capacity to employ people was dropping to the extent already noted that during the Second War, Scots labour was transported to England for war work. Only after 1935 did the value of construction for manufacturing rise above the lowest level of the Twenties.

The industrial condition of the country was surveyed vividly by an industrial psychologist lecturer, Charles Oakley, who in 1937 toured the country on behalf of the Scottish Economic Committee[183] observing the changes in types of factory, their location, their attitude to their workers, and their workload. It is perhaps sobering to realise that the entire industry of a country could be subsumed within one slight volume despite the fact that, judging by the size of two gigantic munitions factories in Bishopton and Irvine, rearmament was already becoming dominant. Oakley visited breweries and biscuit makers aplenty, as well as manufacturers of alloys, castings, electrical goods and surgical supplies. One particular growth industry he observed was that dealing in milk and dairy products—clearly expoiting the opportunities from school milk and the public's new concern with health and beauty. Carnation Condensed Milk had opened their Dumfries factory in 1935, and the Scottish Milk Powder Company did likewise in Kirkcudbright the same year. United Dairies followed in Kirkmichael in the next year, as did the Milk Marketing Board with a huge depot at Hogganfield, Glasgow—all designed by Alex Mair.[184] The Scottish Co-operative Wholesale Society opened creameries in Shettleston (1930s) in Dumbarton and Galashiels (1935). The SCWS was prominent in the creation of new industries during the 1930s, and again during the War—once again mainly in the service industries. In addition to creameries, they ran soapworks, furniture making factories, linoleum factories, an electric lamp making factory and canning factories. When the War arrived, they mostly went over to munitions.[185]

The industrial psychologist in Oakley was particularly interested in the increasing concern industrialists were displaying for the well-being and welfare of their employees. He approved the "special consideration that has been given to spaciousness and to environmental conditions" in the

W Dick

Weir's amenity building, Cathcart.

[181] Between 1924 and 1935, agricultural output delined by 20%, mining by 30%, manufacturing by 20%, iron and steel by 25%, engineering by 21%, textiles by 32%, food and drink by 12%, and construction by 27%: the service sector rose, however, by 30%. Harvie op. cit. page 36.

[182] G M Thomson op. cit. page 72.

[183] C A Oakley: *Scotland's Industry* (1937).

[184] Alex Mair's Mauchline Creamery was almost apocalyptic in its vision of giant white shapes dominated by an immense concrete canopy.

[185] SCWS archive.

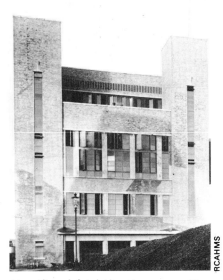

Above. **The new industrial architecture, near Alloa.**

1934 extension to Patons and Baldwins by William Kerr and found "the colour scheme in green being among the pleasantest which I have ever seen in an industrial works". The splendid new Welfare Building for Weir's of Cathcart by Wylie Wright and Wylie, right up to fashion with its clock tower and glazed curving staircase, included a library, rest-room, canteen, lounge, cinema and gymnasium. He commended Templeton's Carpet Factory in Glasgow "for the attention which they give to the well-being of their employees" and for having built a large club and a concert hall. Templeton's extended twice during the period, to complete its gigantic hollow square, with two stylish infill blocks by George Boswell.

Oakley observed a new concern with image as industrialists perceived the necessity to provide their factory with an impressive entrance or a new façade. In that respect, he was particularly taken by Morris's factory, Dobbies Loan, Glasgow, and the "handsome new entrance hall" at Thomas MacIntyre nearby.

THE INDUSTRIAL ESTATE

Although industries had always grouped around sources of power or transport, the Thirties saw the consolidation of the purpose-planned industrial estate; and the transformation of that idea into a 20th-century answer to New Lanark—the social experiment at Hillington.

An industrial colony had existed beside the Forth and Clyde canal at Anniesland since the turn of the century, but the arrival of motor transport relieved its dependence upon the canal; there was plenty of space, and a good labour supply in Glasgow's showpiece housing estate in Knightswood. It was also well-located by the new Boulevard which linked Glasgow to Clydebank and Dumbarton. Thus, when Oakley visited Anniesland in 1937, it contained—in addition to the original sawmill—the glaring new red brick factory of Barr and Stroud (optical works), loco Rubber, engineers, carbon paper manufacturers, laundries, suite manufacturers, "Collars", and dairies. The new industrial estate at Shieldhall established by the Clyde Navigation Trustees was in time largely occupied by the SCWS; but its first two oc-

Right. India of Inchinnan tyre factory by Wallis Gilbert.

cupants were a soya meal manufacturer and "Gyproc" Products. No heavy industry here. In Edinburgh, industrial estates were established at Gylemuir (the largest factory being a printing works although the main survivor, Securex, with its "storm prow", at least made dye-castings), Maybury, and Sighthill. Location near a new road, boulevard or by-pass was particularly important, but Scotland never seems to have accumulated the Thirties factories which so lined the arterial routes out of London, notably the A4 to Heathrow, the Southend arterial, and the Kingston by-pass. Consequently, that type of stylish headquarters factory is a rarity in Scotland. The exception, however, tests the rule. The splendid India of Inchinnan tyre factory by Wallis Gilbert and Partners is the country cousin of London's Hoover factory by the same architects. Opened in 1930, it had an excellent site near Renfrew Aerodrome, facing the main road from Glasgow down the coast. Even today, the quality of its construction and detail surmounts its almost total dereliction.

THE GARDEN INDUSTRIAL ESTATE OF HILLINGTON

RIAS Collection

Saturn oxygen factory, Hillington.

Sir Stephen Bilsland's Scottish Industrial Estates Company,[186] founded in 1937 on government money, needed to show quick results—for morale if nothing else, since only 16 new factories had been established in the Scottish Special Areas during the previous three years.[187] 320 acres of farming land at Hillington, Renfrewshire were bought in June, and architects Wylie Wright and Wylie were appointed to draw up plans for an industrial garden city eventually to expand to 120 factories. By November, progress was sufficient that the site could be formally opened by the Secretary of State, Walter Elliott with the words "Scotland is on the march again". 11 months later, 75 new businesses had taken up premises employing over 1000 people. That in itself seemed to provide ample justification for Hillington's technical, social and economic experiments.[188]

The economics were based upon new financial inducements, which were considerable. Rents were based on a non-profit making basis, set at the level solely on the basis of repaying government interest and covering standing charges. A standard factory of 5000 square feet cost only £208 per annum, and a "nest" unit of under 1200 was as little was £1 per week. Loans were available for the purchase of machinery, and for the remission of charges for up to 5 years; and the Nuffield Trustees offered further

[186] The Scottish Industrial Estates Company was the direct forebear of the Scottish Development Agency.

[187] Mary Fleming: "Hillington: a romance of modern Scotland", *SMT Magazine* (October 1938).

[188] By another irony of the Scots economy, progress at Hillington was hindered by the fact that the new steel-framed factories were competing for scarce steel with the re-armament programme.

Right. Seaforth Canteen, Hillington.

SABJ

189 The Seaforth canteen offered a lunch of soup and bread, meat and vegetables, sweet and cup of tea for the price of 10p.

190 An analysis of the first factories in Hillington in 1938 makes instructive reading. They included Watson's Whisky, Brunella Cream Filling, Neo-Films Ltd, a furniture company, a school supplier, clothes manufacturers, ice cream, fruit juice and sweet manufacturers. Apart from pipework contractors, only one factory would be making dye-castings. Hillington had indeed gone for light industry. Those results are uncannily similar to those in Glasgow's East End Renewal (GEAR). In place of heavy industry like Beardmore's Forge, the new industries · include kiltmakers, bagpipe and pizza makers.

Below. Gas building, Alloa, by William Kerr; rather like a cinema.

Swan

loans for the establishment of totally new businesses. The factories were laid out along broad tree and flower-lined avenues, and offered a variety of sizes and combinations of floor-space. With only two exceptions, all the factories were wide-span, steel-trussed, single-storeyed buildings, with standardised lighting and heating provided from a central boilerhouse. Each factory was faced with a simple office and main entrance in red brick and yellow render which comprised the aesthetic of the entire estate. A rare exception was the two-storey Saturn Oxygen Company, prominently sited on the corner of one of the avenues, and distinguished by its giant semi-circular drum, glazed stairtower.

It was the broader social aims, however, which attracted international attention to Hillington. Together with the new, neighbouring housing estate, shops and churches at Penilee, the entire operation was akin to the scale of the post-war New Towns. The symbol of those social aims was the only other two-storey building on the estate: the Seaforth Canteen, opened in December 1938 by Lady Douglas Hamilton who, as Prunella Stack, had been the President of the Womens' League of Health and Beauty. Originally planned as the first of several centres (before the War intervened) the Seaforth provided two communal restaurants, a roof garden, a smoke room and a small swimming pool. The canteen could also be used for dances. The Seaforth was set in "a delightful garden bright with flower beds". The estate was also provided with tennis courts, a playing field, a communal garage, branch banks, a post office, bowling greens and a labour exchange.[189]

Both the Saturn Oxygen Company and the Seaforth Canteen survive, albeit in altered circumstances. In the case of the canteen, cars now park on the former ornamental garden. Yet both could be restored appropriately, as a fit sign of the second life into which Hillington is now entering.[190]

The Scottish Industrial Estates Company proceeded with three other, much smaller, industrial estates at Carfin, Larkhall and Chapelhall, which shared with Hillington the same architect, the same approach to layout, and the same aesthetic.

THE ARCHITECTURE OF INDUSTRY

It is in the nature of industry that most of the buildings visited by Charles Oakley in 1937 no longer survive—or at any rate in their original form. For example, much of the Shieldhall Industrial Estate is now derelict, whilst most of that at Anniesland has been turned over to new houses of the Home Counties type. Such factories of the period as do survive are now 50 years old, and in general are either severely decayed or have been mutilated by the necessity to bring them up to date.

In general, industrial architecture of the Thirties was a matter of tacking a stylish head office or entrance onto a nondescript building behind, to which the new "functionalist" approach to architecture seemed peculiarly appropriate. In towns, new machinery, the less demanding space requirements of light industry, and new construction and handling technology combined to produce a flatted factory aesthetic of long, horizontally proportioned buildings, with strips of window alternating with strips of brick, each floor identified often with a strip of concrete. The technique proved as adaptable for virulent red bonded warehouses in South Queensferry, Markinch and Leith, as for breweries and Barr and Stroud in Anniesland. Occasionally these buildings would have a main entrance, placed symmetrically at the centre, and emphasised by a brick tower above. A delightful little example of a more creative use of brick can be seen in John Laird's offices for Robertson Dunn Sawmills at Anniesland, the front element of which, designed to impress passing motorists, is a combination of the most up-to-date motifs: portholes, a projecting semi-circular tower capped with a square pediment and a flagpole. Factories in suburbs or the new estates could be much more spacious, and opted for large, simple, single-storey sheds with corrugated iron or asbestos roofs serrated into ranks of pointed, north-facing rooflights. Such buildings would be fronted by simple, usually utilitarian office blocks, often in brick and given presence by a tower or capped by a flagpole. The opportunities for architectural distinction were less than those available to their big city counterparts, but the better lighting, ease of goods handling, and improved working conditions may have compensated.

Robertson Dunn offices, Anniesland.

Former dairy, Greenock.

There are naturally one or two exceptions. The Swedish Luma Factory, later Caravanland, in the Shieldhall Industrial Estate in Glasgow was erected by the SCWS in 1936, designed by their staff architect Cornelius Armour. It provides an interesting example of how a straight forward three-storey flatted factory can be visually transformed. In this case, the means is a slightly projecting staircase tower, which smashes through the roofline and is capped by a bulbous, entirely glazed, conning tower more appropriate to an airport. This building, facing the main road south west out of Glasgow,

Luma light factory, Shieldhall, 1936, the original brick front now rendered.

would have been an effective built advertisement for electric lamps. Factories of lesser pretension deployed the simplest methods to obtain a minimum level of respect: the entrance through a chamfered corner, lined with green tiles and a flagpole above, as in Bowaters, Pilrig; or a fancy front, complete with fashionable motifs of black plinth, Thirties lettering, plate glass windows, chrome and portholes in the doors—capped by a parapet which steps up toward a tower with flagpole—as can be seen in George Henderson's, Gorgie Road, Edinburgh.

The model milking complex at Fenton Barns, 1938–40 by J Inch Morrison is unusually vivid. Standing in the rolling East Lothian landscape, Fenton Barns is a plain, two-storey, flat-roofed, horizontally proportioned box, enlivened by a great off-centre projecting semi-circular glazed staircase. Large windows of the original design have been blocked in. The Bexhill Pavilion has travelled to Scotland and beached itself as an agricultural experiment by craft architects.

Fenton Barns, East Lothian: an experimental industrialised farm in the style of a seaside pavilion.

FIRE STATIONS AND OTHER UTILITIES

Few buildings for utilities were constructed during the Thirties. Most Fire Stations preceded the first War; and most modern postal buildings post-dated the Second, as did most Hydro buildings. There was the occasional electricity showroom (an example surviving in Dunfermline) and a series of plain, reasonably elegant, cubist sub-stations by John Wilson Paterson. Wiliam Kerr's Gas Building, Coal Wynd, Alloa has considerable quality, combining, as it does, a modern wing complete with tower and strip windows, with a frigid neo-classical shop facing the main road on the other side.

One or two new Fire Stations were built—the outstanding one being in Dunfermline, designed in 1935 by James Shearer and its Kirkcaldy clone, plagiarised by George Duffus in 1938. Shearer was an unlikely designer of a modernist masterpiece: the architect to the Carnegie Trust, a craft architect with a gift for communication (William Dey considered Shearer taught him more than anyone else in only six months in his office)[191] and later a planner. The Fire Station was his only building that could be accused of modernism; and even then, may not have been a design wholly of his choosing. The disposition of the station, with its tall hose-drying tower, followed the standard brief (save that Shearer, noted for a sharp architectural wit in his normal commissions, cranked it at 45 degrees) and the flat roof (which gave immense trouble) was a condition imposed by the client. Dey recalls Shearer regarding the carved Scots stone details in the building as a deliberate attempt to make modern architecture more specifically Scots. It is the composition of the main block with its slender tower which ennobles this building, however, no matter how modern (the windows) or how Scots (the carvings) the details may be.

A different utility approached differently was the hydro-electric scheme in New Galloway and Glenlee, from 1933. Designed by engineers Sir Alexander Gibb, the architectural results (principally the pumping stations) were stark, fairly cubist white blocks with tall strip windows, indeed, not unlike some military architecture of the Second World War.

Left. Dunfermline Fire Station. *Top.* Buckie Police Station. *Middle.* Glenlee Power Station, New Galloway. *Above.* Kirkcaldy Fire Station.

191 Interview William Dey.

Polkemmet pithead baths. The plan *(below)* shows how the transformation from dirty to clean was achieved.

RIAS

PITHEAD BATHS

The creation of pithead baths represents a combination of advanced social provision and advanced architecture. That the majority were constructed in the Thirties, in the circumstances that they were, says little for the private mine owners. A Royal Commission into the Mining Industry in 1919 led to the establishment of the Miner's Welfare Fund the following year, initially with educational and social objectives. In 1926, the Mining Industry Act, following the recommendations of the Samuel Commission, instituted a levy of one shilling in the pound on coal royalties, the purpose of which was to "secure, as far as reasonably practicable, the provision, at all coal mines, of accommodation and facilities for workmen taking baths and drying clothes".[192] The levy was first collected in 1927; but even then the programme for pithead baths received less than total support from the miners, since they had to pay for the operation and maintenance, the average cost of which to each miner was 6d per week—a significant factor in view of the fact that miners' real wages fell by 4.5% between 1913 and 1938.[193]

The United Kingdom programme was under the direction of their chief architect J H Forshaw, but in Scotland the general direction seems to have come from J A Dempster: with the result that very different pithead baths were produced for Scotland from England—at least in their external appearance. The purpose, in addition to providing first-aid rooms and canteens where required, was that of transformation: transforming dirty miners entering from the pit on the one side, into clean members of the public, exiting on the other. Pit entrance and the clean entrance were at opposite ends of the building: each miner having a pit locker. Once stripped, his clothes in the pit locker, he would pass through the bathhouse to clean himself: and out the other side into the clean locker area where his clean clothes would be stored: and then out the clean entrance. Otherwise the building simply had to contain a boiler room, a water tank, urinals, a plenum room (which contained the machinery), and a calorifier. Some had canteens. Most of the Scottish pithead baths were distinguished by towers: being a convenient and practical way of storing the water, storage, filter room, plenum room etc, in addition to any symbolic function. The main accommodation of these pithead baths was in sheds—more or less well designed—to the rear. Thus their architecture was very comparable to contemporary industrial architecture with a classy front office, fronting practical sheds behind.

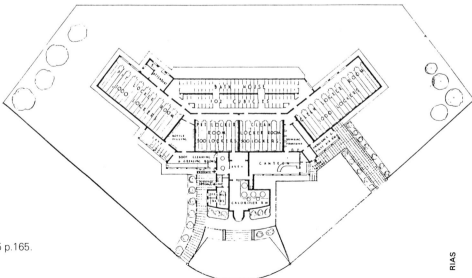

RIAS

192 *Architect and Building News* 9.8.35 p.165.

193 Harvie op. cit. page 41.

194 *Quarterly* no 52 (1936).

RIAS

Cardowan pithead baths: the similarity to Hilversum Town Hall is striking.

Writing in the *Quarterly* in 1936, J A Dempster laid down the philosophy of the pithead baths' architects:

> We, as architects, do not feel justified in allowing expenditure in ornament and decoration in such buildings, and strive to achieve results of architectural worth through the use of line, with well proportioned surfaces and fenestration. Economical buildings need not be mean, but building solely for cheapness, without regard to design, would be unworthy. The Miners' Welfare Committee aims to effect, from the external appearance of a building, a distinctive note of design suited to a natural setting or existing grouping.[194]

The programme was quite remarkable. In under nine years, almost 50 (and maybe more as yet unknown) pithead baths were constructed, each refining its predessor. The only comparable '80s programme would be supermarkets. Most pithead baths have disappeared with the pits. Cardowan, Lanarkshire, was one of the grandest: an arrangement of brick geometrics, culminating in tower, set in the midst of a formal garden with its own pool, a miniature echo of the Town Hall at Hilversum. Many others were white cement rendered, with striking towers such as Kames and Auchincruive (Ayrshire), and Preston Links (Lothian). An outstanding one—surviving but derelict—is that of the Frances Colliery in Fife. Its tower, less dominant than Auchincruive, has a glazed, slightly bowed window, and the main block, with its oversailing flat roof and projecting circular and square corner windows, has a crisp clarity and architectural presence in advance of its fellows. As an advanced monument to institutional philanthropy, as well as an architectural milestone, the Frances Colliery baths deserve reconditioning for some new use.

The buildings seem to differ from their English counterpart in that the majority of Scottish pithead baths were white, usually cement rendered, usually dominated by a higher tower, the windows punched out in brick-lined strips. There is, therefore, a formal quality in the Scottish inherently different from the heavy, brick shapes of English collieries (e.g. Silksworth in Durham) which look more like contemporary power stations. That probably reflects the personal skills of the Scots, first J A Dempster, who was primarily responsible for the Scottish Pithead Baths until he was succeeded in 1938 by D D Jack.

Frances Colliery, Fife. The surviving concrete tower.

Fife Region

117

Whether the decrease in the number of children and the exodus to the suburbs will enable municipalities to replace their great three-storey council schools on congested sites by one-storey glass-houses of the latest German pattern remains to be seen. Sunshine everywhere – if you can get it, all staircases abolished or replaced where necessary by an occasional ramp, bright colours, smooth surfaces.   Martin Briggs

INTRODUCTION

In one respect, the social context of the Thirties is as far from modern times as King Alfred's cakes: it was in the pre-penicillin age. There was determination to get to grips with major infectious diseases and, in the absence of the miraculous medicine, the methods adopted were through health, fitness and education.

HEALTH

Expansion in all types of hospital and sanatorium provision took place between the wars, as techniques of medicine and the mechanical services required to support them, improved. (After 1929, Local Authorities in Scotland were able to build public hospitals.) Concepts of cleanliness and fresh air, first introduced in the late Victorian period for tuberculosis treatment, pervaded hospitals as other building types; and the new materials and construction techniques of the Thirties allowed those in hospitals to peel the walls back, to bless the inmates with full enjoyment of the Scots climate. As the decade progressed, new hospitals would be provided with balconies, sun terraces, and wards opening out onto them—as for example in Canniesburn. Another factor influencing hospital design was the development of the isolation hospital, so that infectious diseases could be kept clear of each other.

The late career of architect James Miller illuminates changes in hospital design. He had been responsible for Stirling Royal Infirmary in 1928, a country house complete with pilasters, pitched roof, and prominent chimney stacks, and he tackled Perth c.1931, with a series of red brick and white linked pavilions of a neo-Georgian sort in a rolling landscape. In 1932, Miller was appointed assessor in the competition for the Infectious Diseases Hospital at Hawkhead which he awarded to Thomas Tait. Tait's approach was to dematerialise the wards, as it were, so that when the elements permitted the patients could be in the open air. Tait's views clearly influenced Miller in his 1934 design for Canniesburn Hospital near Glasgow. Canniesburn, on a superb site with trees to the south and views over to the northern hills, consists of a number of separate buildings—all long, low, and brilliantly white, provided with balconies along the wards, and great curved glass staircases. The exterior walls being glass, patients could lie in their beds and watch the rabbits in the undergrowth outside. The principal entrance is located at the centre under the square stumpy tower of which Miller was so fond, and used elsewhere (e.g. Stow College). His next hospital, two years later, consisted of extensions for the Larbert Mental Colony. The basic arrangement of wards and rooms seems to be similar, but the

Opposite. Dental Hospital, Glasgow.

external appearance has become more streamlined again, with the roof over-sailing the walls in a way not at all visible at Canniesburn. His final hospital was in Greenock: and drawings survive showing the changes of design from the original 1935 scheme to that built in 1943. As the design develops, so does it become more streamlined, the side wings change from being square-ended to having curved ends, and from having inaccessible roofs to having roof terraces.

Above. Canniesburn Hospital, Glasgow.

A significant amount of inner-city hospital rebuilding was undertaken, with new departments in the Royal Infirmary and Simpson Memorial, Edinburgh and in the Western Infirmary, Glasgow and the Deaconess Hospital, 1935 by Kininmonth in Edinburgh. Aberdeen built a number of new medical buildings including a new city hospital, a somewhat plain two-storey building with a tower. Glasgow received a stylish, large new dental hospital, in Renfrew Street, from the hand of E G Wylie in 1932. It is of unusual grandeur for a medical building: consisting of a four-storey metal frame, flanked by two stone pylons linked, across the top, by an almost continually glazed clerestorey, it displays (yet again) the influence of Burnet and Tait (e.g. British Museum). The interior was so designed as to make possible almost any variation in the location of partitions or services.

Below. Nurses Home, Gartloch. *Bottom.* Nurses Home, Gartnavel.

With the expansion in medical care, there was a like expansion in the provision for nurses. The decade opened with a competition for a nurses' home in Montrose, won by a fairly traditional design by J Ogg Allan; and it closed with another competition for a large nurses' home in Falkirk, in 1938, won by Kininmonth and Spence (but never built because of war). Norman Dick's nurses' home in Gartnavel, Glasgow is worth serious study. It is a large, purple-brick building of a remarkably crisp geometric precision (neither the bricks, nor their bonding, nor the construction techniques being British); a cruciform composition of interconnected blocks, symmetrical at the gable, but entered mid length up a flight of steps. Some of the details, particularly the tall corner windows, are very similar to those seen later in St Andrew's House, and the doors are flanked by Dudok pillars. Dick also produced several buildings for the Western Infirmary, including a curiously modern L-plan nurses' home with rounded corners and corner windows, all clad in stone. Glasgow City's 1939 Nurses' Home in Gartloch is the most self-conscious of all such. A large four-storey, horizontally proportioned brick and render building, it is entered beneath a tower and flanked by two huge glass lounge windows, protruding like frogs' eyeballs at either end.

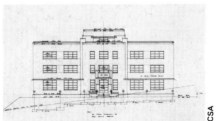

Only the larger of the health buildings have survived. Of the inumberable works carried out by many architects at clinics, maternity homes and the like, little survives in its original form, altered in consequence of the changes that have occurred in medicine in the last fifty years.

Perhaps the clearest illustration of the conjunction of innovative modern architecture and the new type of isolation hospital is the competition-winning Infectious Diseases Hospital, Hawkhead, Paisley, won by Sir John Burnet, Tait and Lorne in 1932, and completed in 1934: ten main buildings set in sloping parkland supplemented by five minor buidings (lodge gates, a mortuary block, power buildings etc). Measles, whooping cough, diphtheria, scarlet fever, and pneumonia each merited a separate pavilion, and wards in these pavilions open out onto a slightly raised terrace, sheltered by an overhanging canopy. The cubicle block is a two-storey T-plan version, the cubicles on both storeys opening onto verandas.

Now in dire need of whitewash and upgrading (it was originally brilliant white), this hospital is a monument both to its type and to its architecture. The horizontality is emphasised by cantilevered concrete canopies, by roof terraces with tubular iron railings and with projecting, semi-circular bays. The influence of Lloyd Wright is apparent in the use of coloured, yellow, blue, and black tiles along the main entrance; and of Dudok in the blue tiled mullions, the canopies, and the massing. As one of Tait's assistants, Esme Gordon has observed, "for Tait, Dudok was a very infectious disease".

Above. Hawkhead Infectious Diseases Hospital. *Below*. Lennox Castle Hospital. *Bottom*. Infectious Diseases Hospital: Cubicle block.

THE OPEN-AIR FAD: NEW EDUCATIONAL BUILDINGS

A fair number of schools were built between the wars, partly as a result of new legislation which, in 1918, replaced the old educational administration with new comprehensive Education Authorities responsible for the entire school population in each county and each large Scottish city. These new bodies were faced with the steady transfer of population from the inner cities to new suburbs, with the consequent demand for new schools. Most, as the newspapers recorded approvingly, were "of the open-air kind". The first such school had been built in 1904 in Charlottenburg, Berlin.[195]

The problems facing those designing schools for the poorer sections of the population were crude and harsh: large numbers of school children came from insanitary slum dwellings in bare feet and carrying disease. Regular medical inspection of children in Scotland had been introduced in 1903, from which date as much attention was spent upon cleanliness as on teaching. Provision was made for feet washing, for the protection against infectious disease, and for the dissipation of smell—largely through cross-ventilation. Between the wars, new schools were given significantly larger sites and built against the northern perimeter, to optimise south-facing playgrounds and fields.[196]

RIAS Collection/Wylie Shanks

Hillhead School – competition-winning design by E G Wylie.

The "open-air" school was one so designed that icy gusts of through draught could sweep through classrooms as and when the teachers thought it necessary: and their execution differed whether they were in central or suburban sites. Schools forced by the constraints of tight city sites to go to several storeys, could only achieve the requisite quantities of open air by providing corridors which were roofed but not walled. As children moved from one class to the other, they would be cleansed by the beneficent blast. The plan-form would either be a radiating one (Wylie Wright and Wylie's virulent red brick Hillhead High School is a double Y-plan) or one of a hollow core with the school pressed out against the edge (as in W W Friskin's Lochee 1933, in an equally unappealing brick).

Suburban schools could afford a more spacious approach to "open-air" planning and that is apparent in single-storey courtyard schools, two of which were built in Edinburgh (but not repeated because they proved so

[195] Dr W M Stephens. Thesis on the development of schools in Edinburgh.

[196] Ibid.

expensive). Wardie Primary School, Granton, was designed by J M Johnston in 1930 around a large courtyard enclosed by two single-storey side wings, along which ran open, but glass-roofed, corridors; closed at each end by two-storey buildings—one the hall, and the other a curved, T-shaped administrative block. Wardie was overtly modern in style: flat roofed, with a striped façade of alternate white cement render and bands of brick. In September 1931, Edinburgh Corporation proudly opened an "experimental" primary school at Prestonfield, for whose architect they had gone shopping to Derbyshire, and their County Architect, Bernard Widdows. The resulting school had the distinction of being the only Scottish building included in the RIBA's *Modern Architecture* exhibition, with which it celebrated the opening of its new headquarters in 1934.[197] Prestonfield Primary was constructed in a brash English brick in the English fashion, and was distinctive for the fact that all the classrooms faced into the courtyard with glass walls that could be pulled back. The Scottish weather soon dealt bracingly with both schools: they were closed in.

One of the most famous Thirties schools was the École de Plein Air, by Beaudouin et Lods in Suresnes (one of the new suburbs surrounding Paris, specially visited by the Scottish Department of Health in 1934). Designed as a series of pavilions opening off a long spine, the school was truly open-air since each pavilion had glass walls which could simply be rolled back if the weather permitted. No direct comparison exists in Scotland, but a comparable aim is clearly intelligible in Tullos School, Aberdeen designed by J Ogg Allan in 1937. The entire ground floor of this large school is glazed, sheltered by a glazed canopy. The structure is such that, if (or when) sufficient sun ever comes to Aberdeen, the pupils could indeed sit with the illusion of being in the open air, looking out at the view of the cement works, industrial estate, (and now the new oil developments at Altens).

Not every school project, however, lent itself to an open-air experiment, and not every School Board wanted one. J R Peddie gave the view of an educational official:

> since the War, every Scottish Educational Authority, in greater or lesser degree, has striven to house its schoolchildren in buildings that are calculated to bring health and happiness. In the modern schools now springing up in every locality, the building is so adjusted to get the maximum of sunlight. Warmth and ventilation are matters to which utmost technical skill is devoted. Classrooms and corridors are brightly painted, pictures of interest—vivid and arresting—hang on the walls, while every effort is made to ensure the ease of working on the part of the teacher. Children receive medical and dental inspection, there is feeding and clothing of those poorly circumstanced, a milk supply is given daily at fractional cost or no cost at all, and attention is given to physical exercise and games.

Even the anonymous teacher, responding adversely to the remainder of Mr Peddie's essay on the educational system, felt constrained to agree that:

> the best modern school buildings are a tremendous improvement upon the older ones. Light, air and colour have been admitted to the rooms. Sometimes there are even baths. The idea has got around that minds work better in pleasant surroundings and that green grass and bright paint may be as stimulating as fear.[198]

It would be wrong to presuppose that all schools built in the Thirties were pioneers of modernism. Logie Central School, Dundee, for example, a 1931 competition winner designed by Maclaren Soutar Salmond, is a large school of the old-fashioned sort, set in a hillside in a very grim part of old Dundee. It consists of a huge U-plan block entered beneath a cupola of vaguely Swedish design, with subsidiary entrances through projecting, stone-fronted pedimented stair towers which emphasise each corner. The private sector schools of the time were also traditional. J B Dunn and Mar-

Top. Wardie School. *Middle.* Ecole de Plein Air, Suresnes. *Above.* The English-imported Craigmillar Primary School.

[197] By thus displaying that the only good Scottish building was one designed by an English architect, the RIBA illuminated an attitude to northern Britain which has changed little since.

[198] *Scotland 1938.*

Niddrie School.

tin's competition-winning George Watson's school, Colinton Road, Edinburgh (1932) is a frigidly classical design, complete with pilasters: a pomp appropriate to the pupils it wished to pull. In its first year of occupation, some pupils at least found the building sterile in character and almost insupportably hot as the sun beat through the windows.[199] Reginald Fairlie's St Nicholas Boarding House for St Andrew's Girls School (1931) is a quadrangular building, its principal face being a three-storey essay in old Scots. It was so successful in this regard that of it, the *Architect's Journal* wrote: "by using Scottish materials in a straightforward manner, the architect has imparted to the house a national flavour far more sincere than can ever be given by the uninspired ornament of its neighbours".[200] Perhaps as a result of his experience with the weather in Wardie, when J M Johnston came to design Ainslie Park School, Pilton, in 1937, he reverted to a tall, dominant main block, with a central entrance, and two circular glazed staircase projecting from each wing. It is not entirely clear what parts of the design were modified since, war interrupting, the school was not completed until 1948.[201] Keppie Henderson won the RIBA Bronze Medal for Cloberhill School, Knightswood, Glasgow, in 1937, a relaxed, orange brick building (for there was plenty of land to build on), none of it more than two storeys in height, consisting of two extenuated wings linked to a central entrance pavilion. Although the staircases are modern in concept, the remainder is traditional in style, particularly the colonial "Georgian" entrance block.

Inverness Academy (1934).

199 Interview Robert Smith OBE.

200 *Architect's Journal* (6 April 1932).

201 Stephens op. cit.

Kelso Academy.

The works of the Edinburgh architectural practice of Reid and Forbes, and that of the Aberdeen School Board architect Allan Ogg Allan, stand out. Reid and Forbes attracted attention when they won the competition for Leith Academy in 1928, in which they had placed a roof garden, reached through opening windows from the library, above the Hall. *The Scotsman* enthused that "pupils in fine weather can experience to the full the benefits of sunshine and fresh air". Leith Academy exemplifies other open-air features. With a plan like the Pentagon enclosing a central rhomboid open yard, the classrooms faced out, with the corridors on the inside overlooking the yard; however, the roofed corridors have a lower ceiling than the classrooms, so that air could pass above the corridor straight through a clerestorey into the classroom itself.

In 1932, Reid and Forbes won the competition for Inverness Academy: which they tackled with verve flavoured with Art Deco of the sort usually found in contemporary factories on the arterial roads out of London. Entered through a marginally projecting seven bay block, emphasised by a square topped recessing pedimentcapped with a centrally placed flagpole and a balcony at first-floor level, the main classrooms are in two-storey wings spread in each direction, terminated by narrow stumpy towers decorated with Art Deco motifs. Those motifs appear much more forcefully in their next competition winning school—Niddrie Marischal (now called the Castlebrae Annexe) Edinburgh (and barely a stone's throw from the English,

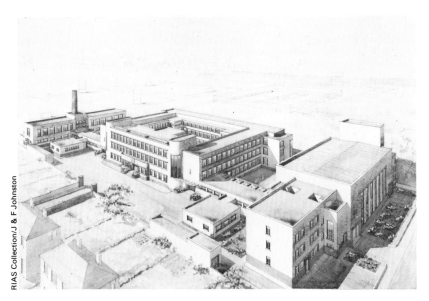

RIAS Collection/J & F Johnston

202 Alan Reiach's memory of the profession's welcome for the building.

Left. Ainslie Park School, by J M Johnston.

Below. Chirnside School by Reid and Forbes. *Bottom*. Tullos School, Aberdeen.

David Brown

brick, pitched-roof Prestonfield). H-shaped in plan, the two wings present entirely different characteristics and images. That to the north, facing the courtyard, is entered through the middle underneath a great squat tower, richly decorated with carved stone details of motifs not unlike Frank Lloyd Wright's re-intepretation of American Indianism. A separate building, containing rooms above and offices below, is like a little, self-contained, Continental house—flat-roofed, and rounded corners. The south-facing wing, overlooking the playing field (now derelict), comprises two continuously glazed, streamlined storeys, emphasised at the middle with the addition of a third storey. Behind these great towers is the staircase, which, in the details of its ironwork and stonework, continues the redskin imagery.

Their next building, Kelso Academy (1936), is considerably more accomplished. It comprises a group of buildings with a different architectural approach for different parts. The main block has the dominant central tower and carved decoration seen at Niddrie, but the decoration for the lower part of the tower much more explicitly implies the influence of Frank Lloyd Wright's Midway Gardens. The science block is more relaxed and abandons symmetry in favour of a more modern composition focussed upon the tower.

That block provides the clue to their next building: the small village school at Chirnside, Berwickshire (1938). On a windy hillside, set some way below a historic village, this schools stands like a beacon which the profession considered rather overdone for a tiny Borders hilltop village.[202] One enters beneath a tower (mostly stripped of its decoration) on the right wing of a Z, which leads into the main stem of the Z containing the hall: another block of classrooms comprising the top left wing of the Z. It looks as modern now as it must have done the day it was opened.

OTHER EDUCATIONAL BUILDINGS

The Thirties does not seem to have been a major period of reconstruction in Scottish universities, the only significant developments—in terms of scale—being the construction of laboratories by John F Matthew at King's Buildings, Edinburgh at the beginning of the decade, and the construction of Glasgow University's Reading Room and Chemistry Building, as part of a much grander development, by Professor T Harold Hughes at the end of it.

Above. Experimental school at Kilsyth for the Scottish Council (1938), by Basil Spence.

Design on the Sanderson Engineering Laboratories, and the Grant Institute of Geology, was begun sometime slightly after 1926, under the hand of Robert Lorimer, although executed by his successor John F Matthew. Lorimer's obituarist, Leslie Graham Thomson, wrote in 1929 that from the blocks of geology and engineering, it would appear that Sir Robert Lorimer's modernism was maturing rapidly, and here he was combining the purely practical excellence of the zoology building with the refinement and grace of design we associate with all his other work"[203]. The Sanderson Laboratories consists of a main symmetrical, stone fronted block, backed by large sheds. Entrance is up a flight of steps beneath an imposing tower (adorned with a sculpture by Alexander Carrick) into a coldly imposing hall and staircase. The vaguely classical Grant Institute of Geology, a U-plan building, is designed as a totality: no sheds round the back here. Its entrance is a curiosity between a pair of projecting two-storey towers. There is a stern plainness about both buildings which belies any frivolous use: but both are designed with a sense of proportion and symmetry not inappropriate to a country house or open prison.

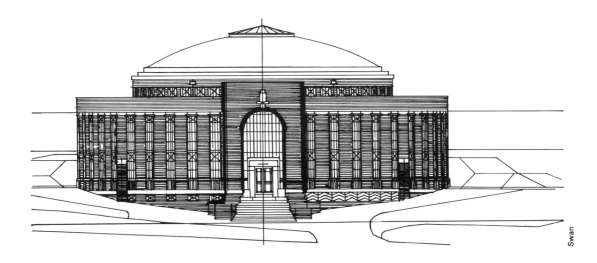

Right. Glasgow University Reading Room.

T Harold Hughes used brick in his buildings for Glasgow University in a way novel for Scotland. The Chemistry Building is a composite of three buildings—a large central block with two wings projecting at an angle. The junctions are graced by two huge spectacular, semi-circular glazed staircases of a most stylish sweep. Each floor is clearly differentiated by the concrete banding, thus positively defining the structure, and a glazed clerestorey runs immediately beneath the roofline. The Reading Room, completed with D S R Waugh in 1938, and winner of the RIBA Bronze Medal in 1950, is a giant, concrete-domed, brick rotunda, entered through a full-height rectangular porch. The conjunction of the two invokes distant memories of the Pantheon. In its setting on University Avenue it has always been somewhat isolated, probably explained by the fact that the original proposal consisted of a very much larger complex, including blocks (complete with tower) facing University Avenue, of which this building would have been the centre in the middle of a courtyard: There is no attempt in the University Reading Room to use any overtly modern motifs. Hughes eschewed the fashionable horizontal sweeping windows and soaring white curves. The windows in the Reading Room are vertical, each one rising through two full storeys, lighting the spacious and faintly antiseptic interior.

[203] Many of those interviewed spoke of the arrival of facing brick from England as a key feature in the Thirties.

[204] Ex. info R Mervyn Noad.

[205] William "Conky" Paterson was also the designer of the Edinburgh Savings Bank, Hanover Street (1939).

9 ▮ CHURCHES

While the "Old Guard" condemns many of the new churches as resembling power stations, the "Youth Movement" jeers at its elders for reproducing obsolete ecclesiastical forms and pseudo-Gothic carving.

Martin Briggs

Thirties churches displayed the old-fashioned architectural virtues: craftsmanship, spirituality, proportion and massing; often in startlingly new settings as the mass movement of people out from the centre of Scottish communities created a substantial demand for new kirks in the housing estates and the suburbs. A reduction in central church congregations (a process that had begun fifty years before) some of whose buildings were themselves threatened by slum clearance, also impelled the construction of some churches in the older, wealthier suburbs.

Most denominations met the demand by Church Extension Schemes, led by the Church of Scotland which held a competition for King's Park Parish Church in Glasgow as a prototype. It was won by Hutton and Taylor with a multi-coloured brick Romanesque design. The brick was significant. The new churches were built to low budgets and in locations with no predetermined character. Brick was a new material in Scotland, and created new architectural opportunities, open to a broader range of influences than Scots Arts and Crafts.[203] The Church Extension Scheme was accompanied by the religious crusade of Dr John White, who believed that a church should be constructed in every new housing scheme, and led the crusade with the slogan: "No Historical Copies Please. Let Our Churches Represent—Today!"[204] The first of the new churches in Edinburgh was St Aidan's, Saughton, designed by the craft architect J Inch Morrison in 1933, in multi-coloured brick, with Art Deco shaped windows and chunky proportions.

The churches following the relocation of an existing congregation (with more money to spend), were quite distinctly grander than those in the council estates and almost always built in stone. The church of St John's, Renfield, on a bluff overlooking Great Western Road, was constructed 1927—31 to designs by James Taylor Thomson (who spent several years with Bertram Goodhue in America). It is a remarkably fine Gothic stone building with a central flèche giving the composition something of the proportions of the Sainte Chapelle. The Reid Memorial Church, designed in 1928 by Leslie Graham Thomson, on the corner of Blackford Avenue, Edinburgh, is constructed in excellently crafted stonework; its horizontal emphasis and sturdy tower in contrast to J Taylor Thomson's vertically proportioned building. The craftsmanship in carved stone, stained glass and timber work, and the quality of light and space inside, provide a soaring, vertically proportioned, well-lit modern Gothic interior of great quality. Another relocated church but of rather less pretension is the Bristo Baptist Church, relocated to Queensferry Road in 1932, realised by William Paterson, of Oldrieve Bell and Paterson[205] in an L-plan, brown harled, vertically proportioned building, with rather pleasant Dutch gables. The new Synagogue in Salisbury Road,

Top. St John's Renfield, Glasgow. *Above*. St Aidan's Saughton – Art Deco window.

White House

McKean

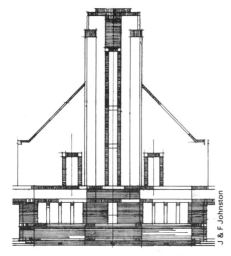

J & F Johnston

Top. Reid Memorial Church, Edinburgh. *Middle.* Fairmilehead Church. *Above.* United Free Church, Portobello. *Right.* St Margaret's Knightswood.

designed by James Miller in 1931, is a formal composition of brick geometric shapes surmounted by a dome.

One of the oddities of the inter-war period was the extent to which Scotland was thought to have an "Irish" problem. Few of those writing about Scotland at the time could afford to ignore it. By 1936, Clydeside had an Irish population of about 600,000, and one in six Dundonians was Catholic: proportions which led the Scottish National Party of the time to propose immigration controls in the pamphlet *Scottish Reconstruction*. The Catholic population brought a demand for churches and also for church schools which, since 1918, had been granted a sectarian place in the education system. Thus it was that Reginald Fairlie was commissioned to design his galaxy of little brick echoes of Westminster Cathedral (see Chap.2) and that Archbishop Donald MacIntosh had the opportunity to commission Jack Coia.

Church construction also followed the re-unification of the Church of Scotland in 1929: and, in true Scots fashion, the breakaway movement of yet another sect—the United Free Church. J M Johnston's two odd and strangely interesting Edinburgh churches were for this new client. The Wilson Memorial Church, Portobello, is a graceful composition with entrance tower, in red brick and white render (a combination he had used successfully in Wardie Primary School). The much smaller, multi-coloured brick and render, flat-roofed United Free Church at Blackhall, hidden behind an ungainly extension, is curiously worth a detour. A small number of buildings were designed within what might be called the old Scots tradition. Lorimer's relic, the firm of Lorimer and Matthew, completed St Margaret's, on the edge of the new housing estate of Knightswood, an attenuated rectangular stone barn, signalled by a somewhat Baltic crow-stepped gable tower at the east end. Pilton Parish Church, Boswall Parkway (1934) shows a freedom and a remarkable similarity to Leslie Graham Thomson's extension church at Fairmilehead (1938). In Aberdeen, A G R Mackenzie produced two churches of specific note, one in Mortlach, which observers thought to be the best modern church in Scotland, and Pittodrie Parish Church,

White House

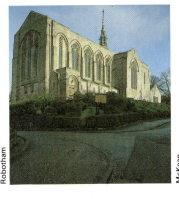

Above and left. Reid Memorial Church designed by Leslie Graham Thomson (drawing 1928 probably by Basil Spence): original perspective of the east end; and the interior today.
Far left. St John's Renfield, Glasgow, designed by J Taylor Thomson.

Ewing

RIAS Collection

Top. Bungalow in the Comiston estate, Edinburgh by Kininmonth and Spence. Note the flat-roofed house with ladders to the flat roof just behind. *Middle.* Bungalow, Newton Mearns, Glasgow (1933), by Launcelot Ross: in reality a grand house arranged principally on a single floor. *Right.* James Carrick's second prize-winning entry in the 1936 competition for semi-detached homes.

RIAS Collection

McKean

Left. Council houses, Dunbar (1935), by Kininmonth and Spence.
Below. Ravelston Flats (1935), designed by Norman Neil and Robert Hurd. The expectation of better weather is indicated by the roof garden.
Bottom left. Miss Reid's house, Easter Belmont (1934), designed by Basil Spence. This odd design not only had a roof garden, but an open courtyard at the centre.
Bottom right. Lucy Sanderson Homes, Galashiels, by Mears and Carus-Wilson.

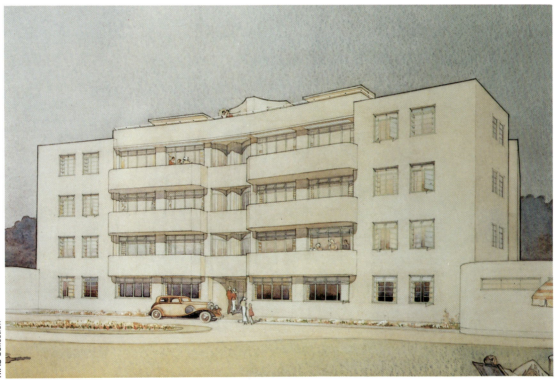

RIAS Collection

Ewing

McKean

Lady Nairn Avenue, Kirkcaldy
(c.1934): the best terrace of Art Deco
houses in Scotland.

Cluny House, Culduthel Road,
Inverness.

Below. Sandringham Avenue,
Broom Estate, as illustrated in the
1938 marketing brochure. The house
was designed by James Taylor.
Below right. 9 Carse View Drive,
Bearsden, one of eight "Sunlight"
houses by John R H MacDonald.

132

RIAS Library

Left. Our Lady, Star of Sea, Tayport. *Above.* Oban Cathedral proposal by Sir Giles Gilbert Scott.

King Street (1939) which in its diminutive way, presents an almost entirely blank gable of multi-coloured granite to the street front. In Dundee, Allan and Friskin provided some exquisite brick patterning in the tympanum of St Elizabeth's Chapel, Graham Street. Sir Giles Scott was tempted north of the border to produce a cathedral in Oban, and a church in Restalrig, of which only half was built. His approach, like that of his grandfather, was to adopt forms already used in England, varied slightly for Scottish sensibilities by the use of stone and crow-step gables.[206]

Towards the end of the decade, there seems to have been a reversion to more specifically Scots buildings in reaction to the rash of brick Romanesque which had appeared all over Glasgow and parts of outer Edinburgh. Launcelot Ross's 1938 church in Drumchapel is pleasantly white harled, with a slated roof and neatly proportioned gables. Reginald Fairlie's church, Our Lady, Star of Sea, Tayport (1939) is quite beautiful in its simplicity: a single-chamber, pitched-roof building with a Gothic window in its east gable, entered through an octagonal, spired tower set on one side.

[206] Scott's ersatz Scots details attracting the scorn of serious Scots like Harry Hubbard.

Drumchapel Church (1937) by Launcelot Ross.

RIAS Collection

Right. St Columba's, Hopehill Road, its ribbed, vaulted interior strangely at odds with its classic façade. *Below.* St Columcille's, Rutherglen: detail. *Bottom.* St Anne's, Dennistoun, Coia's favourite.

207 Unpublished notes for Royal Gold Medal Speech. RIAS Library.

It is now apparent that one of the most consistently interesting church architects of the 1930s was Jack Coia. Looking back later, he said: "the church is, to me, the most admirable exercise in building design. Its abstract and plastic qualities appeal greatly, and its variables are infinite. The architect has to work on every aspect of his creation. No other creative man expressing himself in any other form of art—such as sculptor, painter, musician, or poet—has to produce such a complex performance."[207] About 1937 he was joined in partnership by T Warnett Kennedy, to whom much of the design of St Peter's in Chains in Ardrossan has been attributed.

All Coia Thirties churches display a fusion between architecture and craft, the craft details conveying specific iconography; and most have a west front unrelated to what was happening inside—a good Italian tradition, but not particularly modern in approach. The first, St Anne's, "the first flower of my impetuous and exuberant youth",[207] Whitevale Street, Dennistoun, was begun in 1931, a brick, Italian pedimented building with white stone dressings and carved reliefs by Archibald Dawson. It was followed two years later by St Patrick's Church, Greenock, on a hill above the town. The western entrance gable is almost triangular in form with twin staircases leading up to a twin door. Bisecting the façade is a strong vertical feature which, lower down, contains a stone carving of St Patrick by Archibald Dawson, but which leads up, via twin slit windows, to a cross which projects through the parapet. His next building was St Columba's Church in Maryhill not very far from Charles Rennie Mackintosh's Queens Cross Church. The west front is a hefty rectangular tower in patterned brick, flanked by two lower wings. The entry is emphasised in carved stonework, above which a gigantic cross is cut through the brickwork itself to illuminate the interior. This was the first of Coia's churches to include sculpture by Benno Schotz.

St Peter's in Chains, Ardrossan (completed 1938) marks a departure. An off-centre, Swedish-influenced tower is an essential part of the composition; the church roof has a much shallower pitch, and the craft details are not superimposed in stone (as in the other churches) but take the form of cut bricks emphasising an almost Gothic tympanum, and similar brick detailing surrounds the two flanking windows. Last of these brick churches of Coia's was St Columcille's Church, Main Street, Rutherglen, finished just after the War began. Coia wrote:

> many of my churches were essentially transitional structures. I was anxious to break with the red stone neo-Gothic. I tried to build more freely, and in brick. Fortunately, the Catholic Church was less addicted to Gothic by that time, if anything more influenced by continental idioms. Although conscious of its rich past, the Church was actively aware of its role as patron of the arts.[208]

The Empire Exhibition in Glasgow produced a number of churches. Mervyn Noad designed a very Scandinavian A-frame timber church for the Episcopalians, J Taylor Thomson a less successful, crow-stepped creation (á la Knightswood) for the Church of Scotland, and Jack Coia the Roman Catholic Pavilion. Only Coia grasped the architectural opportunities of the exhibition's construction system—steel frame and prefabricated white asbestos panels. The result was a plain, tall, white box with semi-circular curving apse, all in glowing white, save for huge murals. Coia admitted that the exhibition format compelled him to be "modern" as though he had been reluctant; yet the result had a presence and drama (a wee bit too florid for the Presbyterians) unmatched by the others.

RIAS Collection

RIAS

Top. St Peter in Chains, Ardrossan. *Above*. St Columcille's, Rutherglen.
Left. Roman Catholic Pavilion by Coia at the Empire Exhibition. *Below*. Episcopal Church, Empire Exhibition.

208   Ibid.

RIAS Library

EX.894.

RIAS

Left. "The house that Jean built" – the winning design in the 1932 *Daily Mail* competition for an "Ideal Home", conceived by Mrs E M Reid, and drawn up by the assessor, Douglas Tanner. *Below, Over and Above,* Culduthel Road, Inverness, designed by Donald Fowler (1936) of Carruthers Ballantyne, Cox and Taylor, for himself. *Bottom.* Tenements proposed for Howwood Road, Johnstone by Burnet Tait and Lorne.

Swan

Marion Gracie

Swan

We must prepare for the activities that will arise when the war is over. The Institute of Architects in Scotland of 1850 gave much attention to housing and sanitary questions; we must do the same, and aim at a higher standard than ever. The foundation of this question of housing is that of getting cheaper land for building on. Before that difficult question is equitably solved, progress in this direction will be slow.

THE SCOTTISH HOUSING PROBLEM

Thus said Sir Robert Rowand Anderson in his presidential address to the first Annual General Meeting of the Institute of Scottish Architects in 1917. Almost exactly eleven years later, his pupil, the equally celebrated craft architect Sir Robert Lorimer, told his first Annual General Meeting of the RIAS that he regarded housing as "the most pressing architectural problem", combined with the clearing of congested areas. One would not have expected that housing the working masses would have been such a preoccupation of two such eminent Edwardian craft architects. But they were being no more than observant and, if anything, understating the case, for the 1917 Royal Commission into housing had identified that the want of housing accommodation in Scotland was "undoubtedly a serious cause of unrest".

Official recognition of the Scottish housing crisis dates back to a deputation from the Scottish Miners Federation to the Scottish Secretary, Lord Pentland in 1909. It warned him of potential serious social consequences from the disgraceful state of so many of the rows of miners' cottages.[209] Pentland instructed the Local Government Board to make enquiries, but not until 1912 was a Royal Commission appointed into the Housing of the Working Classes in Scotland: and not until 1917 that it reported. The picture it painted was quite appalling:

> Unspeakably filthy privy-middens in many of the mining areas, badly constructed, incurably damp labourers' cottages on farms, whole townships unfit for human occupation in the crofting counties and islands . . . gross overcrowding and huddling of the sexes together in the congested industrial villages and towns, occupation of one room houses by large families, groups of lightless and unventilated houses in the older burghs, clotted masses of slums in the great cities.

The Commission calculated the shortfall of houses to satisfy immediate shortage at 263,000.[210] In 1919 the Government accepted the necessity of State intervention in house provision, by offering to pay 75% of the estimated annual loss resulting from the construction of new housing schemes. The design guidelines accompanying the offer of subsidy were very specifically *garden city* :

> Street frontages should be considered as a whole, and an endeavour made by recessing certain of the groups . . . to avoid the monotony of a long straight building line. The disposition of houses should obscure, so far as possible, the view of back gardens and drying greens . . . attention should be given to the possibility of grouping a number of houses round three sides of quadrangle or other open space . . . not more than twelve houses should be placed on an acre of land.

[209] Gibson op. cit.

[210] Thus revealing that, *pro rata*, conditions were far worse in Scotland than in England.

That housing legislation was only the first of 18 such Acts of Parliament in the next 20 years. The 1923 Housing Act subsidised the construction of council houses by the private enterprise builder and the 1924 Wheatley Act broadened the scope of possible local authority house building. In 1925 the Government supported the creation of the Second Scottish National Housing Company, with the specific brief to build 2000 steel prefabricated houses.

Although Local Authorities were allowed to guarantee to Building Societies the proportion of a mortgage that the occupier was unable to provide, the opportunity was little used in Scotland. Glasgow Corporation, for example, assisted only 428 houses in this way out of its programme of almost 70,000 houses. Builders' own guarantees were used much more frequently. The Housing Acts also offered subsidy for housing "for let to persons of the working classes", but yet again it was little taken up, with barely 3000 erected in Glasgow of this type.

It was probably the availability of mortgage finance, and the Government subsidy to each new private house, which caused the immense explosion of suburban private development in Scotland. Policy makers regarded the expansion of the private sector as a useful means of releasing existing buildings for people lower in the social ladder. The first housing campaign during the Twenties was aimed primarily at tackling the actual shortage of houses; and the second and subsequent dealt with rehousing caused by slum clearance, and the necessity to reduce overcrowding. It was to this constantly changing Government policy, exacerbated by what was seen as a lack of zeal by many local authorities and a lack of adequate powers in central government to make up the difference, which Sir William Whyte attributed the "woefully disappointing" volume of houses built between the wars.[211]

There is a paradox here. Whereas Whyte concluded that Scotland's re-housing effort, compared with England proportion for proportion, was far poorer, virtually no community in Scotland remained unscathed from one or more new council estates. The country went through perhaps the biggest surge of building in its entire history, as a consequence of which the character of most Scottish localities changed almost beyond recognition—at least insofar as their outer approaches were concerned; and the majority of that building was publicly subsidised.

Private sector house construction in Scotland was almost still born representing barely 30% of total housing construction, as compared to 70% in England.[212] That may explain the relative absence of the blocks of mansion flats so common in the southern parts of England. Despite offers of Government subsidy, there was very little private building of houses to let; the assumption being that rented flats would be provided by the public authorities. Even before the war the provision of rented houses had become increasingly uneconomic for the private investor or builder.[213] After it, many architects found that their client had become the public sector. Yet the tenants within that sector in Scotland expected to pay less than their counterparts in England.[214] If housing income was to remain static, and yet higher standards were to be achieved for reasons of health, increased subsidies would be required. Those subsidies cost a great deal, and limits were soon imposed. The amount of subsidy pumped into each house decreased over time. Many of those who benefited from subsidised housing constructed following the 1919 "Addison" Act, were what became known as the "better class" tenants (classified in the 1935 Consultative Council report as "better off" with family incomes above £250 per annum) not the worst housed, but that changed after subsidies were redirected towards slum clearance. Since housing shortages and slums were concentrated in

211 Sir William Whyte: *A Housing Policy after the War* (1941).

212 Ibid.

213 Professor Roy Campbell. Speech to Thirties seminar.

214 Ministry of Labour analysis of working class expenditure during the Thirties revealed that the Scottish working classes expected to pay only 9.1% of their income on rent and rates, as compared with a general level of 12.7% in Great Britain.

the old, decaying industrial areas, it soon came about that before long, some towns—such as Airdrie and Coatbridge—came to have over 80% of their houses built by the council, as compared to a mere 5% in places like Bearsden.[215]

Pressure to reduce costs, then as now, compelled the use of novel building techniques and cheaper building materials (such as brick) and also explain why the Councils built high density in the Thirties, as opposed to the low density cottage schemes of the Twenties. And costs were indeed kept low. Whilst a "better off" bungalow in Edinburgh could sell for £750 or more, the new semi-detached houses in Kilsyth designed by Sam Bunton for the council had to be constructed for half that cost, in an attempt to extract as many houses as possible out of limited funds.[216]

House building was the most important single factor in the Scots economy and represented probably about three quarters of all building in Scotland (as compared to two-thirds for the UK as a whole). Since only a quarter of that was in private housing, it is probable that 60% of the entire Scots economy was devoted to mass public housing for most of the decade, although by 1939 (if the Edinburgh area is anything to go by) that had been reduced to only 45% of the architect's workload. The proportion of private housing to public (by value) was less than one in 20. Although for other reasons, the speculative villa, the block of flats, and the individual private house are culturally as important (if not more so) as mass housing schemes, they represented only a tiny minority of the total output. There are, for example, probably fewer blocks of Thirties mansion flats in the whole of Scotland than there are in Putney or St John's Wood.

[215] Gibson op. cit.

[216] Glasgow Corporation spent £719 per three-apartment house in 1919, and only £384 in May 1937: 17 years later the investment per flat had halved. Even the reduction in building costs could not explain such a fall as that (Glasgow Corporation ibid.). Every effort was made to contain costs. One innovation was to place the basin above the bathtub, discharging into the bath, so that bath and basin could make do with less space, one set of taps, and one set of piping and drains. A builder in Stirling boasted he had constructed a four-in-a-block for £1000.

Unbuilt scheme of terraced houses in Tillicoultry (1934), by Arthur Bracewell.

MASS HOUSING

In 1930 there was still a huge shortage of houses. Since the end of the First War, predominant house construction had been in great suburban estates and architects had been employed to design only a few of them. Although there was immense popular support for the housing programme, by 1930 public opinion was beginning to object seriously to the consequences. In 1934, Sir John Stirling Maxwell criticised the "thousands of houses built or subsidised with public money since the War" as being "more worthy of Margate, or Brighton, than the land of Burns and Scott". The following year, he addressed the RIBA Conference in Glasgow:

Glasgow has stretched out its new dormitories far into the country, and a very pleasant country it was. One would have thought that such an extension of the city could hardly have helped to absorb something of the charm of the countryside. Not at all. Trees and hedges, cottages and farm buildings have all been swept away and replaced by the stock plan, and the stock house, exactly like all the others. The country is completely blotted out.[217]

That great planner, Sir Frederick Osborne, saw fit to reinforce Stirling-Maxwell's warning three years later:

Twenty years ago, what struck me as the superiority of Glasgow over London was that it was easier to get out of. It is less easy today. Since then, Glasgow has gone on adding suburbs to itself, and has begun to rebuild its business centre at a great height and density. For the people that must still live in central Glasgow, the country and the hills are receding: and that is a terrible thing.[218]

The growing criticism put the housing authorities on the defensive, not all of them being quite so oblivious to the merits of good architecture and planning as Glasgow. That City's Lord Provost was on the defensive when he addressed the RIBA Conference in Glasgow: "I believe you will have been condemning the many municipalities for the want of foresight, and the want of thought, and the want of making use of you. Glasgow has built something like 50,000 houses. Some of you who are architecturally minded, will say that is 45,000 abortions, and 5000 houses. But after all is said and done, we have improved the situation to what it was."[219] Provision at all costs was the thing: and as late as 1939 Lord Provost Dollan still expressed enthusiasm for the appointment of a City Architect without taking any action to achieve it.[220]

INNOVATION

The Thirties was a period of optimistic development in labour-saving devices and machinery and more efficient layouts for kitchens and bathrooms. At the very height of the social scale, kitchens and bathrooms became art objects in themselves, as witness the attention given to the bathroom of Tilly Losch in London.

Houses and flats with experimental poured-concrete walls, designed for the SSHA by Sam Bunton.

SABJ/Edinburgh District Libraries

RIAS Collection

Timber-faced, concrete-panelled houses in Polbeth by Carr and Howard.

Experimentation in methods of construction and with new materials was continuous. Innovations ranged from Mactaggart and Mickel's automatic bricklaying machine to wholly new structural systems. Of the latter, two predominated: the timber kit house, and the house with walls of poured concrete. The Swedish Government, spotting a likely market, despatched Cyril Sjostrom[221] to Scotland with a present of two timber houses which were erected in five weeks at Carntyne Road. The Swedes proffered five other house designs in their booklet, emphasising the twin merits of cheapness and speed of construction. The following year the timber suppliers rammed home the message at the Empire Exhibition, with a very Scandinavian timber pavilion designed by Robert Furneaux Jordan.

The principal exponent of poured concrete houses was architect Sam Bunton, first on behalf of Kilsyth Burgh Council, and then for the Scottish Special Areas Housing Association. The development of poured concrete houses was encouraged since they could be constructed by unskilled labour—usually redundant miners. The material lent itself to a modern aesthetic, which Bunton exploited in some of his SSAHA houses, particularly in Kilmarnock.

THE SCOTTISH SPECIAL AREAS HOUSING ASSOCIATION

These house-construction experiments became wrapped up in the formation of the SSAHA, founded in 1937 as another initiative by the Secretary of State for Scotland Walter Elliot. The Association was intended to act in tandem with the Scottish Industrial Estate Corporation and shared some Board Members. Its brief was to produce as many houses as possible, as quickly as possible, in the distressed areas, using new methods which would allow the construction to be undertaken by unskilled workers.[222] Within a year, the Association was permitted to extend its boundaries beyond the distressed areas, and reduced its title to the SSHA, which it holds now. It appointed A H Mottram,[223] as consultant architect, with a panel of young architects which included Carr and Howard, Sam Bunton, and Kininmonth and Spence. Its early minutes reveal a lay misunderstanding over exactly how long it took to construct buildings, recording constant irritation from one meeting to the next (which took place every two months) that various

[217] *Quarterly* no. 50 (1935) p. 15.

[218] *Quarterly* no. 53 (1935) pp. 5-11.

[219] *Quarterly* no. 50 (1935).

[220] *Scottish Architect and Builders Journal* (June 1939).

[221] Cyril Sjostrom stayed, changed his surname to Mardall, and became a founding partner with F R S Yorke in Yorke Rosenberg Mardall (now YRM).

[222] Charles McKean: *A Mirror of Scottish Housing* (SSHA 1984).

[223] Mottram had come to Scotland in Parker and Unwin's office to build the garden village of Rosyth 1909–21: and stayed. His son James subsequently became RIAS President.

Prototype cottages and flats for the SSAHA by Carr and Howard.

housing schemes given programme approval at the previous meeting were not yet completed and occupied.

The SSHA concentrated on two types of construction: timber houses, for which they imported the material from Sweden and Canada; and poured concrete houses. It built many pretty timber cottages in places as varied as Douglas, Lanark and Biggar. Carr and Howard undertook a number of studies for the SSHA of different types of houses in different forms of construction. Most of these studies were for more advanced houses than they got a chance to build pre-war, mainly terraced housing of the sort built in Sighthill after the war. One of the first schemes which they completed for the SSHA was a group of timber houses in Polbeth, Midlothian, seemingly built of red cedar from Canada. In fact, the walls are constructed of solid, pre-cast block walling, and were essentially prefabs. The cedar is merely cladding. The only craft work done on site related to the roof since everything else consisted of the assembly of prepared units. Everything was designed to the lowest possible cost. Each house in Polbeth had to provide a four-apartment dwelling for £500, and a five-apartment dwelling for under £700. The skirting boards had be be provided for 3/8d per square foot.[224]

The SSHA had no overt interest in architecture as such, so far as one can judge from the Board Minutes. Their only attempt to hold an architectural competition failed to materialise. But Kininmonth and Spence were going to show what really could be done. Commissioned to design terraces of housing in Forth, a terribly remote village in the central uplands, they produced a scheme of timber, mono-pitched roofed houses that put the Association's Council into a terrible flurry. There was nothing folksy here: the influence being modern, principally Swedish. Originally designed to be brown, the Forth houses were painted in various shades of blue and anxious Council members made special visits to the site to recommend that the houses be decently concealed behind trees.[225]

THE PROBLEM OF ARCHITECTURE

The public attention drawn to architects by their campaign to introduce the Architects Registration Act in 1931 had the result of focussing the attention of the major public bodies upon the skills architects could offer: skills which could prove useful to assuage the growing public indignation at the lack of architectural quality in the huge new estates.

In 1935, two remarkable reports were published by the Department of

Controversial houses in Forth, 1939, by Kininmonth and Spence.

224 Interview: David Carr.

225 SSHA Minutes 1930 and 1940.

McKean

The austere architecture of Pilton, Edinburgh.

Health for Scotland. The first reported a trip by its Permanent Secretary at the instigation of the Secretary of State, to examine working-class housing on the Continent, and the second provided an overview of architectural design standards in Scotland.[226] The Permanent Secretary, John Highton, accompanied by the chief architect to the Department John Wilson, the senior depute medical officer of health for Glasgow Dr W G Clark, and the City Architect of Edinburgh Ebenezer J McRae, visited schemes in Rotterdam, Amsterdam, Hamburg, Berlin, Frankfurt, Prague, Vienna and Paris. They considered how tenants were selected, cleanliness, supervision of tenants, the problem of undesirable tenants, housing standards, and the design both of individual blocks and entire estates. They concluded that the internal planning and servicing of Scottish buildings was better than much seen on the Continent: "In the matters of adequacy of individual room space, solidity of construction and the provision of internal sanitary fitment and conveniences, our houses are probably superior to most of those we saw abroad".[227] But as far as architecture in the environment was concerned, the travellers were scathing:

McKean

Tullos, Aberdeen: these modernist bungalows could have been either public or private.

> We found that on the continent, much more attention is paid to the social and aesthetic aspects of housing schemes than is paid here. Insofar as this involves additional expenditure, the cost is willingly faced. In Scotland, we are, I think, too much inclined to regard any expenditure which is not purely utilitarian as unnecessary luxury . . . We should aim at a more imaginative architecture, and a more imaginative planning, a brighter and more colourful layout, and the provision, in an immediate proximity to the houses, of improved facilities for rest, recreation and social intercourse.

The second report (issued virtually at the same time) was the report of the Scottish Architectural Advisory Committee to the Department of Health for Scotland. The members of the committee shared with the travellers the presence of John Wilson: but it also included the architects John Begg, Frank Mears, James Miller and Thomas Tait. Their conclusions were equally stern:

> "There is a general, probably unconscious, tendency in Scotland on the part of administrators and inhabitants alike, to regard working class houses as merely measurable units of accommodation, to be judged solely by standards of internal space and comfort, and to be provided upon a purely quantitive basis, and in whatever location happens to be the most convenient at the moment".

[226] 1. *Working Class Housing on the Continent* (HMSO 1935). 2. *Report of the Scottish Architectural Advisory Committee* (HMSO 1935).

[227] Ibid.

Council houses in Sauchie.

They excoriated the use of cheap materials, raw concrete, poor brick, never-ending grey or brown roughcast, absent amenities (especially for children) dreadful landscape, and the problems of smoke, which they regarded as "the great enemy to the preservation of brightness of appearance in urban areas". Its strongest recommendation was that, in urban areas, existing types of Scottish tenemental development be abandoned in favour of "the style of architectural treatment associated with modern blocks of flats seen on the Continent". Looking at the built results of mass housing schemes of the later Thirties, it is possible to spot some influence from these two reports: and a Continental influence can be spotted in places as various as Renfrew to Rutherglen, Aberdeen to Arbroath.

THE BUILT RESULTS

Much of the criticism of housing estates was well merited. Yet some low-density schemes of considerable charm had been constructed, and for these, "garden-city" imagery was predominant. The vast majority lacked that charm. Harled, with slated or pantiled roofs, with plain dormer windows and plain doorways, the majority of the houses were semi-detached and examples can be seen in Stenhouse (Edinburgh) and Knightswood (west Glasgow) and Carntyne (east Glasgow). Stenhouse was more urban in layout, and attracted praise thereby, whereas estates like Knightswood failed to achieve any identity other than that of a large suburb.

Few early schemes were designed in what might be called a modern style. Arthur Bracewell's adventurous flats in Tillicoultry (1934) never got further than design. Thomas Tait's 1935 estate off Howwood Road, Johnstone, is a majestically modern combination of flats and semi-detached houses, some formerly flat roofed, with balconies and fashionable horizontal metal windows. Sam Bunton's designs for the Barrwood and Balmalloch estates in Kilsyth have the corner windows, white cement render, and projecting bays of the private sector. The Burgh boasted of the estate's features: "spacious balconies, sun-trap windows, flat panelled doors, oak bedsteads, and bathrooms decorated on the most modern lines". [228] A mixture of traditional style and overtly modern buildings (two-storey, flat-roofed, semi-detached houses or four-in-a-block flats)—can be found in Kemp Street, Middlefield, and Tullos, Aberdeen, possibly demonstrating the strong influence of Convenor Tom Scott Sutherland. Some housing in Ferryden by W M Patrick is even more daring—sporting not just projecting, flat-roofed, strip-windowed drum towers, but very Viennese corner blocks in striped brick and harl.

Given the possibility of low density on a large site, the preference was

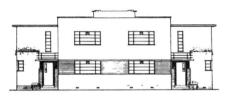

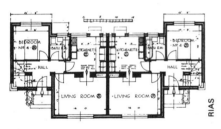

Above. S McColl's competition-winning design for a 5-apartment, semi-detached cottage. *Right.* West-quarter Garden Village, by John A W Grant.

[228] *Building Industries* (September 1938).

still for a return to a garden-city arcadia, amply illustrated by John A W Grant's winning model village for miners at Westquarter, near Falkirk. The estate of flats and semi-detached houses was carefully designed around existing natural features such as hills, burns and bridges, and the white-harled, red-tiled houses are linked by walls screening back drying greens. Its ancestors are the English Garden Cities (such as Letchworth) rather than anything specifically Scots, but it overcame this hurdle to be commended in the Saltire Society Housing Awards of 1937. Schemes by other architects in less dense locations, particularly those by the County Architect of Dunbartonshire, Joseph Weekes, displayed the tartan a bit more, with the use of Scots historic details around the doors, windows and roofs. [229] Robert Hurd, inspecting a Weekes scheme at Milton Corner in Bowling for architectural patriotism on behalf of the Saltire Society, found it good.

The desire for a modern "Scottishness" intensified as the decade progressed, and demonstrated that designers of some the suburban schemes had faced the Stirling-Maxwell criticism of characterlessness, and had met the challenge. The denser, central area schemes had, by contrast, switched allegiance to Vienna.

THE PROBLEM OF PERIPHERY

A problem already appreciated in the Thirties, but not acknowledged adequately for fifty years thereafter, was that of isolation in the peripheral housing estate. The housing pioneer Elizabeth Denby (who had been the real promotor of Maxwell Fry's housing scheme in Ladbroke Grove, London) identified the problems of the new estates to the RIBA in 1936. "The income level is low; rents, repairs and the cost of journey to work high. Although those estates are often the size of a town, they are purely dormitory, and contain no facilities for companionship. The tenants have no margin of income from which to equip the necessary buildings, even when space has been reserved for them."[230]

It is not surprising that when Cicely Hamilton visited new estates in both Glasgow and Dundee, she found resentment: "one family, newly established in what seemed to be a most eligible flat, was frankly disgruntled by its distance from the centre of the town; a disadvantage that seemed to outweigh a bathroom, good cupboards and excellent heating arrangements. The inhabitants of Dundee—a good many at least—still consider it a hardship to dwell a tram journey from their work."[231] Yet Sir Patrick Dollan, Lord Provost of Glasgow, used to boast of Knightswood: "30,000 people—the size of Inverness. No pubs and only one policeman."[232]

INCREASING DENSITIES

Later housing schemes became denser which, although appropriate for inner city locations which had been slum cleared, were built in suburban locations as well. The emphasis more upon flats than semi-detached houses was symbolised by the 1936 competition for a four-in-a-block sponsored by Glasgow Corporation, one built result of which can be seen in the unlikely location of Montrose. A consequence of higher densities was the re-affirmation of the tenement form, largely propagandised by E J MacRae, City Architect of Edinburgh. It was not the "traditional" tenement, in that the blocks were usually three storeys in height, and rarely had shops at the ground floor. (Blocks got taller towards the end of the decade, the Advisory Panel recommending increases to five storeys—although four was more normal.) The flats were thoroughly serviced. So the tenement survived remarkably well under the scrutiny for its adaptability to the 20th century, even to the extent of Greenock Burgh Council instructing Frank Mears to design an "experimental block" in 1936.

Below. "Modern" council flats, Middlefield, Aberdeen. *Bottom.* 4-in-a-block, Montrose, to J G Tedcastle's 1937 competition-winning design.

[229] Joe Weekes, as he was known, won the first Saltire Award in 1937 for his "very nice ideas" at Milton Corner, Bowling.

[230] *RIBA Journal* (1936).

[231] Hamilton op. cit.

[232] Professor Sir Robert Grieve: interview.

Wishart

McKean

Thus the scale of mass housing became more urban, and the style more Scots. In what were otherwise three-and four-storey blocks with a great pitched roof, the Scottishness was conveyed by carved, bolection-mouldings or Gibbsian details around the main door and the tall stair windows above, (often provided with viewing balconies). Good examples can be found in Crieff Road and Muirton in Perth, and in Piershill (1937–8), Edinburgh in which MacRae re-used ancient Scots details he had first used in the Grassmarket. Piershill goes over the top, trying to create a Grassmarket urbanism in the fields between Abbeymount and Portobello, by means of stone staircase towers projecting into the street in true old Scots fashion. J McLellan Brown's scheme for Morgan Place, Dundee shows a tighter grip of scale for stone tenements.

Yet it was not all old Scots. Beechwood, north-west Dundee (1936) affected a smart dress of contrasting brick dressings, yellow harling and Art Deco balconies, and an unusual lozenge-shaped scheme in western Bo'ness is distinguished by Art Nouveau-esque chimney towers above the entrance, and rhomboid-shaped windows that imply the hand of Matthew Steel.

The *Quarterly* noted in late 1938 that Glasgow had at last been infected with the "flats for the workers on the Viennese model" that Tom Scott Sutherland had been advocating in Aberdeen for the previous two years. The huge development bounded by Larchgrove Street, Springboig (1946) seems to be a built embodiment of that. The block encloses an entire square like the traditional tenement, each corner of which is marked by twin flat-roofed, semi-circular towers, with horizontal metal-framed windows. At the centre of each of the long flanks the scale, proportion and materials change to indicate the location of shops and associated facilities; brown in contrast to the yellow of the rest of the block, vertically proportioned and identified by twin semi-circular thin, spindly towers, rising up almost like cinema advertising towers or beacons, in contrast to the horizontality of the remainder. It is a very long way out of Glasgow for such a high density development. A range of two-storey shops and houses in Porterfield

RIAS Collection

Top. Morgan Place, Dundee. *Middle.* Bo'ness. *Above.* Piershill housing, Edinburgh. An attempt to create old Scots urbanity in a suburb.

Road, Renfrew, by James Steel Maitland distinguished by grand curving stair towers (1938) conveys a comparable sense of mid-Europeanism.

In Aberdeen, Councillor Tom Scott Sutherland finally overcome the coalmen's resistance to four-storey flats with Rosemount Square designed by city architect Albert Gardner in 1938. Rosemount Square is an immense D-plan enclosed estate of council house flats, entered on three sides through great eliptical arches. Above the south entrance, a superb carving is laid into the granite of a boy on a winged horse. Air-raid shelters are provided in the basement. The sheer façade of Rosemount Square reverses the normal tenement pattern: no staircase from the street. You

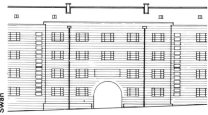

Left. Rosemount Square, Aberdeen. *Above.* Elevation of Rosemount Square. *Top.* Larchgrove, Springboig, completed after the War.

have to penetrate the private courtyard to reach those. Almost fifty years after construction, it still seems to be in reasonable condition, although it is an old, high density, inner-city estate. All that is missing from putting Rosemount Square in the pantheon of pioneering British schemes is the fact that, in pursuance of a council dictate, the walling of the scheme is in granite block and not white harled. Yet the local profession, in the *Quarterly*, thought it "distinctly foreign in form and feature . . . domesticity lost behind a veneer of civic grandeur. Only a few have noticed the allegorical sculpture by T B Huxley Jones above the arches, and still fewer understand it."[233]

Just before the war, Edinburgh District Council began work on West Pilton, which continued during the war and after it; establishing a clone in Broomhouse in 1946. Pilton is of an architectural formality which only great care could make work. Two-storey, flat-roofed, semi-detached houses, with twin rectangular projecting bays, the horizontal windows boxed out in post-war fashion. These dwellings would have done well enough (with better roofs), if painted brilliant white with scarlet windows and occupied by university professors; in mud brown, and remote from services, they provided a rather unsympathetic housing form for the people, and are now being privatised with pitched roofs and brightly coloured harl.

[233] *Quarterly* (1947).

Above. The privatisation and restyling of Pilton.
Right. Niddrie, laid out with a formal symmetry.
Below right. The Empire Exhibition's prototype
working class flats: the ground floor of a 3-storey
block designed by Mervyn Noad.

In 1938 the Scottish Council for Art and Industry commissioned Mervyn Noad to design prototype working class flats "demonstrating the most modern practice at home and abroad which is, at the same time, suitable for our climate"[234], the ground floor of which was built in the Empire Exhibition. The purpose was to "show good design in architecture and in the things of everyday use in the home"[235]. Surveyors' costings indicated that a four-bedroomed flat would cost £480 assuming the construction of a block of twelve. Lady MacGregor of MacGregor, convenor of the Exhibitions Committee of the Council (sponsors of the building) identified the key features in the new thinking: by expanding upwards instead of outwards, such buildings would liberate space for gardens and children's playgrounds; flats would save money for workers by enabling them to live near their work; bricks surrounding the windows and used for the base were cheap, and could be painted in any cheerful colour (bright blue in the exhibition); the cement would have a brilliant white finish; each flat had a balcony wide enough to take a pram supervised through the scullery window; and there would be proper organisation of the scullery, including a folding iron board, and a back-to-back grate between the living room and the scullery. Natural wood was used for furniture and beech or birch for the floors.

234 *Building Industries* September 1938

235 Sir Steven Bilsland *SABJ* November 1938

236 *Flats* (Ascot Gas Water Heaters) 1938

237 *Building Industries* September 1938. McNab was a hard, senior official of the old mould.

238 *RIBA Journal* 1952.

McKean

Left. Obertal, Largo Road, Leven.
Centre. Lamburn, Old Edinburgh Road, Inverness.
Bottom left. Sunningdale, West Ferry. *Centre*. 46a Dick Place, Edinburgh. *Right*. Drummuie, Portpatrick (1936), A MacLean Goudie.

Gracie

Wishart

McKean

Hodge

Colour was as an important component of the Empire Exhibition, but little accurate colour record survives. *Left*. The tower of Empire at night. *Right*. The Scottish Avenue. The Palace of the Arts closes the vista, flanked by the two, two-tone blue Scottish Pavilions. Note the discreet advertising hoardings on the left.

Cigarette cards, *left to right from top*: the Concert Hall, the United Kingdom Pavilion, the Garden Club, Colonial Pavilion, West Africa Pavilion, Agriculture, Fishery and Forestry Pavilion, City of Glasgow Pavilion, Australia Pavilion, Industry, Shipping and Travel, Palace of Industries (north), Scottish Pavilion (north) and the Press Club.

Topping

Wren

Far left. Palace of Industry drawn by David Harvey. *Left.* As it is today, re-erected in Prestwick. *Middle.* The Atlantic Restaurant, the ocean-liner metaphor made manifest. *Bottom left.* Plan of the Exhibition. *Bottom right.* View uphill to Garden Club.

RIAS

RIAS

RIAS

151

Tait's tower.

"The manufacturer will repeat any piece immediately. If large numbers of pieces were required for housing schemes, it would make a reduction in the price. The furniture shown illustrates that it is possible to obtain ready, well made, well-designed furniture at a reasonable cost for working class homes".[236]

The flat attracted enormous attention, official visits from Housing Authorities, and immense correspondence. The Council established a committee with Housing Authorities to exert its influence on future house design. But there was some dissent. Glasgow's director of housing, W B McNab predictably dismissed the flats on the grounds of cost, the absence of direct access to the front, wooden skirting boards instead of cement, the absence of picture rails and the steel framed windows[237]. As if to demonstrate its haughteur, it proceeded to construct an old-fashioned series of 3-storey red standstone tenements facing Anniesland Cross, the only concessions to Noad's scheme being balconies (albeit with neo-Mackintosh details). The War compelled a change of heart, and Glasgow's 1940 scheme in Penilee had metal windows, flat roofs, skirting of either latex or similar compound, balconies for prams, portholes and canopies over the main door. To some, this scheme represented Glasgow being dragged screaming into modern times. To others like James Steel Maitland, national characteristics were being "blended into one vast international commonplace of uninspired and flat-faced mediocrity"[238].

Emerson

McKean

Above. Plan of the Empire Exhibition flats. *Left.* Glasgow Corporation flats in Carntyne, 1938. *Below.* Veterans' Homes, Callander; picturesque stone neo-Scots housing thought appropriate for rural areas.

THE RURAL HOUSE

Rural housing had been a standing offence even longer than the urban tenement. Its improvement had been one of the first tasks of the APRS; and in 1931 Leslie Graham Thomson and Frank Mears produced six prototype houses, with the approval of Secretary of State William Adamson. The designs ranged from single-storey cottages to 2-storey detached houses, and were offered to authorities at £2 per house. In 1938, the Department of Health under the radical influence of Robert Matthew joined the RIAS to stage an architectural competition for the design of rural housing, the winning prizes once again being cottages with a pitched roof. In 1943 the RIAS approached the Government enquiring how the Government could help unemployed architects unable to join the services, and also how the

McKean

153

Above. RIAS Standard House Plan 16: four-apartment rural cottage – modern version.

profession could assist reconstruction. Tom Johnston, the Secretary of State replied in May 1944, inviting the Scottish profession to produce a series of house types, which could be offered to rural Local Authorities without in-house expertise, for an agreed sum. Some 38 house types were thus prepared, and offered to Local Authorities in a booklet illustrated by Jack Coia in 1945. The house types included individual cottages, semi-detached cottages and semi-detached houses, to four-in-a-block flats. The styles varied from traditional, single-storey pitched-roofed cottages, to two-storey flat-roofed houses with horizontal metal windows. Sixty-nine Burghs and 16 County Councils took up the offer, employing some 71 architects; and the designs were realised in tens of thousands from one end of Scotland to the other. Such was the legacy of the smaller Thirties house.

Different conditions prevailed post-war. Speed of reconstruction—particularly in view of the shortfall of 500,000 houses—took priority over all other considerations, leading inexorably to "the erection of temporary, pre-fabricated houses such as Arcon, Tarran and the USA type, also Swedish houses and others built on the Orlit system".[239] In the post-war housing rush, architecture and a sense of place ranked low in the priorities.

BUNGALOWS

"Their ceilings are so low that all you can have for tea is kippers."

In 1934, Robert Chalmers, a printer's artist, moved from a tenement flat to a bungalow in Priestfield Road, Edinburgh. "A bungalow", said young Chalmers' teacher at Boroughmuir, "is an Indian word for a flimsy shelter. There is little else. It will blow down before Christmas." His friends were even more knowing: "if you ever lock yourself out, you can put your hand through the window at the front to unlock the back door". As like as not, these disparagements were caused by envy: for the Chalmers family was doing what tens of thousands of other Scots families did between the wars: flitting from a tenement to a fashionable bungalow. 81 Priestfield Road is a good example of the bungalows built by Sir James Miller

Below. Mactaggart and Mickel bungalow, as built in Hillpark, Edinburgh, designed by Stuart Kaye.

in 1934. At £640, it was of a better sort, its status signified by imitation stone walls.[240] It cost a deposit of £65 down and a joint repayment of mortgage and rates of £1 per week. The young Chalmers' attention was caught by the excellent cupboard space (large enough for bikes), and by a room solely used as a kitchen. Such luxury had been unobtainable in a tenement flat. It was also caught by the cold. Compared to the warmth of a tenement flat surrounded by others, bungalows were perishing, "you put clothes on to go to bed, not take them off". Exactly a year after purchase, Miller's men returned to do "maintenance" which included making good all movement cracks, and the complete redecoration of the interior of the building in a two-colour sponge stipple. The cost to the Chalmers' family of the mortgage of this bungalow was slightly more than 1/6 of Robert Chalmers salary. It sold recently for over £50,000.[241]

BUNGALOW ANCESTRY

The use of the word "bungalow" in Scotland seems to have had marketing origins. The term was indeed Indian, associated with a single-storey house with outdoor spaces such as a covered veranda and the notion of rocking chairs and "Punkah Wallahs".[242] Translated for introduction to England in the late 19th century, it made the novelty of single-storey living respectable. It did not need such a complicated justification in Scotland. This poverty-stricken country had a tradition of single-storey cottages in rural areas, usually in terraced form but occasionally, particularly from the 19th century onwards, on separate plots. Such cottages were usually rectangular, with a room in the pitched roof, and occasionally distinguished by stone bay windows. Victorian and Edwardian lodges to great estates usually elaborated on this form, frequently L-plan with assumed ornate bay windows: and these formed the prototype of countless of thousands of Thirties bungalows. (That is fortuitously illustrated in the curious story of the Stirling Provost who so admired Basil Spence's lodge at Gribloch (1938) that he had a replica built for him in Bannockburn Road, Stirling. At Gribloch, it looks like a lodge: at Bannockburn it looks like a "moderne" bungalow.)

Top. Bungalow, Hillpark Road, Edinburgh. *Above*. The same bungalow, as built and later extended. *Left*. Earlier, grander, semi-detached bungalow in King's Park, Stirling.

239 *Quarterly* (1947).

240 Cheaper bungalows of the £425–£500 range had to make do with an external finish known as "Dorset pea" rather than imitation stone.

241 Chalmers' income, as a publisher's artist, was £4/12/6d per week. He obtained a 90% mortgage from the building society, which cost him 16/- a week over the newly extended period of 20 years, to which he added 4/- per week for rates.

242 Scotland had more than its fair share of Empire Builders wishing to retire from India back to Scotland, who may have encouraged the trend. But the Scots versions lacked the extensive servants' quarters which lay behind the Indian ones.

McKean

Baxter

The connection between the Lodge and the Bungalow. *Above.* The bungalow, Bannockburn Road, Stirling, is the Provost's purchase of a reproduction of Spence's Lodge at *Gribloch* *(right).*

The bungalow, therefore, is the traditional, Scottish single-storey rural house, translated and mass-produced in suburbia: and as such it first appears in Scotland just before the First War. Immediately after it, the Department of Agriculture built a number of T-plan single-storey houses on small holdings as "Homes fit for Heroes". Recognising, that for economic if for no other reason, the bungalow was likely to be the dominant building form in the newly colonised areas on the fringes of great Scots cities, the *Daily Mail* organised a competition in 1922 for a prototype bungalow. It was won by S N D Henderson from Ayr, with a fairly grand plan: a large E-shaped bungalow entered through the centre, the wings enclosing a patio. It also contained quarters for maids. Although a number of these, or ones like them, were built, they did not constitute the enormous bungaloid growth which soon affected both Scotland and England, with competitive cost-cutting and high-pressure sales techniques. In Scotland, in particular, the growth seems to have started about 1930.

THE BUNGALOW BUILDERS

The enormous spread of bungalows was an economic phenomenon, fuelled by the availability of easy mortgages. It virtually created new building companies, or at any rate so diverted existing building companies that they were utterly transformed. Sir James Miller related that when he had constructed his first 12 houses in Blackhall, Edinburgh and advertised them (as yet unfinished) in *The Scotsman* in 1927, all his 12 unfinished houses were sold within the day; but, more importantly, he had been informed by those who came to visit that there was a far greater demand for a smaller house. From that time onwards, he developed his type-A bungalow which remained his principal output until the Second World War.[243] Mactaggart and Mickel, previously builders of railway stations and subsidised council houses, became transformed with the new private property market. In 1931, they bought an entire page in the *Glasgow Bulletin* to announce that they had achieved "the world's record in house purchase" with the sale of 130 bungalows at Merrylee Park, Newlands within 24 hours. The package being offered was a bungalow for £25 cash with a repayment of 21/- per

[243] E A Mowat: thesis on Sir James Miller; also Miller's speech to Edinburgh Chamber of Commerce 1972.

Mactaggart and Mickel

McKean

Left. Two of 1348 similar houses sold by Mactaggart and Mickel in King's Park, Glasgow, during July 1930. It cost £645. *Above.* Hepburn bungalow in March Road, Edinburgh: reconstituted stone, oversailing roof and twin bay windows – one of the better sort.

week, along with free removal, no road charges and no legal fees. Tom Scott Sutherland in Aberdeen, with a similar package, boasted that he had sold three houses in 20 minutes. In south-west Glasgow, James Y Keanie offered well-built homes "built to stand the test of time" on 11 separate sites ranging from the Bridge of Weir to Crookston, whereas Geekie of Dundee advertised their bungalows in a "choice of 7 healthy sites" as "the gateway to happiness". Their deposit, at £25, was £10 less than Keanie.[244]

Only Mactaggart and Mickel produced a bungalow which made a gesture towards its Indian cousin: both in its showpiece Broom Estate in Newton Mearns, and in bungalows in King's Park, they provided bungalows with loggias. That in the Broom Estate was completely enclosed with glass walls which could be folded back should the weather ever prove so clement. The very existence of bungalows in the Broom Estate—some "modern", some with turrets, some with towers and fierce castle-like projections—indicates that, leveller though the bungalow might be thought to have been, there were class distinctions within.

The bungalow providers do not appear to have competed with each other, but to have had an unspoken "no poaching" agreement based on territorial lines. Thus in his own parts of Edinburgh, Miller had both £400 bungalows and his rather more expensive £600 varieties. Mac and Mick built their four-apartment bungalows costing £775 in Silverknowes whereas, barely a few hundred yards away on Craigcrook Road, Hillpark they offered a special modern bungalow for £1080, architect designed in 1937 by Stewart Kaye and Walls (designers of Lothian House). With its central doorway, curved walls, banding of brick, and curved bay windows going round the corners, you feel as though you could take the roof off, put on whirlybird rotor blades and the entire assembly could take flight.

BUNGALONOMICS

The bungalow was the nearest the Thirties got to a mass-produced cheap house, and its costs make constructive comparisons with today. Most bungalows cost £450–£750 in Scotland, although the really posh ones

[244] *SMT Magazine* advertisements throughout 1938.

Top. Maharg, Thornhill, Dumfriesshire. *Middle.*
Hunter bungalow, Dollar Road, Tillicoultry by
Arthur Bracewell (1935). Original elevation.
Above. Hunter bungalow as built. *Below. Edwana*,
Burnside Road, Broom Estate.

cost slightly more than £1000. Assuming the Chalmers family was broadly representative, the mortgage repayments absorbed only 1/6th of salary, and the deposit cost only the equivalent of three months' salary. In the same issue of the *SMT Magazine*,[245] James Y Keanie offered for sale a bungalow the identical price of a Buick Regal Coupé advertised on the page opposite: £535. It was a price just over double that of a Ford V-8 and only 2/3 of that of a Humber Pullman Saloon. To judge by contemporary furnishing advertisements, by Edinburgh's Patrick Thomson's, it was thought by no means extraordinary that people should be expected to spend between 15% and 20% of the price of their new house on their bedroom and dining room suites (in the most fashionable lines with walnut veneer and "beautifully curved mahogany").

BUNGALURBIA

Bungalows were built in their hundred thousands, in astonishing variety and astounding quantity. Falkirk spread uphill to the south; Aberdeen to the west and north; Dundee to the east and west; and Glasgow—in all directions of the compass, but particularly the south-west into Renfrewshire. They tended to follow and line the main roads (at least until the 1935 Ribbon Development Act) whereas local authority housing estates tended to form enclaves of their own away from those roads; indeed, the estates were often lined on the outside by bungalows, either as a guarantee of respectability, or more probably because the private developer could afford to purchase the more favoured sites fronting the main road. Each bungalow had to display its own individuality, no matter how artificial the lengths which were gone to to achieve the effect. It is not unusual to find, as one does in a small area of Brechin for example, a large number of single-storey houses, each one significantly different from the others.

In looking for common characteristics of bungalows (excluding the internal planning), one would have to conclude that there are no common characteristics save a pitched roof and the fact that the building is usually single-storey (although the really classy bungalows had a prominent room with dormer window in the roof). Their idiosyncratic details may well represent popular taste having a chance to express itself for the first time. As one might expect, it is expressed more clearly around the windows and the doors, of

Left. Semi-detached bungalow in Fort William. *Above.* Bungalow, King's Gate, Aberdeen. Some rare adventurism from T Scott Sutherland.

which there is the most astonishing variety: picture windows, metal strip windows, triangular windows, portholes, lozenge-shaped windows, and bay windows of all types including neo-Tudor. Doorways may be enobled by classical columns, cocooned by a circular brick arch, blessed with Arts and Crafts carving and stained glass, dignified by traditional carved stone Scots details, or streamlined with porthole or slit windows, shiny black doors and plentiful chrome. There was no general pattern in plan form, considerable numbers of bungalows being semi-detached, a lot square, a lot rectangular, and a lot L-plan. They might, or might not, have bay windows, might or might not be symmetrical, and might or might not be entered from the side, the front, or in the corner.

Despite these varieties, there were some broad bands of character; the bungalows of Kessington in Glasgow are predominantly red brick; those in Blackhall, Edinburgh are reconstituted stone, whereas Cicely Hamilton commended the bungalows found in Aberdeen for being "granite-grey and sturdy—it would be an insult to place these bungalows in the same class as the pink-roofed, rough cast erections of our English-home counties". The colour of many of the new bungalows was a prime cause of criticism. It symbolised to D H Lawrence the enslavement of the spirit:

> Still more monstrous, promoters of industry today are scrabbling over the face of England with miles and square miles of red brick homes, like horrible scabs. The men inside these little red rat-traps get more and more helpless, being more and more humiliated, being more and more dissatisfied like trapped rats.[246]

Harry Alberry reported thus on one of the RIBA Conference trips in 1935: "here we passed the house that was once the home of Sir Harry Lauder: there we avert our eyes from a red brick building which must blush each dawn in the knowledge that it is a blot on the landscape, and welcome the approach of mantling dusk".[247] The editor of the *Quarterly*, commenting upon the new proposals for the Highlands and Islands, noted with disgust "beneath one of the most spectacular hills of the North West, rugged and grand, an enterprising builder has contrived to erect half a dozen reproductions of *Mon Repos* from suburbia with pink asbestos roofs".[248]

Colour apart, bungalurbia was not a pleasant new phenomenon. Before the First War, most towns and cities in Scotland simply stopped at the

[245]   *SMT Magazine* August 1938

[246]   *Architectural Review* 1930

[247]   *RIBA Journal* August 1935

[248]   *Quarterly* no 61 (1939)

Tullos. There is little difference between the flat-roofed semi-detached houses, and the bungalows in the foreground, save their roofs.

edge: their character clearly defined by a sharp definition between town and country. All those advantages were lost as the approaches became blurred with bungalows. Robert Matthew and his team, considering the phenomenon in their 1937 exhibition in the RSA, pointed out that whereas bungalows provided a perfectly acceptable method of living in the countryside, their concentration in large groups had failed to provide identity. Robert Hurd agreed. "I do not know what picture forms in your minds eye at the mention of the words 'Edinburgh suburb': maybe the south side with its circumspect villas and trim gardens; maybe the tenements of Gorgie; maybe the sanitary gloom of Niddrie; or maybe those chatty, perky bungalows which seem to have cropped up in every direction." Thus he addressed the Saltire Society in 1939. "Many acres of land on the south side of Queensferry Road are controlled by the city authorities, and yet it is one of the grimmest areas of bungalow development in the east of Scotland. As superiors, the city had every opportunity for a decent standard of design for the bungalows and their land, but that district today is one huge, wasted opportunity."[249]

Architecturally the bungaloid areas are indeed hard to like although their rawness, devastatingly dissected by Edward Muir in his description of Prestwick, has now been muted by mature trees and bushes:

> The Main Road which now runs through both towns, strung with houses all the way, is a glaring concrete waste, and the soil round about it has the angry inflamed look one often finds in raw new suburbs. This road and these houses were created to serve the pleasures of industrial man. To such places, the Glasgow magnate retires for the weekend towing his favourite typist, a big balloon attended by a little balloon to enjoy amid concrete, dust and the hoots of motor cars the amenities of love and seclusion.[250]

The absence of any identity or any form of recognisable urbanity in the new bungalurbias, the monotony of the wide roads, and their undeviating remorselessness, stick in the craw. Bungalows were too small to create a new townscape, and too large to be imperceptible: they seemed like a series of boils. People were slow to get to grips with the fact that the rise of the bungalow was an economic phenomenon, and satisfied an immense latent demand: and that the real challenge was to investigate how areas of bungalows could be given an identity comparable to that of earlier, Victorian suburbs.

[249] *Quarterly* no. 61 (July 1939) pp. 11–18.

[250] Muir op. cit. p. 94.

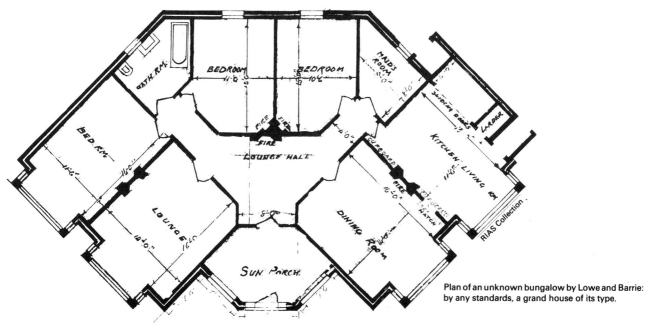

Plan of an unknown bungalow by Lowe and Barrie: by any standards, a grand house of its type.

RIAS Collection

RIAS Quarterly

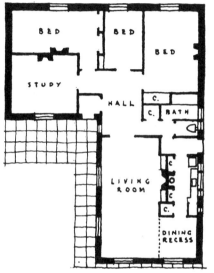

BUNGALARCHITECTURE

A small, single-storey house on a minimal standard plot is not a prime candidate for architectural distinction. Yet few architects felt too grand to attempt the design of these "little villa-type of houses" as Sir Robert Lorimer called them (some of which were only scaled-down versions of his Colinton Cottages). Indeed, in 1935 the RIAS held an architectural competition for a £1000 bungalow, which was won by Robert Matthew with an L-plan, pitched-roof building looking much more like a traditional cottage than a heavy-shouldered bungalow. William Kininmonth, Basil Spence, Ian Carnegie, Launcelot Ross, James Carrick and T Scott Sutherland were amongst the many architects who ventured their hand at it. Architect William Patrick of Dundee, twinned with builder William Black, sprayed the east coast with their version, and architects Gordon and Scrymgeour earned much of their living from bungalows in West Ferry. William Guild designed a number in Cupar—one, complete with curved windows, to live in himself.

The notion of a heavy, pitched roof as an essential component of the bungalow is emphasised by the surprisingly wide scatter of single-storey buildings stripped of their bungaloid character by a flat roof and fashionable details. In Ochil Road, Stirling, there are several such with the Art Deco square-headed pediment. Percy Hogarth built a number of flat-roofed bungalows with curving doors in Ayr, No 151 Prestwick Road being a good surviving example. A better has just been bungaloided out of existence with a pitched roof and replaced windows in the village of Boreland, by

Left. Bungalow at Ratho for the Rushforths. Ian Carnegie, 1937. *Above.* Robert Matthew's winning design for the *1000 guinea bungalow*.

13 Wittet Drive, Elgin, probably designed by J & W Wittet.

Kirkcaldy. A real oddity can be found in Wittet Drive, Elgin, where two near-identical, adjacent bungalows, both vividly white, with cut away corner entrances and horizontal windows, differ only in their roofs: the one pitched, the other flat. The former is a bungalow: the latter is *listed* as a building of architectural and historic interest. It is indeed striking: which simply emphasises the extent to which the aesthetic of hard rectangular shapes overrode simple function. In the pursuit of modernism, the designer of 13 Wittet Drive deprived the occupants of any loft space.

Architectural penetration, as the word is, of the bungalow market was small; and it was in an attempt to try to influence the builders that Robert Hurd suggested criteria for bungalow improvement to the Saltire Society: away with the "chatty and perky" bay windows, dormers and fashionable brick details; back with symmetry, hipped roofs and discreetly tucked chimneys. Yet his plea was made in March 1939: the first great bungalow boom was almost at an end; and he was dead by the time of the second, 25 years later.

Below. Percy Hogarth bungalow in Prestwick Road, Ayr. *Below right.* Robert Hurd's sketch of the "better bungalow" in March Road.

The better Bungalow —
—round the corner

The fact that the tenement edge of the great towns of Scotland was still visible in 1914 is a clear indication that the country had not yet enjoyed the explosion of late Victorian and Edwardian "bye-law" terraced housing that occurred further south: and which produced an alternative to central area living, at reasonable prices, for a wide range of the population. Up to the war, many of the Scottish lower and middle classes had no alternative but to live in one of the better-off tenements—a "wally" (china-tiled) close. Terraced, semi-detached, or detached houses (of necessity in stone) had been the preserve of the richer. The coming of the mass-produced bungalow changed all that.

In a speech to the Edinburgh Chamber of Commerce in 1972, Sir James Miller welcomed the fact that one of his £400 bungalows was by then worth over £12,000. The fact that it is currently worth possibly over £50,000 is an indication that the single-storey house or bungalow was no inter-war aberration but provides a convenient arrangement of accommodation, on a conveniently sized plot, at a convenient location for the city centre.

MANSION FLATS

Life in a mansion flat is an image inseparable from the inter-war period, mainly as a result of P G Wodehouse's Bertie Wooster; young, upper-class twits and flappers, on the razzle in town during the week, escaping to the Home Counties at the weekend. But the Home Counties are a long way from Scotland. Few blocks of mansion flats were built in Scotland, the majority of residential Thirties building catering, by contrast, for people trying to escape from flat life into a house with a garden. Furthermore, tenement flats were still being built (e.g. Comely Bank, Edinburgh).

The difference between a mansion flat, and a modern tenement was that access to a mansion flat would be by lift rather than stair, the common areas would be private; living-in caretaking or a service would be provided; and each flat would have its own servants' quarters.

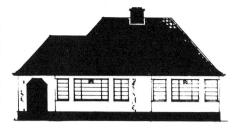

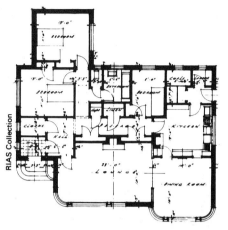

RIAS Collection

Above. William Guild's own house in Brighton Road, Cupar.

Kelvin Court, Glasgow: caretaker's house on the left.

W Dick

251 The tenement staircase, traditionally concealed at the centre, or projecting to the rear of the building, thus takes its place in the main façade and becomes part of the designer's vocabulary. A 1936 Sir James Miller block in Bruntsfield Gardens develops this idea by emphasising the staircase as a tower, standing forward, proud and slightly higher than the rest, with Art Deco modelling.

252 Ex info: Peter Robinson.

253 Douglas Mickel.

254 Facing brick was more expensive than white-rendered common brick: thus economics contrived to lend the caretaker's house a spurious modernism denied to the flats.

White House

Right. Flats, Napier Road, Edinburgh, with their spacious balconies.

Learmonth Terrace mansion flats. Note the car park entrance on the left, and the glazed staircase tower behind.

McKean

Tenement flats were still tenement flats with an open stairwell; but a good example of how they changed in the Thirties is the huge block in Falcon Avenue designed by J R MacKay (the architect of Binns) for the proprietor of the Falcon Garage, Edinburgh. The fresh air fad had penetrated even tenement design: there are strip balconies and tall triangular windows lighting the stairwell. The blocks' old-fashioned construction of a solid brick wall is slightly counterbalanced by the modernity of reinforced concrete floors and staircases and the façade of precast cement slabs. Presumably the "wrot" iron fence—now missing—was also a gesture.[251]

A block of flats on Napier Road, designed by John Jerdan in 1935 probably represents Edinburgh's first brush with mansion flats. The innate rectangular form of the building is disguised by bands of brickwork and cutaway open corner balconies.

In 1935 T Bowhill Gibson extended Learmonth Terrace, Edinburgh with a long block of old-fashioned, artificial stone-fronted mansion flats, whose only Thirties characteristics are the entrance halls, the glazed semi-circular curved staircases projecting from the rear, and the peculiar curvilinear concrete entrance canopy to the underground car park. A larger, later development by Sir James Miller downhill to the north, aspired to be Edinburgh's grandest mansion flats and was designed to be faced in stone. War prevented its full realisation, and it was completed in brick with only a limited use of stone around the principal entrances.[252] The interior, particularly the hall and corridors, is brisk, but hardly grand. Tom Scott Sutherland was unsuccessful in persuading Aberdeen to permit any of his proposals for mansion flats. In the west, there were no such reservations. Bill Gladstone designed two smart blocks with underground parking in the Broom estate (see page 169) into which house occupiers were encouraged to move when their houses or gardens got too big for them.[253] Each flat had a large dining room, a lounge, two bedrooms and maid's quarters, for a rent and rates of £250 per annum (i.e. two years rent would purchase a Keanie bungalow just along the road). The stairwell had smart streamlining details not unlike parts of the Beresford Hotel, the rear of which was enclosed in a curved, glass block wall to conceal the servants' stairs behind. The brick exterior and pitched roof was comfortable rather than adventurous, as was appropriate for Broom.

Kelvin Court, facing the Boulevard at Anniesland, was the largest private flat development in Scotland during the Thirties: over 100 flats in two enormous 11-storey blocks. Despite sneers of Bearsden villa-dwellers that the development was vulgarly "arriviste", it was a clever, popular development in an expanding industrial area with excellent communications by

Mactaggart and Mickel

Below. Sandringham Flats, Broom Estate, by Bill Gladstone, 1938. *Bottom*. The Ravelston flats motif.

train, tram, bus and car to central Glasgow. Both architect J N Fatkin and his developer, hailed from Newcastle, which may explain an English aesthetic of brick and stone bands emphasising the horizontality of the blocks, punctuated by vertical stair towers. The south (private) front is transformed by its curving brick balconies accessible, in the approved fashion to two rooms, and overlooking a little white, flat-roofed caretaker's house.[254]

Neil and Hurd's Ravelston Garden, 1935 (and thereafter known as the Jenners Flats in tribute to the managing agents) is the most self-conscious mansion flat design in Scotland. As is evident from the original perspective, the architect (thought to be Andrew Neil rather than Robert Hurd) saw these flats as one of a piece with cloche hats, roof gardens, limousines, and sun terraces. The three large blocks, each linked to single-storey curving garage

Right. Ravelston Flats: plan.

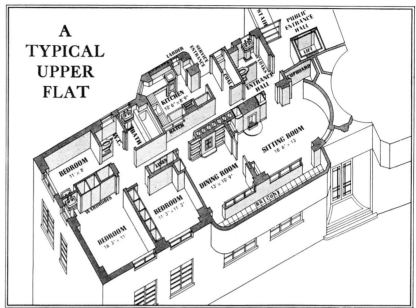

A
TYPICAL
UPPER
FLAT

Above. Kelvin Court doorway.

wings are designed on a butterfly plan. The servant entrances, service access and rubbish are disposed centrally in the building, invisible to residents and their guests. The flats were planned as interconnecting suites of rooms, cupboards and recesses in the principal living room opening right through into the hall. Robert Hurd had an architectural nationalist vision which he considered was realised in the Ravelston flats. He aspired after buildings as truly Scots as the architecture of "that most national period" of 1600, by taking the architecture of that period and stripping it of period details like turrets and crow-step gables; by such means arriving at the basis of a modern Scots aesthetic. Unfortunately, this good polemical point is at variance with the sweeping curving balconies, distinctly not a feature of 17th-century Scottish tower houses, but rather of blocks of flats found in some profusion on the south coast of England, and seaside hotels in places from Saunton to Morecambe.

Right. Ravelston Flats.

McKean

SPECULATIVE ESTATES

Previous to the First War, villas in Scotland were faced with stone (often red sandstone), and, where not terraced, were usually on reasonably spacious sites. The post-war equivalent on a small site was virtually a new building type, and, in the early days, the inspiration was English; north of the Border flowed red roof tiles, tile-hung bays, and mullioned windows—the only concession to Scotland being a preference for render for the side and back walls in the place of English brick. Echoes of Kent in Caledonia.

Into the Thirties, the predominant style changed: houses would be given pyramid roofs of thick orange or green pantiles, and be white harled. Crittal's horizontal windows would be used for protruding, curved corner bay window for that newly titled room, the "lounge". Where the houses were joined as semi-detached, the lounge bay windows of each would be fused together into a billowing, glazed belly with the porch canopy taken right across the top tying the houses together visually as a single design.

Discussing house building to sell in 1936, Gordon Allen described what motivated the private buyer:

> What the average person wants as regards the elevations of his house is a question of psychology rather than art. It is safe to say he desires his home to look different to his neighbours and, above all, unlike the municipal house, owing to his sense of social dignity. In many instances, the modernist elevation, with its freshness and breadth appeals to him a great deal. This kind of design lends itself to bright colouring, and can include large windows and the ever popular bay—without too many glazing bars. The absence of ornamention promises a low bill for repairs.[255]

Allen was writing about England: and the techniques used in Scotland undoubtedly derived from southern England and the prototypes displayed in the various Homes Exhibitions.

In some respects, Scottish speculative villas are not dissimilar to counterparts in Enfield, Park Royal, Mill Hill, Bournemouth or Bromley or Bude. The

McKean

Above. Lady Nairn Avenue, Kirkcaldy. *Below*. One of the Lady Nairn houses in detail: note the stairtower, recessed porch, and sunburst motif on the door.

[255] *House Building* (1936).

167

Aberdeen's *Modern Homes* in Broomhill Avenue, all the original windows removed.

Craighouse Avenue, Edinburgh. Semi-detached on a hillside, possibly by Sir James Miller.

singular difference lies in the proportion: these Scots houses are smaller, taller and more squeezed than those further south. Perhaps the largest single concentration can be found in Whitecraigs/Giffnock, Clarkston and King's Park in Glasgow, most constructed by Mactaggart and Mickel; though smaller, such developments—such as the street of semi-detached houses in Evelyn Street, Perth—were quite widespread. They were very cheap. Mac and Mick (not to be outdone by John MacDonald's "house that Jean built" at the 1933 Ideal Home Exhibition) built a modern semi in Central Station in 1934 of the type selling for £500 in Clarkston "modernistic in design, special attention given to health and sunlight". They were good at their marketing: this house was known as the Colour Home: "some had glazed green pillars, and roof tiles, others had natural green roof slates, and if not green, bases and features were red rustic, all giving this contrast".[256] Their subdividable house (3 or 5 rooms according to occupier choice) was known as the Super Unit.

These were the "moderne" houses that Lionel Brett condemned retrospectively, when inviting the public to distinguish between modern houses and poor imitations[257].

The trouble is that it takes a trained eye to distinguish the modern from the modernistic. With earlier styles it was easy: the genuine was old, the fake was new. In our day, the two go on together, and the creative Jekyll is dogged by a clumsy Hyde who picks up the more superficial aspects of the modern manner (the flat roof, the corner window, the strong horizontal) and attached a jazzy version of them to his otherwise quite conventional building. The novice is advised to look for simplicity, and for the time being to treat smartness, streamline and luxury with suspicion.[258]

Thus spake the purist. Yet even such noted London architects as Welch, Lander and Cachemaille-Day, designers of a number of inter-war churches in London, and the Park Royal Tube Station, lent their design skills to the creation of a series of semi-detached "moderne" villas, unified by single green tile, pitched roof. The publicity given to such creations may explain the near-identical houses designed and built by Sir James Miller in Morningside Drive, 1936. As with bungalurbia, the environment of these new villas consists of wide curving roads with little vegetation, forming the setting for rank upon rank of tall, white-harled pitched-roof houses, with curved bay windows, the occasional corner window, and some jazz-recessing detail

256 Interview: Douglas Mickel.

257 Lionel Brett: *Houses* (Penguin 1947).

258 See W A Miller's interesting thesis: *International Style Housing in Scotland* (1979).

around the doors. It should be borne in mind that these are speculative houses of a fairly low price on small plots: and their inability to be more truly modern, in the ways desired by a purist is caused as much by its cost as by any artistic failing.

There were some exceptions to these trends—the experiment of Balfour Builders (in Fife), Mactaggart and Mickel (in Glasgow and Edinburgh), Modern Homes (Aberdeen) and Sunlit Homes (Glasgow). In 1933, Douglas Mickel was dispatched to Edinburgh, beginning their private-sector development with a series of semi-detached houses in Silverknowes, designed by William Gladstone, their "in-house" architect, with corner windows, cut away porches with green glazed brick columns, and triangular projecting windows lighting the staircases. Hillpark, a few· hundred yards away, begun two years later with the construction of No 409 Queensferry Road and adjacent bungalows, was to be the better estate, where the builder himself would settle; and its inspiration derived from Mac and Mick's new flagship on the west coast—the Broom Estate, Newton Mearns. In September 1936, Douglas Mickel took a Mr Denholm (purchaser of No 409), through to the Broom to see No 1, designed by James Taylor. He bit, and for £1485 Mickel got Stewart Kaye to design and build its mirror image in Hillpark. So what was the Broom?

THE BROOM ESTATE

The Broom Estate became a byword for smart, fashionable living in the Thirties for those in the west of Scotland, the 20th-century answer to Bearsden. Carefully marketed by Mac and Mick for its seclusion, its trees, water, burn and landscape, and its distance from the city, smog, slums and smoke, it earned its title "Estate" since each house was set in its own grounds, and the roads were curved around existing landscape features. It was at the top end of the speculative market, and a world away from the mass villas of Whitecraigs. Mac and Mick were selling an English con-

Wishart

Mactaggart and Mickel

Swan

Top. Before and after: *Sunnylea* and *Kalinga*, Largo Road, Leven, possibly designed by Lawrence Rolland. *Middle.* 5-apartment semi-detached villas, Braehead, Glasgow. *Above.* The semi-detached aesthetic transformed into triple-detached. A 3-house terrace by Arthur Bracewell, Moss Road, Tillicoultry (1937). *Left.* 409 Queensferry Road, Edinburgh (1937), by Stewart Kaye.

McKean

cept, English from the red-brick garden walls to the tile hanging on some houses, symbolised by the fact that they called their loch a lake.

The Broom is divided into different sections. Area A was to be overtly modern. "The adoption of modernism", trumpeted their *Glasgow Herald* advertisement of April 1935 "does not always bid goodbye to beauty" (note the *not always*!). In that area of Broom, Mac and Mick offered in-dividually designed houses in "striking modern architecture", each designed by James Taylor, an architect with whom Frank Mickel had trained. The same advertisement, illustrated by flat-roofed cubist design by Taylor, em-phasised that no two houses in the Estate would be identical, and that the "harmony of the estate and its natural amenities" would be respected. There is no evidence in the Broom that any of Taylor's flat-roofed houses were actually built; Area B was for houses and bungalows with pitched roofs. It is clear that the mass houses and bungalows erected by Mac and Mick subsequently derived from these designs, prepared by their architect Gladstone or by Taylor himself.

Broom Estate houses were generally large: double-fronted instead of single-fronted, and bungalows with pillared loggias enclosed in glass which folded back. Living and dining rooms were generally linked to each other by sliding glass doors; the kitchens and bathrooms were fitted with the most up-to-date equipment; and the light fittings, fireplaces and light de-tails were pure Art Deco. The notion of providing an individual architect to design for plot purchasers was possibly unique in the Scottish speculative market, only John R H McDonald of Sunlit Homes coming close (see below).

Messrs Balfour of Kirkcaldy provided speculative, small, semi-detached houses, based, it seems, on prototypes they had seen in exhibitions in London.[258] They deviated considerably from the norm in Lady Nairn Avenue on the Dysart side of Kirkcaldy. Some of the houses were examples of what can be seen from Broughton (Edinburgh) to Burnside (Rutherglen): semi-detached, pitched-roofed villas, with projecting, flat-roofed window bays. Three pairs in the middle are flat-roofed, white (not mud brown), cement rendered, two of them having a fretted parapet linked by tubular railings. One is still sufficiently undamaged to show how very distinctive these houses were intended to be: a solid white cube, with bands (cur-rently blue) emphasising the horizontality—save for the stair tower which projects both from the plane of the side wall, and above the roof line to emphasise verticality. The porch is cut away from the corner, and the door has a sunburst motif.

Four pairs of houses and a singleton face Largo Road, Leven designed by Lawrence Rolland for Andrew Cook of Leven. Two are capped with a pitched roof, but have (or had) horizontal windows, cut away porches and a recessed bedroom balcony at first-floor level. Two pairs have the flat roof of Lady Nairn Avenue. Obertal is an oddity: a two-storey and roof garden villa, very similar but smaller (single rather than double-fronted) to the "house that Jean built" of the Daily Mail Ideal Homes Exhibition of 1932: and for the story of *that* oddity, we must move to John R H MacDonald, in Hillfoot, Glasgow.

CARSE VIEW DRIVE

Carse View Drive, Hillfoot, deserves a niche on its own because of its completeness, and because of the broader aims of those who built it. The promotor was John R H MacDonald, son of Sir John MacDonald, builder of Burnside, Glasgow, who, in 1924, had patented a flat-roofed, semi-detached house prototype to profit from the new council house boom, its only distinguishing feature being the flat roof itself. Many were built in Carntyne for Glasgow Corporation (all now having received pitched caps on

Mactaggart and Mickel

Opposite. James Taylor's adventurous houses in the Broom: no-one was tempted. *Above.* Broom Estate interiors.

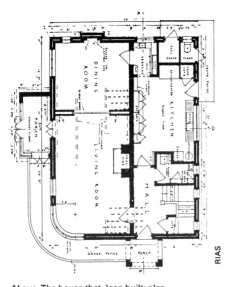

Above. The house that Jean built: plan.

RIAS

top). MacDonald *père et fils* visited modern Continental houses, particularly the 1927 housing estate at Weissenhof, Stuttgart.[259] The result of that trip was a book by the younger MacDonald entitled *Modern Housing*[260] whose publication aroused considerable partisan feeling. The reviewer in the *Quarterly* dismissed it contemptuously as an expensive 25/- advertisement of his father's firm; whereas the *RIBA Journal* found it valuable and informative "which would do much to arouse the interest both of laymen and architects".

Unfortunately, the *Quarterly* had the better judgement. MacDonald selected from any contemporary Continental house key attributes for which he wished to propagandise in Scotland: the ultra-modernity of cubist shapes, flat roofs for sun terraces and roof gardens, advances in light and "air space", speed of erection, and standardised steel windows. But the book was really a propaganda document for flat roofs and cavity walls written for consumption by lay councillors.

In 1930, his father established a subsidiary company, Sunlit Homes Ltd, in order to build such houses, with little success until the construction of a home in the 1931 Ideal Homes Exhibition in the Kelvin Hall. Called the "Sunlit Home" after the name of the company, it had a flat roof, a roof garden, and an orientation towards the sun. It thus predated Wells Coates' Ideal Home "Sunspan" house, with its south-facing, glazed bay by two years. The following year, the *Daily Mail* sponsored a competition for an Ideal Home which was won by a Glasgow teacher Mrs Reid, her design being christened "the house that Jean built", and built within the exhibition. Sunlit Homes offered to erect that house at sites in Bearsden, Burnside or Hillfoot for £1000. It was a large, double-fronted, two-storey house with roof garden, top conservatory and corner windows. The only house in Scotland, so far discovered, that even approximates to this prototype is Obertal, Largo Road, Leven. It is not as adventurous as its original: there are no windows going smartly around corners, and the house is single-fronted. But what it does share is the characteristic of being a two-storey, flat-roofed house, with a roof terrace entered from a third-storey, glass-enclosed room.

Mrs Reid explained that her house was modern

> to give the maximum of comfort with the minimum of labour. There are no mouldings, and the doors are of smooth wood, without panels, their beauty depending entirely upon the veneer. The house is all-electric with the exception of one coal fire, which gives a homely feeling to the principal sitting room.

The house was really designed around the kitchen:

> A well designed kitchen is as necessary to the smooth running of a house as a well designed engine is to the smooth running of a motor car. The kitchen is the engine of the house, and a good kitchen is equivalent of several servant power just as a car engine is equivalent of several horse power.

The MacDonalds claimed that the construction of a two-storey house was cheaper which, bearing in mind that a full two-storey house was being offered for £1000, whereas Mac and Mick's Hillpark bungalows cost more, was evidently correct. What is odd is the difference between the designs of "the house that Jean built" and the houses in Carse View Drive—one of which (at least) was bought at the Ideal Homes Exhibition itself. Eight two-storey houses were built in Carse View Drive, Bearsden, between 1933 and 1936, together with MacDonald's own house round the corner. Seven of the eight are two-storey buildings, square or rectangular in plan, with the exception of one rounded, glazed corner facing south. Most have projecting porches, and No 9 has a canopy at first-floor level, which, once faced with a railing, may have been a balcony. Only No 1 has access to the roof, and that is by an outside staircase. There was little attempt to

Below. Obertal, Leven.

Wishart

exploit the flat roof to give a free plan inside, and most of the roofs have given trouble at some points.

MacDonald was no architect. Yet he demonstrated architectural ideals in his houses, and produced engineer's architecture of great impact but little subtlety. Those white drum towers stand like pre-historic monoliths on their site: and are rapidly acquiring an appropriately totemic significance in the history of modern architecture in Scotland.

Top. 1 Carse View Drive – the only one with formal access to the roof. *Top right*. No. 10. *Above.* No. 2. *Above middle.* No. 5. *Above right*. No. 8.

[259] Lindlay Nelson thesis: *John R H Macdonald and Sunlight*, to whom some of the information in this section is indebted.

[260] *Tiranti* (1931).

THE INDIVIDUAL PRIVATE HOUSE

THE
DAILY MAIL
ALL-SCOTTISH
HOUSE

Below. Broadmeadow, Symington, Ayrshire, 1933, designed by Noad and Wallace.

Despite the evaporation of the private house market that had prevailed before 1914, there remained a residual demand for architect-designed residences. Their size and type tended to depend upon whether the houses were in the country or on the outskirts of a town. The latter were very much smaller, designed for the upwardly mobile, whereas some fairly large establishments with ancillary offices were provided for the former.

Gribloch, near Kippen, designed in 1937 by Basil Spence in association with Perry Duncan of New York for the steel family Colville, was probably the only large country house to adopt the modern style (and even then, muted with Hollywood Regency overtones) complete with swimming pool, water sculpture and double-height glazed hall. Inverewe House, built in 1937 to replace that earlier destroyed in fire, displays certain modern elements, the plain whiteness and horizontality of the windows, modified by a calmly swept roof and prominent chimney stacks. Generally however, the larger private houses were designed either in craggy Scottish carved stonework, or in the vaguely Dutch South African style adopted by Leslie Graham Thomson (and many others elsewhere) in his own house at West Linton and Ardnasaid, Easter Belmont. In 1932, the *Daily Mail* held a competition for a Scottish country house that had to combine the amenities of modern living with native Scots characteristics. The winning design by J W Laird and Napier was a medium-sized L-plan house, in cement render with stone dressings, distinguished by a large, round stair-tower in the internal corner with a Lorimer cap. It provided 4 bedrooms in addition to maid's quarters, and cost slightly over £2000. Faint whiffs of Mackintoshian modernity could

RIAS Collection

be detected around the main entrance. There were aberrations: James Miller designed an occasional classical house, Noad and Wallace ventured into lavishly flamboyant Tudor in Broadmeadows, Symington (1933)[261], and Basil Spence produced two wholehearted forays into old Scots, one of which the huge Broughton Place (from 1934) is neo-17th century. "The client wanted a mediaeval keep" says Kininmonth of Broughton, "so we gave it her."[262] She received, rather, a 17th-century tower house with 13 bedrooms, bathrooms, 3 dressing rooms and, amongst other services, a picturesquely crow-stepped servants hall. One looks in vain, at Broughton, for any hint of a Mackintosh influence ex Hill House; or even a baronialising of modern

[261] Broadmeadows is the house that all readers of the *Honeywood File* must have in their mind's eye when reading that book.

[262] Interview.

Baxter

Swan

Stokes

Top left. Greywalls, Perth Road, Dundee, 1929–33; an English Arts and Crafts manor house by Patrick Thoms. Above. Gribloch. Left. Broughton Place. Below left. The Pines, Dollar, designed by Patrick McNeil. Below. Drawing room, Littleway, Bieldside, designed by David Stokes, The partition to the Dining Room is folded back.

RCAHMS

Right. Ardnasaid, Easter Belmont, designed by Leslie Graham Thomson. *Below. Moderne*, off Slammanan Road, Falkirk: note stair window, and porch hood derived from the Beresford Hotel.

McKean

W Dick

Above. 42 Pendicle Road, Bearsden, 1938, built by John Lawrence.
Right. Littlecroft, Paisley, the house of James Steel Maitland.

attitudes toward indoors/outdoors. The house is in the direct Lorimer tradition, massing from Balmanno and roofs from Formakin. Kininmonth and Spence had already designed a pleasant, 18th-century Scots houses in outer Edinburgh, Glenburn, Glenlockhart, a number of cottages in Comiston.

Areas of Thirties suburbia in Scotland are usually recognisable by their road layouts, their verdure and white rendered boundary walls lining the pavement. The houses erected behind are almost impossible to characterise, being in as many styles as there were clients and architects. It is in these areas that most of the flat-roofed modern houses are to be found, mostly overwhelmed by houses with pitched roofs in red, black or green, and an indiscriminate variety of motifs from Stockbroker Tudor to Art Deco. Nonetheless the *avant-garde* seems to have clung together for comfort in Bearsden, Carmunnock, Roddinghead Road Whitecraigs, Barnton and Cramond. Fashionable motifs ranged from concrete balconies with Art Deco details (as in Carradale, Mary Street, Dunoon), great octagonal, glazed staircase towers (Kilmardinny Avenue, Bearsden) to the house by Cecil Stewart in Perth, the location of whose staircase is indicated by a sequence of four portholes rising like ducks on the wall. Most of these new houses had utility rooms instead of maids' bedrooms, symbolising the change in the clientèle for the single private house.

RCAHMS

Left. Carradale, Dunoon, designed in 1935 by Jack Reid.
Below left. 23 Rubislaw Drive, Bearsden. *Below*. Upton, Corsebar Road, Paisley, with its newspaper perspective. Possibly designed by Basil Spence.

MODERNISMUS[263]

It is often only in the purpose-designed private house that one can see the unadulterated architectural culture(s) of the time, untramelled by problems of finance, location and complicated operational requirements. Consequently, here is where we can see the nearest Scotland approached to the "white architecture" of the Continent; the pleasure of plain geometric shapes interacting in sunlight; and thereby a distant echo of Cubism.

No Thirties house in Scotland approximates to Maxwell Fry's Sun House in Hampstead, or to Le Corbusier's Villa Savoie in construction, plan, or money. The concepts of free plan, exploitation of new construction techniques, merging of outdoor and indoors, and raising the house off the ground, were considered carefully by Scots architects, but largely rejected (see Chapter 3). One can suggest a number of reasons. First, only one modern house in Scotland matched the Sun House in size, and that was Gribloch. The remainder were smaller, and some very much smaller. Some of the glories of the modern house such as the double-height halls, curving staircases and generous balconies were very expensive and, being the preserve of

[263] A word coined by Sir Reginald Blomfield to indicate that modern architecture was the creation of foreign (and probably European) intellectuals, and therefore had no place in England.

Scotsman

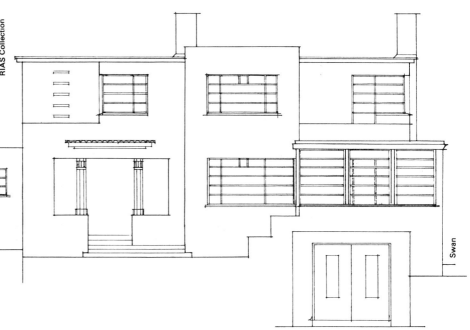

RIAS Collection

Right. House, Broadstone, Stranraer, 1936, designed by A. Maclean Goudie. *Top. Lishmor*, Easter Belmont, Kininmonth and Spence. 1933. *Above.* Gysels' house, Brighton Road, Cupar, 1936, designed by Wiliam Guild, now reroofed.

the very wealthy, stayed south of Hadrian's Wall. Flat roofs, for small private houses remained suspect until at least 1937 on the grounds that the technology was insufficiently known. Ironically, the climate seems to have rendered a successful flat roof on a small private house in Scotland a rich man's option, thus contradicting Le Corbusier's notion that the flat roof should form the basis of a universal, mass-produced house for the people (furthermore, people who could afford to be deprived of loft space). That such suspicions were not purely reactionary prejudice is evidenced by the number of Thirties flat-roofed houses subsequently blessed by the pitched, pantiled variety, thus destroying much of their aesthetic attraction.[264]

[264] See note 138.

Swan

Are the considerable numbers of flat-roofed, modern-styled houses built within Scotland mainly between 1933 and 1938 simply traditional houses with a fancy modern facelift, or do they represent something more fundamental? As was pointed out in Chapter 3, they are generally built in rendered brickwork rather than mass concrete, and little opportunity has been taken to create the free plan and introduce the other features of Le Corbusier's *Five Points* of a modern architecture. That was probably a reaction to the climate and economics of Scotland. Although many houses, such as those in Carse View Drive, Hillfoot, and James Taylor's houses for Mactaggart and Mickel in the Broom Estate, had sliding partitions between the main public rooms none was completely open plan. There was probably cold climate resistance in those pre-central heating days.

The mere fact of opting for a flat roof was adventurous (if not impractical in Scotland) in the implications it had for internal layout. Although MacDonald propagandised tirelessly for roof gardens, and planned them for his houses in Carse View Drive, he never realised his vision. There was no direct access to a roof terrace from inside the houses. That contrasts with, for example, Obertal, Leven, Ingle Neuk, Arbroath, 46a Dick Place,

RIAS Collection

Left. 4 Glenlockhart Bank, Edinburgh, designed in 1938 by George Lawrence for artist Helen Thornton *(below)*. *Below left.* 15 Roddinghead Road, Broom. *Middle.* 13 Roddinghead Road, Broom. *Bottom.* 44 Pendicle Road, Bearsden.

W Dick

W Dick

W Dick

Gracie

McKean

Top. 89 Culduthel Road, Inverness, 1937, by Donald Fowler of B. Carruthers-Ballantyne, Cox and Taylor. *Middle. Ingle Neuk*, Arbroath. Designed in 1935 by Gordon and Scrymgeour for a client with a homesick English wife. *Right. Noridlo*, Peatman's Brae, Thornton, 1937. The scrap-dealer occupation of the client is commemorated in the name read backwards.

Edinburgh and Lamburn, Old Edinburgh Road, Inverness, in all of which there is provision for a roof terrace reached from inside the house. The view out to sea from Ingle Neuk is matched, in style, by the gangway ladder up to the roof enclosed by tubular railings. If the presence of such railings at roof level is indeed indicative of a roof terrace, Noridlo, near Thornton (1937), the houses in Largo Road, Leven, and their clones by the same builder, Balfour, in Lady Nairn Avenue, Kirkcaldy, share this blessing. Lamburn is something of a curiosity. For the *National Builder*, an architect called Stewart Lloyd produced designs for a "modern house", which was to be built in Essex, and it was published in some detail.[265] The similarities of the exterior to Lamburn are so great that there can be no coincidence. Lloyd expressed his philosophy thus:

> We live oppressed in dark forests of houses, and we all mostly exist indoors. The modern style seeks to get back to light and freshness, and to express affinity with the scientific and intellectual advance of life.

Timid as they may have been or appear to be, these modern homes show that considerable efforts were made to puncture the white harled box, and to provide recessed or projecting balconies, bay windows, porches, with terraces or balconies above. But these holes are mean; and intentionally so. The climate in Scotland is 300% more severe than that in Buckinghamshire[266] and Scots architects were cautious about offering the weather too much fun at their clients' expense. Each protrusion conveyed information about the function inside: a circular glazed bay window almost always projected from the drawing room, and the roof terrace above was almost always entered from the principal bedroom.

To appreciate these modern Scots houses one must accept that they are for the most part smaller than their contemporaries elsewhere in Europe, considerably more solidly and traditionally built, and adapted to the local climate. They are usually white or pink geometrical sculptures in space, plonked firmly in the ground, windows as holes punctured through a white skin and, as such, were entirely appropriately highjacked by Messrs Hurd, Reiach, Spence, Lindsay, Forbes and Mears, as representing not a Continental import wished upon Scotland as recommended by John Summerson, but a reawakening of an indigenous native tradition brought up-to-date.

[265] *House Building* (1936). There is some evidence that W Carruthers Ballantyne disliked the modern style of architecture and was anxious to dismiss this commission quickly. The availability of a crib must have been a godsend (ex info Marion Gracie).

[266] SDD Memorandum on dampness (1983).

McKean

W Dick

Metcalf

J G L Pate

Top left. 17 Roddinghead Road, Broom. *Middle left.* Bennochy Drive, Kirkcaldy (1934), designed by Williamson and Hubbard. *Left.* Old Kirk Road, Corstorphine (1936), designed and built to the horror of surrounding bungalow owners by Sir James Miller. *Top. Hethersett*, Cramond in its original state: competition-winner with strong similarities to MacDonald's Carse View houses. *Above.* One of the legacies: *Edgemont*, Dunoon (1946), not unlike the face of a robot.

McKean

McKean

Lawers Road, Mansewood (1937), designed by Bill Gladstone.

W Dick

No architect specialised in their design, as was the case down south, and the impetus to go modern was as often a client demand as an architect's preference. The profession therefore never had the opportunity to be really practised at the idiom. That may account for some of the real peculiarities that were produced—pre-eminently Carradale, Dunoon (1946). Probably the most sophisticated was the earliest, Kininmonth's own house at 46a Dick Place (1933) built in the grounds of F T Pilkington mansion. Reminiscent of a house by Sven Markelius in Sweden, it conjoins a cylinder (the drawing room with terrace above) with a two-storey rectangle. Its original cladding was whitewashed brickwork, until the weather suggested a rendered overcoat. Its success may be judged by the fact that he lives in it still.

Above. 6 Arnhall Drive, Dundee (1936), designed by Lowe and Barrie. *Below*. The garden elevation. *Right.* 46a Dick Place.

11▌ THE EMPIRE EXHIBITION

The Distillers' Building was very interesting indeed, and had one of the
finest interior displays of any building in
the Exhibition. After hanging about for a
long time, a man managed to steal some
bottles and took them behind the building to drink. Afterwards he was told that
they contained acid, and he was taken to
hospital; but he recovered—it was only
coloured water.

Thomas Tait, *Quarterly*

The Empire Exhibition, which opened in Bellahouston Park, south Glasgow in May 1938, was the last time that Scotland featured large on the international stage; and—to many people's clear surprise—acted its part with flair.

International exhibitions were quite the thing between the Wars—Paris (1925), Brussels (1927), Stockholm (1930), Barcelona (1930), and Paris (1937). To these exhibitions, the cultural community (predominantly of Western Europe) looked for inspiration. An exhibition from the British Empire represented something entirely different: for it would be far more cosmopolitan in content, and more parochial in culture. The *Architectural Review* had the worst forebodings: "an Empire Exhibition in a country as architecturally backward as Britain cannot expect to draw on the same richness of architectural talent as an international exhibition"; and the magazine retrospected grimly to the Wembley Empire Exhibition of 1924. Yet by the time it left Bellahouston, the *Review* had been compelled to revise its assessment, and to admit that the achievement in Scotland was worthy of comparison with the best.

What most of those who attended remember are the sensual items: the appalling crush, and crowds, and endless queues for teas; drinking Kia-Ora in the Kenya Pavilion; listening (willy-nilly) to the "Lambeth Walk" over the loud-speakers; the disappointment caused by the pallid reality of the Victoria Falls representation in the Kenya pavilion after all the publicity; the Butlin's amusement park, the Crazy House and the roller-coaster; the great revolving globe against the starlit sky in the engineering pavilion; the wondrous, full dairy ice-cream; the colour—(particularly at night); the train and the little motor-carts that transported visitors around the site (one of which Queen Mary drove into a ditch); the trees which poked through the floor of the Treetops Restaurant which had been built around them; and—unfortunately above all else—the rain. Not a few visitors were also aware of the coincidence of the exhibition, a major Air Raid Precaution conference, and the Munich Crisis (the exhibition number of the *Scottish Field* featured a review of the "Dictator at home": Adolf Hitler). The Peace Pavilion (by Ramsay MacDonald's cinema-architect son Alister) was relegated to the far end of the site as though, intuitively, everybody had begun to realise that the peaceful aspirations of the exhibition were being overtaken by the reality.

That recollection of crowds is curious. The organisers had budgeted on gate money from 17 million visitors, whereas only 13 and a half million transpired (forcing the organisers to call in some 3/- in the £ from the Scottish guarantors). That implies that either the exhibition was poorly attended—scarcely a tenable thought in the light of those memories of

Above. **The Clachan.** *Right.* **Palace of Engineering: Butlin's fun park was immediately behind.**

crowds, and the fact that the attendance was only marginally less than three times the entire population of Scotland; or that the organisers had over-estimated the capacity of the exhibition site, a reasonable proportion of which had been left unmolested as a wooded hill.

The notion of a Government-aided exhibition emerged from the Scottish National Development Council, driven by Cecil (later Sir Cecil) Weir, and enthusiastically supported by the Secretary of State, Walter Elliot. It started with the intention of surveying Scottish life, and ended by aiming to illustrate the progress of the Empire, to display the resources of that Empire to new generations, to foster Empire trade, and to emphasise to the world the peaceful aspirations of that Empire (something Neville Chamberlain, Joint Honorary President of the exhibition, took with him to Munich). To the Scots, the most important object of the exhibition was to stimulate Scottish work and production. By curious paradox, this extravaganza to promote modern Scotland opened by presenting the King-Emperor with a Barra widow ululating a Gaelic lament in an ersatz Highland slum, with which his mother, Queen Mary, professed herself enchanted.

The Exhibition was designed in the form of a bent "U", the hill, capped by the Tower of Empire (much better known as Tait's Tower) in the middle. The northern wing's allegiance was signified by its title, the Scottish Avenue, enclosed on the east by Launcelot Ross's heavily classical Palace of Arts, and on the west by J Taylor Thomson's surprisingly inventive concert hall (which harked back to Helsingfors, and looked forward to the Royal Festival Hall). The Avenue was flanked on either side by Basil Spence's rectangular, spicy, dark and light blue Scottish Pavilions. Beyond the Palace of Arts to the east, lay the intellectual's corner: you could pay to enter Dr Colin Sinclair's carefully reconstructed Highland Clachan, with its shawl-covered, black-clad, weaving, singing widows, its cottages walled with plaster casts taken from real highland cottages, its wholly unreal castle, and its lochan enclosed with a naturalistic mural of an infinite highland perspective beyond. Only the pipers were allowed to walk on the grass.

Alternatively, you could exercise in the curvilinear Physical Fitness Pavilion (an adventurous design by T W Marwick), examine Mervyn Noad's prototype working-class flats, enter Basil Spence's cottage for Art and Industries, avoid Alister MacDonald's peace pavilion, or be persuaded that timber houses represented the future of Scotland in Furneaux Jordan's Swedish-looking Timber Pavilion.

Normal people probably went the other way: down Kingsway. Kingsway represented the heel of the U—past Herbert Rowse's United Kingdom pavilion, a gigantic production with drum towers and fins; past Margaret

"The Empire Exhibition was a refreshing piece of nonsense. Our aim was to produce eye-catching pavilions. In the search for inspiration and suitable cribs, many architects looked to the 1937 Paris Exhibition." Mervyn Noad.

Brodie's Women of the Empire Pavilion (opposite Alexander Mair's temples to milk) and Jack Coia's huge pink Palace of Industries (North); eventually to arrive at the main avenue. The southern limb of the U ran from the Palace of Industry (West) to the even more enormous Palace of Engineering at the east, consisting of a broad avenue split by water and fountains faced by the Colonies on the south, Dominions on the north. Discreetly tucked behind the Palace of Engineering was Butlin's amusement park (for which you had to pay). About twenty smaller buildings were scattered around the lower slopes of the hill, occupied by various businesses such as newspapers, railways, commercial companies, whisky firms and churches.

An exhibition of over one hundred large structures—some of them truly gigantic—could easily have been a mess; and that was most commentators' expectation, bearing in the mind the less-than-spectacular Empire Exhibition in Wembley in 1924. That prognostic was increased by the fact that the entire enterprise had to be created from nothing in eighteen months, in conditions of exceptionally poor weather, and a builders' strike.

As soon as the Scottish profession got wind of the exhibition in 1936, it lobbied for an architectural competition. Instead, the Government appointed Thomas Tait. So the profession lobbied instead for work to be shared out amongst Glasgow architects. Tait's response was threefold. First, he permitted the Colonies and Dominions to choose their own architects. Secondly, he provided the opportunity for industries and interest groups to have their own pavilions, bringing with them their own architects if necessary (he himself being appointed for Distillers and several others): thus appeared Joseph Emberton (Railways), Basil Spence (ICI), James Miller (Automobile Association), Launcelot Ross (RAF), Gardner MacLean (Gas) and W E Dickie (Scottish Steel). Tait's third response was to gather around him Scots architects of the younger school to work upon individual projects under his overall control and within his guidelines. These architects (some not quite so young) were Launcelot Ross (the Palace of Arts, the Treetops Restaurant, and the Tower); Spence (the Council for Art and Industry, and both Scottish pavilions); Jack Coia (the Palace of Industries North with Gordon Tait); T W Marwick (who produced a truly notable series of buildings in the Physical Fitness Pavilion, the Garden Club, and the Atlantic Restaurant); Margaret Brodie (Women of the Empire Pavilion); James Taylor Thomson (the Concert Hall, and the Palace of Industries West); and Esme Gordon with William Dey (the Transport and Travel Pavilion). Those architects, many of whom were partners in their own firms, some long established,

Night architecture.

Top. **Inside the Royal Suite.** *Middle.* **The Garden Club – resort of the élite.** *Above.* **Women of the Empire Pavilion.**

[267] *Quarterly* no. 60 (April 1939).

[268] *Scotland 1938*.

[269] Mackenzie op. cit.

"Altogether a very fine exhibition"
King George VI

would travel through to Glasgow once a month during construction for a fifteen minute briefing on site. Tait was in charge of everything, from the floodlighting to the lavatories. Apart from the broad concepts and outline design of the Tower and Pavilions, Tait himself concentrated on consistency, and a certain number of the smaller incidental buildings—the main entrances, the advertising hoardings, the Press Club, the Coal Pavilion, the Travel Pavilion, and the Bandstands.

Construction and organisational problems were immense. The team faced a project whose total cost was estimated at £11.5 million (possibly £150 million at current prices), with a construction programme of barely twelve months ending in a Royal opening. Pre-fabrication being the only way of achieving the target, Tait devised a constructional system of steel or timber framing, and cladding with asbestos sheeting in pre-fabricated sizes of four-foot multiples (only a few buildings—a church, the Timber Pavilion, and the Treetops Restaurant escaping into timber). The decision was a total success. John Summerson wrote for the *Architect and Building News* :

> Suffice it to say that asbestos cement sheeting, corrugated and plain, scores a real triumph and establishes itself as one of the most important recent additions to the architect's repertory of skin materials.

To the *Architectural Review*, the exhibition was distinguished by its aesthetic unity, attributed to the controlling hand of one man.

> To the fact that every detail was either the direct invention of his pencil, or in some degree under his personal control, is due the consistency of which we have spoken. It is easy enough, given reasonable architectural competence, to achieve the consistency amongst the major buildings ... but one knows so well from past experience how the appearance of unity is destroyed by the litter, as it were, of the foreground: by signs and advertisements, kiosks that sell picture postcards or exhibition rock, and the assorted oriental styles with which the commercial gentlemen embellished their wayside stands at Wembley ... with the enlightened co-operation of the authorities, (Mr Tait) has played the role of the architect in its widest sense. He has made himself fully responsible for design through the exhibition, and has succeeded in imposing his own standards so that only here and there does commercial ambition break out into obtrusive ostentation ... all accessories are neat and harmonious.

A feature picked up by most visitors to the exhibition was the cheerful colour of the pavilions, the road surfaces and the night-lighting. That had been a primary aim of Tait:

> Scotland, to my mind, has probably the most instinctive feeling for colour ... I made every effort to prevent any feeling of drabness, solemnity or sadness ... even in northern industrial towns, it is possible by judicious use of colour to achieve a spirit of happiness and life.[267]

A number of the pavilions were coloured in pink pastel shades, to complement those major buildings in brilliant white: all the roadways had a pink hue and some of the buildings—notably the two Scottish pavilions—were dramatic in dark blue. Some of the most striking views of the exhibition buildings are night-time ones.

The Empire Exhibition was the largest single construction project in Scotland of the late Thirties; and almost certainly one of the last of any significance to be built before the War. In its buildings one can see a number of Thirties motifs begin to mature. The modernist belief in prefabrication had been truly realised in this vast project, and the choice of structural system lent itself to the creation of "white architecture". The function of each pavilion offered designers the chance to explore the magic of juxtaposed geometric shapes seen in light (and rare sunshine): sphere and rectangle, curve and straight, vertical and horizontal. The effects ranged from Herbert

Topping

Topping

Topping

Top. Garden Club, Cascade and Rotunda Shopping Centre, by T W Marwick. *Left*. Palace of Industry, North, by Jack Coia. *Above*. Country house for the Scottish Council, by Basil Spence. *Below*. Concert Hall, by J Taylor Thomson. *Bottom*. Fitness Pavilion.

Rowse's establishment monumental in the UK Government Pavilion to the whimsical drum towers chosen by Esso, Distillers and the Railways. The exhibition layout was very British: using the site to the best effect, in the most informal way so that only rarely was there the notion of inexorable vista. By contrast, there were flights of steps up hills; churches, restaurants and pavilions vicariously perched at various levels, and water and fountains everywhere. It was, in effect, grand planning striving successfully to conceal that fact.

Basil Spence's ICI Pavilion, which Robert Hurd considered the best exhibit,[268] was remarkably similar to some of the film sets being designed for films about the future; and in a similar way, Tait's Tower, as it stood dominating the entire exhibition from every view, its searchlights flashing out at night, can now be seen to have had some uncomfortable symbolism. Yet its pedigree was good, ancestors possibly including Walter Gropius' entry for the Chicago Tribune competition, and definitely Robert Mallet-Stevens' design for the Tourist Pavilion in the 1925 Paris Exhibition. The tower theme throughout the exhibition, however, probably owed more to Dudok's inspiration, a connection observed by many visitors to the exhibition who considered it "Dutch".

The *Review* considered a major achievement of the exhibition was not solely that it demonstrated the potential of modern architecture to Scotland but that its modernism was dynamic, producing an architecture that was exciting and fun, and not purely cerebral. It gave Scotland "an air of gaiety and chic, in colour and grace of proportion and festival lights . . . providing an important step on the road to recovery".[269] The connection between the Exhibition and Scottish industrial recovery was symbolised by the fact that the King, having opened the exhibition, went on to visit the nearby Hillington Industrial Estate. The contrast between Scotland's bright and colourful future as represented in the Empire Exhibition, and the dark,

Summerson

Transgraphics

grimy and gloomy condition of the rest of Glasgow struck many.[270] John Summerson, revisiting Scotland for the *Architect and Building News* after seven years' absence in London, concluded:

> There are things about Glasgow which, by the lowest standards that can be called civilised, are still quite unforgivable. The Paisley Road is one of them . . . Glasgow, city of engineering, sees for once on its skyline, something which is not a crane or a chimney, nor the hull of liner, nor yet the square cornice-lid of a neo-Grecian bank. Something which is construction, not for money's sake or work's sake, but just for fun. That is good for a place like Glasgow . . . it is well to recognise the vivid impression which the exhibition is making in the north because that, for architecture, is immensely important.

The Palace of Engineering was re-erected at Prestwick Airport where it can be seen yet. The Empire Cinema in Lochgilphead is subject to an unconfirmed rumour that it had been re-erected from Bellahouston. Many attempts were made to save the Tower, or re-erect it elsewhere; but War priorities intervened and it was sold for scrap. A number of buildings remained on the site during the War, acting as a transit camp for Canadian soldiers, German prisoners and the Argyll and Sutherland Highlanders.

Only the Palace of Arts, and the numberless souvenirs like key-rings and lamps in the form of Tait's Tower survive.

As might be expected, once over, the Exhibition was subjected to exhaustive post-mortem analyses. Of those, Charles Oakley and A G Macdonell might be allowed the last words. To Oakley, the undoubted success of the exhibition was vitiated by the absence of many Scots firms, and by a total failure of the organisers to market the exhibition in London and America. Macdonell, equally proud of the achievement, worried lest too many Scots had regarded the Exhibition as an end in itself. "Stands Scotland where it did?" he asked rhetorically: "Yes. But the rest of the world has moved on."

Top. Exhibition Details. *Above.* United Kingdom Pavilion. *Right.* The Scottish Pavilion.

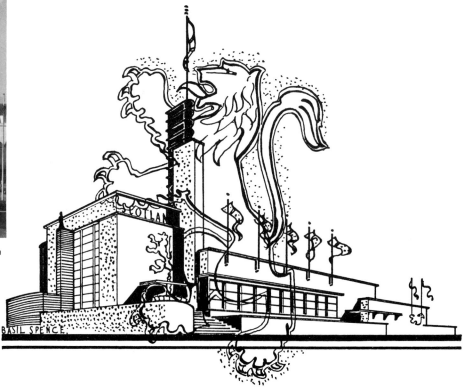

[270] Interview: Robert Smith.

THE EMPIRE EXHIBITION

Provisional List of attribution

1. **Thomas Tait**
   A. Overall plan
   B. Tower and Treetop Restaurant (with Ross)
   C. Union Bank
   D. Main entrance
   E. Press Club
   F. Advertising Hoardings
   G. Distillers Building
   H. Coal Buildings
   I. Shipping and Travel
   J. Garden Club

2. **Basil Spence**
   A. Country House for the Council for Art and Industry
   B. Scottish Pavilions
   C. ICI Building

3. **Launcelot Ross**
   A. Palace of Engineering
   B. RAF Pavilion
   C. Palace of Arts
   D. Tower and Treetops Restaurant (with Tait)

4. **W E Dickie**
   Scottish Steel Pavilion

5. **George Millar**
   South African Pavilion

6. **J A Coia**
   A. Roman Catholic Pavilion
   B. Palace of Industries (North) (with Tait and Gordon Tait)

7. **T Waller Marwick**
   A. The Atlantic Restaurant
   B. The Garden Club and Lucullus Restaurant
   C. The Physical Fitness Pavilion

8. **Gordon and Dey**
   Transport and Travel Pavilion

9. **Margaret Brodie**
   Women of the Empire Exhibition

10. **Alex Mair**
    Scottish Milk Marketing Board Pavilion

11. **Joseph Emberton**
    British Rail Pavilion

12. **Herbert Rowse**
    United Kingdom Pavilion

13. **James Taylor Thomson**
    A. Church of Scotland
    B. Palace of Industry (west)
    C. Concert Hall (based on Helsingfors)

14. **Mervyn Noad**
    A. Episcopal Church

Topping

ICI Pavilion by Basil Spence.

   B. Scottish Council Experimental Flats
   C. Oil and Shellmex Pavilion
   D. Interior of Scottish Pavilion (North)

15. **James Miller**
    A. Beattie's Bread
    B. AA Pavilion

16. **Dr Colin Sinclair**
    Clachan

17. **A L Abbot**
    Australia Pavilion

18. **Alister MacDonald**
    A. Film Theatre

   B. Peace Pavilion

19. **R Furneaux Jordan**
    Timber Pavilion

Attributions of the other pavilions including the Post Office, Times, Glasgow Herald etc have not yet been determined. They tend to be those that attracted opprobrious comment.

189

ACKNOWLEDGEMENTS

This book, like the study, has been dependent on much generosity, support and sponsorship. Foremost thanks must go to Mactaggart and Mickel, not just for financial aid, but for consistent help and enthusiasm in delving information by Douglas and Bruce Mickel.

We are also grateful to the National Library of Scotland, the RIBA Library, Edinburgh Central Libraries, Glasgow School of Art architectural library and the Royal Commission on the Ancient and Historical Monuments of Scotland for their considerable assistance. The value of the RIAS and EAA libraries in this study must be self-evident. Janet McBain at the Scottish Film Council has been unfailingly helpful. Those who contributed papers to the RIAS/Thirties Society seminar in October 1984 provided a base for all further work. Thanks go to Professor Roy Campbell, Alan Reiach, Ian Carnegie, Janet McBain, David Walker, Sir John Summerson and Neil Baxter.

The following people, however, have acted as anchor-points to the entire operation, advising, commenting and contributing their own knowledge and research. Whilst no mistake can be attributed to them, such good as there is, may be: David Walker, Ian Gow, Neil Baxter, Roger Emmerson, Kitty Cruft, Alan Reiach, Ian Carnegie and Anne Riches.

CREDITS

The compilation of this book, and the study which underlay it, has been an enormous team effort to which many people, organisations, local authorities and government bodies have contributed. Whilst reserving to the author all inaccuracies and false judgements, the following list of contributors, sources and reference documents may be of some help to those who wish to delve deeper.

PEOPLE WITH EXPERIENCE OF THE THIRTIES

Mrs Isobel Adams, Margaret Brodie, J D (Ian) Carnegie, David Carr, James Carrick, Robert Chalmers, Mr Castell, Jack Dallachy, William Dey, Archie Doak, Robert Dron, Leo Durnin, Robert Forsyth, Esme Gordon, Professor Sir Robert Grieve, William Guild, Sir William Kininmonth, George Lawrence, Dr J Mackintosh Patrick, Jack MacDougall, Campbell McKay, Stuart Matthew, Laurie McKean, Douglas Mickel, Robert Scott Morton, Robert Naismith, R Mervyn Noad, Alan Reiach, Robert Rogerson, George Singleton, George Smith, Robert Smith, David Stokes, Mrs Inez Scott Sutherland, Alaister Wallace, Arthur Wright.

LETTERS, CORRESPONDENCE ETC

R A Bell, Roger Brown, Stanley Carrie, Jack Chalmers, Keith Chalmers-Watson, Robert Close, T Duncan, T D S Gibson, M Gilgannon, Marion Gracie, Mrs J W Guest, A Harkness, Mrs J King, Kyle and Carrick District Council, Mrs M M Hendry, Gordon Hodge, W Murray Jack, Ninian Johnston, James Lyon, Mr and Mrs Metcalf, Janet McBain, Mrs MacLaren, Eleanor Murdoch, Douglas Nelson, D A Ramsay, William Reid, James Shiell, Stuart Tod. Dr A H L Wilson.

RESEARCH

Neil Baxter, Robert Close, Frank Dunbar, Marion Dunn, Robert Elwall, Roger Emmerson, Gillian Mackinnon, T W McKie, Rudolph Kenna, Lindsay Pate, Peter Robinson, Anne Riches, Adam Swan, Alastair Wilson, George Wren.

PRINCIPAL SOURCES

The *RIAS Quarterly*; the *Architects Journal*; the *Architectural Review*; *Architecture Illustrated*; the *Builder*; the *Architect and Building News*; *Pencil Points*; the *Scottish Architect and Builders Journal*; *Building Industries*; the Minute Books of the RIAS and the Edinburgh Architectural Association; Fellowship application forms to RIBA and RIAS; EAA letter books; the minutes of the Scottish Special Areas Housing Association; and a collection of papers and pamphlets of E J MacRae.

COLLECTIONS OF DRAWINGS AND FURTHER ASSISTANCE

John Thomson (Weddell & Inglis), James Wood (T Bowhill Gibson), Richard Ewing (Rowand Anderson & Paul, Kininmonth and Spence), James Rennie (James Miller), James Carrick and Garry Hutchison (J & J A Carrick), Bruce Mickel (Mactaggart and Mickel), Stuart Paterson (Launcelot Ross), T McKie (Caledonian Associated Cinemas), Ian Carnegie, David Carr (Carr and Howard), Mervyn Noad (Noad and Wallace), William Guild, Mrs I Scott-Sutherland (T Scott Sutherland), David Moir (A D Haxton), Richard Dewar (W M Wilson), J Houston (James Houston), Scott Noble (George Boswell), Larry Rolland (Robert Hurd and Partners) Bill Hunter (Wylie Wright Wylie), Esme Gordon, and Bill Topping (Empire Exhibition Collection).

THE RIAS THIRTIES WORKING GROUP

Charles McKean (Convenor), David Walker, Bruce Walker, Roger Emmerson, John Richards, Susan Cornah, Kitty Michaelson, Alan Reiach, Frank Dunbar, Ann Simpson, Anne Riches, Miles Horsey, Marista Leishman, Esme Gordon, Neil Baxter, latterly Jemina Tindall.

THE STUDY TEAM

The Nineteen Thirties Study was predominantly financed by the Manpower Services Commission, with additional contributions from the National Trust for Scotland, the Saltire Society, the Scottish Development Agency, the Ancient Monuments and Historic Buildings Division SDD, the RIAS, and the Duncan of Jordanstone College of Art. It was also assisted by the award of the Gordon Ricketts Memorial Fund Prize to Charles McKean.

Team: Neil Baxter (Researcher and Leader), Joy Pitman (archivist), Renata Leishman, Lesley Gerrard, Alastair Wilson, Bryan Montgomery, Leslie Stephenson, Marion Dunn, Gillian McKinnon. Thanks must be given to the office of Ove Arup and Partners (Dundee), Ross Lindsay and Partners, and Coleman/Ballantyne and Partners (Glasgow) for affording the photographers premises.

PHOTOGRAPHY CREDITS

Immense thanks must go to the National Monuments Record of Scotland, for their help in photography, particularly in photographing newly discovered drawings. The compilation of the Thirties photographic archive was begun by

MSC photographers, Anne Millin, Ben Robotham and Richard Davies; and since then has been continued by the author and the following people: Shona Adam, Neil Baxter, Bill Brogden, David Brown, Alaister Burnet, Willie Dick, Inglis Stevens, Russell Ferguson, Marion Gracie, Gordon Hodge, Robert Hurd and Partners, Andrew Kelly, Ian McGill, Colin Morton, J G Lindsay Pate, Jim Ramsay, Peter Robinson, Adam Swan, Charles Strang, David Storrer, Frank Walker, White House Photography, George Wren, Colin Wishart and Mrs E J Metcalf.

Edinburgh District Council Central Libraries gave kind permission to copy and reproduce items from the now defunct *Scottish Architect and Builders Journal*; whilst the RIBA Library kindly copied a number of items in their collection. The source of each illustration is noted alongside.

THESES

Life and Works of Thomas Smith Tait, Bruno Sicomori (1982); *Beresford Hotel 1938*, Dorothy Laing (1975); *Thomas S Tait*, Jeremy Gould (1970); *St Andrew's House*, M K Young (1975); *Scottish Industrial Estate Co*, Marion Dunn (1984); *International Style Houses in Scotland*, W A Miller (1979); *J R H MacDonald and Sunlight*, R Lindlay Nelson (1977); *The House that Jean Built*, Daily Mail Scottish Ideal Home Exhibition, 1932; *T Harold Hughes. His Reaction to the Modern Movement*, J B Campbell (1979); *The Oakwood Motel, Elgin*, Brian Edwards; *Klondyke of the Cinema World*, Christopher Doak (1979); *Thomas S Tait and the Glasgow Empire Exhibition*, J Neil Baxter (1982); *Continental and American Influences on the Commercial Architecture of Sir John H Burnet in Glasgow*, Ian Lowden (1975); *Did Sir James Miller's Bungalows show signs of modernism?*, E A Mowat; *Modernising our homes 1920–50*, A W MacLaren; *Suitability of National Library of Scotland for its purpose*, Eileen Watson; *The New Premises, Tranent*, J Logan (1975); *Westquarter Model Village*, R Sharp (1981); Thesis on *Edinburgh School buildings*, Dr W M Stephens; *Open Air Bathing Pool at Portobello*, Janet Medd; *Binns, 146 Princes Street*, R C V Addison (1982); *James Lamont and Co Ltd*, D J M Fender; *The Cinema and the Facade*, James Denholm (1979); *Carnegie's Dunfermline Architects 1875–1935*, Roger Emmerson.

BOOKS CONSULTED

CONTEMPORARY WORKS

(International works: Vers Une Architecture etc, generally excluded)
Scotland 1938, J R Allan; *The Heart of Scotland*, George Blake (1934 Batsford); *Scotland, That Distressed Area*, George Malcolm Thomson (Porpoise 1935); *Summer in Scotland*, John R Allan (1938); *Modern Scotland*, Cicely Hamilton (1937); *Scottish Journey*, Edwin Muir (1935); *Magnus Merriman*, Eric Linklater (1934); *My Scotland*, William Power (Porpoise Press 1934); *My Scotland*, A G Macdonell (Jarrolds 1937); *The Highlands of Scotland*, Hugh Quigley (Batsford 1936); *Scotland in Modern Times*, Agnes Muir Mackenzie (Chambers 1940); *One Way of Living*, James Bridie (Constable 1939); *Tedious and Brief*, James Bridie (Constable 1944); *Scottish Industry Today*, C A Oakley (1937); *Strolling through Scotland*, W S Percy (1934); *House Building*, The Federated Employers Press (1934–6); *Europe Rehouses*, Elizabeth Denby (1938); *Timber Buildings for the Country*, E H B Boulton (1938); *Small Houses and Bungalows*, Frederick Chatterton (1932); *Houses*, Lionel Brett (Penguin 1947); *A Miniature History of the English House*, J M Richards (The Architectural Press 1938); *An Introduction to Modern Architecture*, J M Richards (Pelican 1941); *Modern European Buildings*, F R Yerbury (Gollancz 1928); *Modern Theatres and Cinemas*, T Morton Shand (Batsford 1930); *Twentieth Century Houses*, Raymond McGrath (Faber 1934); *Living in Cities*, Ralph Tubbs (Penguin 1942); *A Key to Modern Architecture*, Yorke and Penn (Blackie 1939); *The Modern House* (Country Life c.1930); *Building Scotland*, Alan Reiach and Robert Hurd (The Saltire Society 1940); *The Modern House in England*, F R S Yorke (Architectural Press 1937); *Fine Building*, Maxwell Fry (1944); *Small Houses £500–£2500*, Myles Wright (1936); *Planning Our New Homes*: Report by the Scottish Housing Advisory Committee (1943 HMSO); *Small Houses*, (Architecture Illustrated); *Houses for Moderate Means*, Randall Philips (1936); *Seaside Houses and Bungalows*, Ella Carter (1937); *The Modern House in America*, Ford and Ford (1940).

MODERN BOOKS

London in the Thirties, Alice Prochaska (London Museum 1973); *Battle of Styles*: London 1914–39, D Atwell and Charles McKean (RIBA 1975); *Guide to Modern Buildings in Cambridge and East Anglia 1920–80*, Charles McKean (RIBA Eastern Region 1981); *The Thistle and the Crown*, John S Gibson (1985 HMSO); *Pictures Past*, Janet McBain (1985); *The Last Picture Shows*, Brendon Thomas (Moorfoot 1984); *Cathedrals of the Movies*, David Atwell (Architectural Press 1980); *The Cinemas of Cinema City*, T Louden (1983); *The International Style*, Henry-Russell Hitchcock and Philip Johnson (Norton 1966); *Modern Architecture Since 1900*, William Curtis (Phaidon); *Rob Mallet Stevens*, (1982 The Archives D'Architecture Moderne); *The Thirties: Recalling the English Architectural Scene*, David Dean (Trefoil 1983); *The Thirties*: Arts Council Catalogue; *Joseph Emberton*, Rosemary Ind (1983); *Glasgow Art Deco*, Rudolph Kenna (1984 Richard Drew); *International Style houses in Britain*, Jeremy Gould (1978 SAHGB); *Jack Coia*, R W K C Rogerson (1986).

Inside the Scottish Pavilion. Sculpture by Archibald Dawson.

Topping

MODERN (i.e. FLAT ROOFED) HOUSES
(so far discovered)

Aberdeen

Auchinlech, Lumsden—probably 1937 by Roy Meldrum
House, Garthdee Road, 1937: Roy Meldrum
2 pairs semi-detached: Annfield
10 pairs semi-detached: Broomhill Avenue. T Scott Sutherland

Aberlady

Luffness Croft. 1935 as holiday house for Chairman, Cement and Concrete Board. J D Cairns and Ford?

Alness

Ardmhor, 43 Obsdale Road

Arbroath

Ingle Neuk. 1935 Gordon and Scrymgeour

Ayr

White Plains, Longhill Avenue. Alex Mair. 1936
51 Prestwick Avenue. Percy Hogarth 1935

Ballater

House, Golf Road

Boreland

Bungalow (now altered)

Bowden

Backett's Field

Brechin

2 pairs semi-detached

Carmunnock

Four houses and bungalows, Cathkin Road

Cupar

Guysel house, Brighton Road. 1937 William Guild (re-roofed)

Dumfries

2 houses, New Abbey Road/Pleasance Avenue. W N Thompson and Co

Dundee

43 Forfar Avenue, Gordon and Scrymgeour
Sunningdale, Ralston Road, West Ferry.
1933. Thoms and Wilkie (Donald Fowler)
5 Arnhall Gardens. Lowe and Barrie 1937
7 Bingham Terrace. Frank Henderson. pre-War and 1950 1st floor

Dunfermline

Bella Vista, Linburn Road. 1950. A B Allan

Dunoon

St Mary Street. 1946

Duns

Harden's End, Clockhill

Edinburgh

Hethersett, Whitehouse Road, Cramond. 1934. C F Reid
Balnagarrow, Kirk Loan, Cramond 1937. James Miller
32 Old Kirk Road, Corstorphine. 1936. James Miller
2 pairs semi-detacheds. East Craigs. 1936. James Miller
538 Queensferry Road, Barnton. 1937. W N Thomson
46a Dick Place. 1933. W Kininmonth
Lishmor, Easter Belmont. 1933. Kininmonth and Spence
Miss Reid, 4 Easter Belmont. 1934. Kininmonth and Spence
40 Camus Avenue (?)
4 Glenlockhart Bank. 1938. George Lawrence
House, Liberton Brae. T Bowhill Gibson
House, by Ravelston Gardens (? Neil and Hurd)
House, Joppa
House, Glasgow Road

Elgin

Wittet Drive bungalow. J & W Wittet
3 houses, Hamilton Drive—post-war?

Gairloch

House

Gattonside

The Keep

Glasgow

6, 13, 15, 17 Roddinghead Road, Whitecraigs
9 Lawers Road, Mansewood. W E Gladstone. 1936
44 Pendicle Road, Bearsden. J E Dallachy
28 Rubislaw Drive, Bearsden
15 Douglas Park Crescent, Bearsden
3 houses, Kilmardinny Avenue, Bearsden
8 houses, Carse View Drive. 1933-6. John R H MacDonald
Caretaker's House, Kelvin Court. 1939. J N Fatkin
2 semi-detached houses, Carntyne Road
House, Eaglesham Cross (re-roofed)
16 Kirkview Crescent, Mearns Kirk

Helensburgh

3 Kidstone Drive

Inverness

Lamburn, 41 Old Edinburgh Road. R Carruthers Ballantyne 1935
Balnabruach, 89 Culduthel Road, 1937 R Carruthers Ballantyne 1935
Clachnaharry (next Delmore). William Taylor of Ballantyne Cox and Taylor 1938
House, Cradlehall. c.1946 Carruthers Ballantyne
Over and above, 145 Culduthel Road. c.1936 Carruthers Ballantyne Cox and Taylor (David Fowler)
Cluny House, 87 Culduthel Road. c.1937 William Allan (of Carruthers Ballantyne Cox and Taylor)
7 Darnaway Avenue. James Johnson and (? Rose) 1936
135 Culduthel Road. Frank Rizza 1947

Kelso

Broomlaw

Kilsyth

Skyrock, Horsburgh Avenue. c.1938. Carmyle Cement Manufacturers

Kippen

Gribloch, 1937. Basil Spence with Perry Duncan

Kirkcaldy

8 Bennochy Drive. Williamson and Hubbard. 1934
5 pairs semi-detached houses, Lady Nairn Avneue. Balfour Brothers. 1934
Kincraig, Peatman's Brae, Thornton. 1937

Lanark

Windsor, Cleghorn. 1934 Stewart Shaw

Leven

3 pairs semi-detached. Lawrence Rolland for Andrew Cook. 1936
Obertal, Largo Road c.1935

Newhouse

House by Griffin Motel

North Berwick

house

Portpartick

Drummuie, Heugh Road. 1937. A MacLean Goudie

St Andrews

44-46 Buchanan Gardens
8 semi-detacheds, Strathkinness High Road. Tom Roger 1946
2 Melburn Gardens

Selkirk

Stabstane

Stirling

Bungalows, Ochil Road, Causewayside.

Stonehaven

Unidentified house (re-roofed)

Stranraer

Hawkesworth, Broadstone Road. c.1946 A M Goudie
The Moorings, Broadstone Road. 1937. A McLean Goudie.

Empire Fountain.

Topping

INDEX OF ARCHITECTS

Abercrombie and Maitland (Paisley)
Thomas Graham Abercrombie had died in 1926. Sole partner James Steel Maitland 1887–1982. Trained with William Leiper. Many buildings by Abercrombie pre-1930 in Paisley. After the arrival of Maitland, note Russell Institute (Paisley) 1926; own house Littlecroft, Stonefield Avenue (1924–36); Cochrane's, Gauze Street (1927); Porterfield Road Housing, Renfrew (1935–1939); Cocklesloan Housing, Renfrew (1940); Church of Scotland, Meikle Road, Pollock (1940); Four Square Factory, Greenhill Road, Paisley (1936–8). **89, 97, 146, 153, 176.**

Armour, W Cornelius (Dumbarton)
Architect to the SCWS. Work includes the Store, Seagate, Dundee (1935), Dumbarton Creamery (1935), Kinning Park Co-op (1935), Warehouse and offices Carnoustie Street, Glasgow (1937), Eastwood Paper mills (1933), probably paper factory, Falklands (1931), and the Luma factory, Shieldhall (1936). **97–8, 113.**

Baird and Thomson (Glasgow)
Old firm going back to 1818; Baird had died as long ago as 1859, James Thomson in 1905. The firm was his son William Aitken Thomson 1871–1947. Bank of Scotland, Crieff, Clydesdale Bank, Ayr, Clydesdale Bank, Hamilton 1935, Clydesdale Bank, Wellington Street 1934, Clydesdale Bank, Falkirk 1933, Clydesdale Bank, Greenock 1932, Clydesdale Bank, Saltcoats 1938. **101.**

Ballantyne, W Carruthers (Inverness)
Born 1891. Trained at AA and with Sir Guy Dawber. Inherited his father's firm in Inverness. In 1930s the President of the Inverness Society of Architects. Buildings include the public hall in Broadford (1933); 41 Old Edinburgh Road, Inverness (1937); Lamburn, Old Edinburgh Road (1935); and numbers 87, 89, 135 and 145 Culduthel Road. **34, 136, 180.**

Boswell, George (Glasgow)
1879–1952
Former chief assistant to James Miller, under whose direction he was designer of the Argyle Electric Cinema 1910. Designer of 14 cinemas and picture houses, only the Argyle reconstruction (1938) in the Thirties. Two extensions to Templeton's, Glasgow (1934–38), Eastwood Secondary School, Williamfield (1936). Designed Parkhead Picture Palace, cinemas in Carlisle, Dumbarton and Paisley, and Newall Ltd Possil (1940). Lived in the White House of Milliken which he converted, and wore orange,

hand-made leather shoes. After the War, the firm became Boswell Mitchell and Johnston. **32, 36, 68, 70, 105, 110.**

Bunton, Sam (Glasgow)
Mainly housing work. Modern estates in Kilsyth and Kilmarnock. Experimental concrete houses for the SSAHA. Pubs in Glasgow (see Kenna). Swimming pool and Cromarty Centre, Kilsyth (1939). Was responsible for revival of Jack Coia in 1945 by inviting him to help rebuild Clydebank. Highly commercial architect who believed he had a mission to rebuild the West of Scotland. **94, 139, 140, 141.**

Burnet and Boston (Greenock and Glasgow)
Continuation of an Edwardian baroque firm by Frank Burnet's (1848–1923) son: W J Boston still in the practice until his death in 1937. Followers but not relatives of J J Burnet. Designer of J R W Laing Showrooms, St Vincent Street; Greenock Ice Rink; Union Bank, Langside (1936); St Columba's School, Kilmacolm (1936); Bank of Scotland, Possilpark; and Maryhill. Architects to the Royal Bank of Scotland.

Carnegie, J D (Ian) (Edinburgh)
Andrew Grant scholar (1932); lecturer at Edinburgh College of Art (1934). Highly commended with E A A Rowse in competition for RIBA headquarters. Worked with Aldjo Jamieson and Arnott. Designed the Rushforth House, Ratho (1937). "Came back from Paris full of Mallett Stevens" (Lawrence). **21, 30, 40–41, 161.**

Carr, David (Edinburgh) died 1986
Trained Edinburgh College of Art. Travelled to Italy in 1923 with Robert Matthew. Returned to Collcutt and Hamp, London. Met Howard in Herbert Baker's office. Redundant. Move to Michael Rosenaur's office, responsible for Arlington House. Returns 1936 to Edinburgh with Andrew Grant Fellowship to study prefabrication. Carr and Howard entered over 27 competitions with great success, winning Kirkcaldy Town Hall (1937) and Tanfield School, Edinburgh (1939). They also undertook many prototype houses for the SSAHA, and built timber ones in Polbeth and Kirknewton. **26–29, 32, 41, 56, 106, 141–2.**

Carrick, J & J A (Ayr)
Established firm of architects going back to turn of century. J. (senior), a craft architect with an extensive home practice.
James Carrick junior, award-winning student famous for draughtsmanship. Winner of Cragburn competition (1935); Rothesay Pavilion (1936). Placed in Glasgow housing competition. Otherwise designer of houses and shops.

President RIAS after the War. **28, 52, 86–7, 130, 161.**

Coia, J Antonio (Glasgow) 1898–1981
Partner in Gillespie Kidd and Coia. Lecturer Glasgow School of Art. FRIAS in 1933. Opponent of architectural competitions as productive of boring buildings. Churches: Whitevale Street, Dennistoun (1933); Duntocher (1936); St Columba's Maryhill (1937); St Peter's in Chains, Ardrossan (1938); St Patrick's Greenock (1935); St Columcille's, Rutherglen (1940). Lanarkshire Ice Rink, Motherwell (unbuilt). Brierlands, Busby, 1936. Roman Catholic Pavilion, Empire Exhibition; Palace of Industry North. Partner: T Warnett Kennedy. **21, 29, 36, 38–9, 40, 42, 87, 134–5, 154, 185, 187.**

Dey, William (Edinburgh)
College of Art 1929–36; town planning course 1935. Worked with John Begg 1936, joining E J Macrae on planning the Royal Mile 1937. With Esme Gordon on Empire Exhibition Transport Pavilion 1938. With Kininmonth and Spence 1933. After War, partnership Gordon and Dey, set up with capital of £150 each. **22, 115, 185.**

Dick, Norman (Glasgow) 1883–1948
Pupil of J M Dick Peddie and Washington Browne, studied in Paris 1905–7. Bought Glasgow partnership 1909 at a time when Burnet needed both money and a Glasgow partner. Red haired and quick-tempered. Partner John Burnet, Son and Dick. President the Glasgow Institute of Architects 1936.

Nurses Home, Gartnavel; nurses home Western Infirmary; collaboration with Merchiston School; Tennant Memorial, Western Infirmary; Holyrood RC School, Dixon Road, Glasgow (1937); Crosshill School (Glasgow) 1931. **120.**

Dunn, J B and Martin (Edinburgh)
James Bow Dunn, 1861–1930; an architect of the old school, pupil of Campbell Walker, began practice 1885. George Watson's School, won in competition. Finished 1932. Murrayfield Ice Rink 1938. **87, 123.**

Fairlie, Dr Reginald (1883–1952) (Edinburgh)
Predominantly church and country house architect. Worked within the Scottish tradition. 29 Roman Catholic churches including Rothesay (1920); Fort William (1932); St Patrick's, Edinburgh; St Mary, Star of Sea, Tayport (1939). Princess Margaret Rose Hospital (1935). National Library of Scotland from 1934. Various school buildings. **33, 34, 106, 108, 124, 128, 133.**

Fairweather, John and Son (Glasgow)
John Fairweather 1867–1942.
W John Fairweather born 1908.

Visited USA in 1923 to study cinema theatre design.
14 cinemas including the Edinburgh Playhouse, and the Green's Playhouses, Dundee and Glasgow—the 3 largest cinemas in Scotland, two of them the largest in Europe. The output of the practice was devoted to "planning of cinemas and private houses" only. They included Largs super cinema (1935), Saltcoats, Rutherglen (1931), Lockerbie (1932), La Scala, Aberdeen (1933); Ayr (1930); and concert halls in Montrose (1933), the East Park Home (1933), and the British Linen Company, Gallowgate, Glasgow (1936). **38, 53.**

Gardner, A V (and Glen and Thomson) (Glasgow)
Involved in 36 cinemas and roller rinks—8 in 1938 alone—and 5 others during the Thirties. The rest were earlier. They included Campbeltown (1935) and Ayr. **39, 61.**

Gibson, T Bowhill (Edinburgh) c.1895–1949
Dominion Cinema (1939); County Cinema, Portobello (1939); Learmonth flats (1935), Roadhouse, Granton; Hillburn Inn; cinema in Baillieston (1939); the Regal, Niddrie (1934); and many other cinemas and private houses. **38, 61, 63–4, 66–7, 80, 164.**

Gordon, Esme RSA (Edinburgh) born 1910
College of Art. Tait's office for one year. Returned to Tait's office, contemporary with Pat Ronaldson, Margaret Brodie. George Lawrence, Andy Bryce, Clifford Strange, Franz Stengelhofen, Gordon Farquharson. Worked on the Freemasons Lodge, Silver End, and the Curzon Cinema. Work: church at Methil; Travel and Transport pavilion Empire exhibition; Lodge and house alterations Kinellan Road. **185.**

Gordon and Scrymgeour (Dundee)
J Ramsay Gordon (d.1938) ex Thoms and Wilkie, began practice 1920; R A Scrymgeour taken on as partner 1927 (d.1939). Architects of Dundee. Work includes housing in Arbroath, bungalows in West Ferry, a cinema in Arbroath and two modern houses: Ingle Neuk (1935) Arbroath, and 93 Forfar Road, Dundee. **161, 180.**

Grant, John A W (Edinburgh) 1885–1959
Formerly at Honeyman and Keppie's. Work included Fountainbridge Library, the Drimery Estate, Clydebank (1939); and the competition-winning Westquarter model village, by Falkirk, from 1936. **27, 144–5.**

Houston, James (Kilbirnie)
Architect of Kilbirnie. Work includes the Moorings, Largs (1935); Radio Cinema,

Kilbirnie (1936); the Viking Cinema, Largs (1939); cinema (?), Dunoon (1939); and several Galbraith stores (eg Milngavie 1939). Many houses and light industrial units. **39, 59, 63, 64, 93.**

Hubbard, Harry (and Williamson) (Kirkcaldy)
William Williamson (1871–1952) was an Arts and Crafts designer who began practice in the mid 1890s. Harry Hubbard was with John Burnet and Son 1910–14; then Watson Salmond and Gray. 1928, Chief Assistant to Robert Lorimer. Popular lecturer in Edinburgh College of Art, and EAA Correspondent for the Quarterly. Joined Wiliamson in Williamson and Hubbard 1933 onwards. Williamson got the jobs, Hubbard designed them.

Work includes: Kirkcaldy Ice Rink (1937); house, Bennochy Road, Kirkcaldy (1934); Cameron Infectious Diseases Hospital (Kirkcaldy, 1939); Westfield flats, designed pre-War for Alexander Glass, and built post-War for Edinburgh District Council; Fidelity Garage, Kirkcaldy (1938); attempted restoration of Sailor's Walk, Kirkcaldy; and a number of housing estates—44 houses, Kinglassie (1936), is an example. He also designed St Mungo's Church of Scotland, Alloa (1936); won the Forth Park Maternity Hospital, Kirkcaldy in competition (1934), produced the library, Loughborough Road, Kirkcaldy (1933); and the unusual savings bank, St Clair Street, Kirkcaldy (1933); "a delightful man". **22, 77, 87, 101, 181.**

Hughes, Professor T Harold (Glasgow)
Born 1887, Staffordshire. Studied RCA. In 1910, age 23, appointed Head of Architecture Department. Robert Gordon's. Organised the new day school, and recognition was received in 1914. 1919 moved to Glasgow, for partnership in Burnet Tait and Lorne. Resigned after one year to become Professor of Architecture in Glasgow. Work includes Merton College, Oxford; Corpus Christi; Regent Park College, London; Chemistry Building, Glasgow University; Reading Room, Glasgow University; Garscadden Sports Pavilion, Glasgow. Work also includes St Matthew Church, Balmore Road, Glasgow; hospital near Eaglesham; Cardonald Association Hall. Married Edith Burnet, niece of Sir John. "Outstanding teacher" (Doak). Significant architectural historian, and contributor to Quarterly. **30–32, 39–40, 66, 72, 88, 125–6.**

Hurd, Robert (Edinburgh)
1905–63. Arrived in Scotland early 30s to write about architecture and investigate national traditions. 1933 enters partnership with Norman Neil. Work includes Ravelston flats, 1935; house for Annie

Swan; and 3 commissions for the Marquess of Bute; the restoration of Acheson House, Canongate; Loudon Hall, Ayr; Andro Lamb's house, Leith.

Nationalist: campaigner for Scottishness and old buildings. Involved in Saltire Society and NTS. Author and journalist. Joint author of *Building Scotland*; contributor to *Scotland 1938*; author of *Scotland in Trust*. Voracious lecturer and speaker.

Survived by Robert Hurd and Partners, merged with Lawrence A Rolland and Partners, Leven—architects of housing schemes, Leven and St Monans and Leven Co-op. **17, 21, 22, 36, 104, 131, 160, 162, 165, 180**

Inglis, W Beresford (Glasgow)
Cinema architect, promoter and owner. Designer of 6 cinemas including Toledo, Muirend (surviving); Boulevard, Knightswood; the Ritz, Cambuslang; and three others. Designer also of some pubs, houses in Whitecraigs, Ferrari's Restaurant (1933); St Charles Roman Catholic School (1934); Rogano's (1936); the Boundary Bar, Springburn; loco Factory, Anniesland. Managing Director, designer and owner of Glasgow hotels, particularly the Beresford Hotel, 1937-8. The firm was Weddell and Inglis; survives as Weddell and Thompson. **24, 64, 85, 94.**

Jerdan, John (Edinburgh)
Died 1947: son of James Jerdan, an architect of the Rowand Anderson school, who had died in 1913. EAA Council member. Head of Building Construction at Heriot Watt. Flats Napier Road, Colinton. Joins J Jerdan and Son in 1904. Several houses in Colinton, house for Annie Swan, Temple Hall, Gogarburn House, strongly Arts and Crafts. **164.**

Johnston, J M 1871-1934 (Edinburgh)
Architect of Leith, Wardie School, United Free Church, Portobello and Blackhall, and numerous warehouses, offices etc, mainly in Leith. Survived by J & F Johnston and Partners, Leith. **123-4, 128.**

Kaye, Stuart (and Walls) (Edinburgh)
Stuart Kay and Son (c.1891-1952) Lothian House; the Hillpark Estate (from 1936); Bonnington Road Factory (1937). **37, 157, 169.**

Keppie and Henderson (Glasgow)
John Keppie (1862-1945) had been manager rather than architect since before World War 1; A Graham Henderson (c.1882-1963) was a hard-headed New Zealander who had been with McWhannel and Rogerson. He made an issue of Mackintosh's departure in 1913 and succeeded him as partner at the end of World War 1 in 1918. Bank of Scotland, Sauchiehall Street (1931);

offices above—sculpture by Benno Schotz. Cloberhill School, Knightswood (1935); RIBA Bronze Medal. Glasgow Cross Building; Pettigrew and Stevens, many churches and church halls, office buildings, Scottish Widows. **38-9, 97, 103, 124.**

Kerr, William 1866-1940 (Alloa)
Pupil of J. Burnet's, thence to Abercrombie's in Paisley, became a partner in John Melvin and Son, Alloa, 1904 to handle Paton and Baldwin's work. Sensitive arts and craftsman who fell under the spell of Scandinavia in the 1920s before becoming a modernist in the 1930s. **105, 110, 112, 115.**

Kininmonth, Sir William Hardie (Edinburgh)
Born 1904. Architect of Edinburgh. Finished Edinburgh College of Art 1931, forms loose association with Basil Spence 1932 onwards. Invited to join Balfour Paul as partner 1934, taking Spence with him. Partner thereafter in Kininmonth and Spence, and also Rowand Anderson Paul and Partners. Earlier apprenticed to W. N. Thompson (Leith) and also having been assistant in the office of Sir Edwin Lutyens. Work includes own house, 46a Dick Place (1933); terrace of houses with Spence in Dunbar (1933); Deaconess Hospital, Edinburgh (1936); Falkirk Town Hall, unsuccessful competition entry; Duddingston Church Hall; Falkirk Nurses Home (1938) winning entry; Dr Allan's house, Glenlockhart (1933); and experimental school for the Scottish Council at Kilsyth (unbuilt).

On RIAS Council; altered the building to provide lavatories. Shared drawing board with Spence. **28, 34, 40, 41-2, 120, 130, 175.**

Laird, J W and Napier (Glasgow)
J Austen Laird, son of J W Laird had been sent to Burnet's as an improver to gain experience; James Napier was at Burnet Son and Dick's in the early 1920s. Working mainly on the University. Winner of *Daily Mail* 1931 competition for a Scottish house. Robertson Dunn headquarters at Temple; Norwood Cinema (1936) and two others. Ladykin School, Greenock (1930); Bay Hotel, Gourock (1938). **82, 113, 174.**

Lawrence, George (Edinburgh)
Died 1985. Edinburgh College of Art: Tait's office 1934. Work on Ravenscourt Park and the Curzon Cinema, and Silver End. 1936 set up own practice. House, Pattulo, Ormiston Terrace; house for Helen Thornton, Glenlockhart Bank (1938); in 1938 joined LCC in planning. **42, 56, 78, 179.**

Lennox and McMath (Glasgow)
Designers of 8 cinemas in Glasgow including Roxy, Tudor, Giffnock and Granada, Duke Street. Designer of the new Bedford Cinema, Eglinton Street (1932). Also Eaglesham School (1940); Globe Cinema, Johnstone (1939); Port Glasgow Cinema (1937); Masonic Temple, Queen Street, Renfrew (1931); and the Regal, Dumbarton. **39.**

Lindsay, Ian Gordon (1906-66)
Studied at Cambridge with Raymond McGrath and fell under the spell of Mansfield Forbes. Worked with Reginald Fairlie before becoming a partner with BNH Orphoot ("Phootie") as Orphoot, Whiting and Lindsay. F E Whiting lived in England where his sole contribution was a modern house for himself ("only met him once: couldn't say I took to him much"). "Phootie" (1880-1964) built some lavish houses in a kind of white-walled American Italianate in Easter Belmont Road in the early 1930s. **32, 35, 36, 40, 42, 180.**

Lochhead, Alfred G d. 1972
Pupil of Abercrombie at Paisley with Burnet until 1914 when he went to Canada to work for Ross and MacDonald. Returned after war service to become Lorimer's draughtsman. Designed Cleghorns, now the Pearl on Castle Street/George Street, Edinburgh, 1929, the second phase being completed by Spence. **29.**

Lorimer, and Matthew (Edinburgh)
John Fraser Matthew (1875-1955); Stuart Russell Matthew; Robert Hogg Matthew (1906-78). Wheatsheaf Inn (1934); Knightswood Church; Pilton Church, Boswall Parkway (1934); Walpole Hall (1933); unbuilt scheme, Canal Basin (1933). **36-7, 125-6, 128.**

MacDonald, Alister (London)
(Son of Prime Minister Ramsay). Designer of several cinemas including Grangemouth, Lumbley Street (1939); Playhouse Montrose; Peebles; 2 cinemas in Glasgow; 3 cinemas in London. Peace Pavilion, Empire Exhibition; with John Patterson, third prize winner in Kincorth competition. **39, 64, 184.**

Mackay, John Ross (Edinburgh)
1895-1961. Apprenticed to Robert Lorimer—fired for accepting an invitation to stay with one of Lorimer's clients, General Aylmer Hunter-Weston. President RIAS 1943-5. Work includes Binns, Princes Street (1934); Dornock Mill, Crieff (1939); flats, Falcon Road, Edinburgh (1936); tenements and shops, Factors' Park, Dalry; National Bank, Inverkeithing (1934); Caley Cinema (1922) with James Richardson (1883-1970), another disaffected

Lorimer employee who gave up his partnership to be Principal Inspector of Ancient Monuments, a position from which he backed Lorimer at the National War Memorial. 97–8, 164.

Mackenzie, Alexander George Robertson (Aberdeen)
1879–1963. Apprenticed to R W Edie, Aston Webb and Rene Sergent in Paris for experience before beginning practice in 1902 as London partner; merging the practice with H H Wigglesworth (an ex MacKenzie employee) after World War I. Leaves London 1936 to return to take over his father's firm Marshall Mackenzie Son and George. Buildings include flats, Spittal (1937); Jackson's Garage (1937); Pittodrie Parish Church, King Street (1939); Aberdeen University Sports Pavilion (1939); house, Chanonry (1936); Northern Hotel, Kittybrewster (1938). President RIAS after the War. 33, 77–8, 83, 90, 101, 128.

McKissack, James (Glasgow)
1875–1940. Cinema architect, of architect's family. Son, same name, also an accomplished cameraman. Over 20 cinemas in Glasgow, including Cosmo (1939), Aldwych (1939), Vogue Riddrie and Govan (1938), and cinemas also in Renfrew (1938), Inveresk (1936), Scotstoun, Empire Dundee, Vogue Dundee (1935); Troon (1935); Irvine; Regal Paisley (1932) and Tudor Cinema, Stockbridge, Edinburgh (1937); work also included St Roch Roman Catholic School extension (1935). 58, 63, 67–8, 73.

McNair, C J and Elder (Glasgow)
McNair, born 1881, licentiate of the RIBA. McNair got the work, Elder designed it. Primarily cinema designer, not short of 50 in number, 6 in 1939. Cinemas include Govan Lyceum (1938); State, Shettleston (1937); State, Castlemilk Road (1937); Cuban Picture House, Kilmarnock (1939); Palladium, Tollcross (1936); and cinemas in Falkirk, Paisley, Coatbridge, Dumfries (1931), Stirling (1932), Hamilton (1932), Galashiels (1937), Cartsdyke (1937), and Motherwell (1936). Also Dennistoun Palais (1937), Glen Moray Hotel, Dunoon (1937), extensions to Yarrow (1936), Ayr Old Church Session House, and the Bellgrove Hotel, Duke Street. 38, 50–1, 63, 73–4.

MacRae, Ebenezer J (Edinburgh)
1881–1951. Trained with John Kinross. City Architect from 1925. 1931–3 design of cast-iron Edinburgh Police Boxes. Work in new Saughton 1932–3; converted Seafield Poorhouse 1931–2; warehouses, Dalry; restoration of Candlemakers Row; rebuilding of Pleasance; Gorgie School Gym; St Anne's School; extension to Heriot Watt;

Westfield Tramway, Gorgie; City Chambers extension; Niddrie; various schools; Piershill Housing. 22, 143, 145–6.

Mair, Alexander (Ayr)
Complete list held in RIAS archive prepared by Frank Dunbar. Prodigious output, based in Ayrshire. Work includes Scottish Milk Marketing Pavilion, Empire Exhibition; creameries in Mauchline, Stranraer, Galloway (1935), Hogganfield; milk powder factories in Kirkcudbright (1934) and Mauchline (1935); administrative building, Prestwick Aerodrome (1935–6); and Grangemouth Aerodrome (1939); extensive houses—both in estates and individual, including modern ones. Responsible for transfer of Palace of Engineering to Prestwick; and designer of Ayr County Offices (1930). 75, 109.

Marwick, T P and Son (T Waller Marwick) (Edinburgh)
T Waller Marwick c.1901–1971; pupil of father. "Funny little man" (W Dey). Buildings include Jays, Princes Street; St Cuthberts Co-operative (1937); Eagle Star Insurance Offices, George Street (1937); Shops Princes Street and George Street; pavilions in the Empire Exhibition. 34, 100, 105, 184–5, 187.

Matthew, Sir Robert Hogg (Edinburgh)
1906–75. Prizewinner Edinburgh College of Art. Travelled abroad in twenties. Joined father's firm early Thirties. Designed Wheatsheaf Inn, 1934. 1936 joins Department of Health. Designs in private capacity house for Dr Kemp Smith (1936). Winner £1,000 bungalow competition 1936. Organiser 1937 Town Planning Exhibition in Royal Scottish Academy. Enters competitions with Alan Reiach, and designs Watford Fire Station. In 1939 winner with Reiach of the Ilkeston Baths Competition. 21, 27, 36, 37, 79, 153, 160–1.

Mears, Sir Frank (Edinburgh)
1880–1953. Lecturer, Edinburgh College of Art. Practised initially with Carus-Wilson producing Lucy Sanderson Homes, Galashiels. Interested in planning and bridge design. 1926, responsible for Association for the Preservation of Rural Scotland. With Leslie Graham Thomson, designed standard rural cottage plans, 71 of which built in Roxburghshire. Restored Gladstone's Land, Lawnmarket, and rebuilt Kirk Wynd, Stirling and Baker Street, Stirling. Founded Scotland's first town planning course at Edinburgh College of Art. Son-in-law of Sir Patrick Geddes (photograph remains of him leading a masque). Represented profession on most planning and housing advisory committees, and was given a number of planning consultancies. "Hopeless teacher, profoundly wise" (Matthew);

"looked old, responsible and avuncular" (Lawrence). Known as "Daddy" to his students. 20, 22, 36, 55, 131, 143, 145, 153, 180.

Miller, James (Glasgow)
1860–1947. Pupil of Andrew Heiton, Perth, rose in Caledonian Railway civil engineering department and secured the confidence of its directors. Celebrated architect. Full list of works exists in RIAS archive. Notable buildings include the Commercial Bank, Bothwell Street, opened May 1935; Perth Royal Infirmary extension (1931); Church of the Holy Rude, Stirling (1936); Greenock Hospital (1943); Canniesburn Hospital (1934); Larbert Colony (1936); Pavilion, South Beach (1937); and Lintwhite School (1900). 25, 33, 37, 78, 101–3, 106, 119–20, 128, 143, 185.

Neil, Hamilton (Paisley)
Work includes houses, Renfrew; 4 cinemas in 1931 including the Florida Cinema, King's Park; a cinema in Stirling; Paisley Co-op Causeyside; Tinto Square Housing, Renfrew.

Nicol, J B (Aberdeen)
Succeeded to practice of William Kelly. Works include Aberdeen University Students Union (1936); maternity hospital Forrester Hill; Holburn Savings Banks; Royal Infirmary (1930); Grand Hotel, Union Terrace; University Union, Upperkirkgate (1930).

Noad, R Mervyn (Glasgow)
Born 1906, Set up practice 1931. In partnership with Alastair Wallace from 1933. Studio instructor Glasgow School of Art 1930–5. Editor of the Quarterly 1933–4. Editor of RIBA Conference Handbook 1935. Winner of Prestwick Town Hall and Baths competition 1933. Buildings include Renfrew Aerodrome (1934); many houses; Broadmeadows, Symington (1933); Broadwood, Gifford; Church of Good Shepherd, Hillington; St Aidan's Church, Clarkston; factories, MacLennan Street, Glasgow and Lesmahagow; and in the Empire Exhibition the interior of the Scottish pavilion; the Scottish Oils and Shellmex Pavilion; flats for the Scottish Council; and the Episcopal Church. 28, 32, 34, 75, 88, 106, 126, 135, 148, 153, 174, 185.

Reiach, Alan (Edinburgh)
Born 1910. Apprentice Robert Lorimer, 1928–32. Student at the College of Art, Winner of the most prizes. Andrew Grant Fellowship. 1934, designed house in Suffolk. Travelled to France, Scandinavia and America. Reputation of being really au fait with Continental and US work, and took time to explain it to fellow students. Worked with Robert Atkinson and Grey Wornum in London 1936–8. Entered competitions with Robert

Matthew—won Ilkeston (1938). Technical Secretary in Scottish Housing Advisory Committee; joint author with Robert Hurd *Building Scotland*. Third prize Tanfield Competition. Designed with Robert Matthew. Watford Fire Station, "Scots rural architecture was always a passion". **21–2, 27–9, 30, 37, 41, 48, 56, 80, 180.**

Reid and Forbes (Edinburgh)
G. Reid; J Smith Forbes. Work includes Leith Academy; Inverness Academy (won in competition 1932); laundry, Stenhouse (1935); extension to Peebles School; Art Deco garage, Dundas Street; Craigmillar Intermediate School (1936); Eyemouth School (1935); Kelso Academy (1936); Chirnside School (1937); Melville Estate School,. Gilmerton; Victoria School, Newhaven (1930); Wilkie's, Shandwick Place. **72, 98, 124–125.**

Spence, Sir Basil Urwin (Edinburgh)
1907–76. Student Edinburgh College of Art. Prizewinner. Loose association with William Kininmonth from 1931. Freelance perspectivist for other architects. Worked with Leslie Graham Thompson on Reid Memorial Church. 1933 works on Lismhor, Easter Belmont for Dr King; the house for Miss Reid, 4 Easter Belmont 1934; row of houses in Dunbar (1934). Glenburn House, Glenlockhart (1933). EAA stand, Waverley Market (1936)—as Basil Spence. Broughton House (from 1934); part time lecturer Edinburgh College of Art 1931–34. Partner with Balfour Paul from 1934 along with Kininmonth. Described in 1937 as "Architect of the Scottish Council for Art and Industry" when describing Kilsyth experimental school. Gribloch 1937 (with Perry Duncan of New York); some evidence that he was involved in Upton, 141 Corsebar Road, Paisley, built in 1935 for Lewis Brennan, a research chemist with J and P Coates. Causewayside Garage 1933. Other miscellaneous buildings. In the Empire Exhibition, the Scottish Pavilions. **36, 38–9, 40–2, 69, 76–7, 126, 129, 155–6, 174–6, 180, 184, 185, 187, 189.**

Stokes, David (Aberdeen and London)
Left AA in 1930. Set up with P Fleetwood-Hesketh. 1933 firm closed with no work. A G R MacKenzie offered the design partnership in Aberdeen to replace Clement George who had died. He worked on the Capitol Cinema, the Stuart House in Banchory, Halifax Building Society offices in Union Street. Glad to return to London in 1935. **34, 41, 175.**

Summerson, Sir John
Born 1904, Junior lecturer, Edinburgh College of Art 1929–31. Freelance contributor to the Architect and Building News. Editor of *Quarterly* 1930–1. Winner *Quarterly* Essay Prize 1931. "Wasted on first year" (Lawrence). Notable architectural historian and Curator of the Soane Museum. **23, 30, 38, 53, 55, 107.**

Sutherland, Eric (Glasgow)
1870–1940. Cinemas, Dunoon, Govanhill, Battlefield. Various Savings Banks in Glasgow including Hillhead (1939) and High Street. Ayr (1935–7). Designer of Mayfield Cinema, Sinclair Drive (1933). **101.**

Sutherland, T Scott
Born 1899. Final degree Robert Gordon's College. 1923—Gray's School of Art. One-legged. Expert bridge player, stalwart Aberdeen Magical Society, fine swimmer, tennis player, cricketer and fisherman. Immense energy. 1934 stands as Progressive in Ruthrieston. At height of election had 80 cars ferrying voters to polling station. Spent £59 on his election—local paper noted the highest sum for a number of years. Was elected and became Housing Convener. Recommended "new houses on the Viennese design". Responsible for Kincorth Housing Competition (1936).

Founder director of Caledonian Associates Cinemas. Director of 39 other companies including Silver City Lido, Tivoli Theatre Company, Inverurie Pictures Ltd, Aberdeen Varieties Ltd, Chairman James Allan and Company Furnishers. Branch manager and architect for Scottish Amicable, Director of Modern Homes (Aberdeen), Chairman Dunblane Hydro, promoter of Aberdeen ice rink. Buildings include Broomhill Estate, bungalows, Peterhead Cinema (1937), Majestic Cinema, George Street Cinema, Victoria Cinema, Inverurie, Astoria Cinema Kittybrewster, Dunblane Hydro refurbishment, Hazelhead Clubhouse, Pooles, Regent Street. **24, 25, 88, 146, 157, 159, 161.**

Tait, Thomas Smith (1882–1952)
Most prominent Scots architect of the inter-war period. Became partner of Sir John Burnet 1920 and dominant principal after 1926. Projects include Silver End (from 1926), Adelaide House (1921–4) *Crowsteps*, Newbury and the *Daily Telegraph* (1927).

Winner of Hawkhead infectious Diseases Hospital (1934) and assessor of Bexhill Pavilion, Waverley Market and Kirkcaldy Town Hall competitions. Appointed to design housing in Elgin, Lincluden and Johnstone, only the latter built. Controlling designer of the Empire Exhibition and designer of St Andrew's House. **12, 28, 34, 36, 37, 47, 67, 98, 106, 107, 119–21, 143, 144, 185–8.**

Taylor, James
Born 1890, began practice 1919. Buildings include British Silk Model Factory, Balloch (1930). Marine Hotel, Oban (1936); perspectives for houses in the Broom Estate including Broom No 1 (1936); head offices for Dalziel Iron Works; Thornwood Pub, Dumbarton Road; cinema, Paisley Road; and the Homeopathic Hospital, Kirklee (1936)—never built. Remembered as an unscrupulous architect who refused to register, and who went to prison for tax evasion after the War. **82, 84, 132, 169, 171, 179.**

Thompson, J Taylor
Died 1953. Trained Edinburgh. 8 years with Bertram Goodhue, USA, returned to Glasgow early 1920s, helped at Burnet Son and Dick's while establishing own practice. Buildings include St John's, Renfield, Glasgow (1931); High Carntyne Parish Church (1931) brick with stone dressing; Tulloch Factory, Bridgeton Cross (1937); Cowlairs Creamery (1937); Cowlairs Co-operative 1934; Possil New School (1935); Clyde Valley Power Station. **127, 129, 135, 184–5, 187.**

Thomson, Leslie Graham
1896–1974. Apprentice and assistant to Robert Lorimer. Left in 1928, taking the Reid Memorial Church. Later joined by Frank Connell, firm becoming Leslie Graham Thomson and Connell. Lorimer's obituarist in the *Quarterly*. Later President RIAS as Leslie Graham MacDougall. Buildings: own house, West Linton; Reid Memorial Church (1928); Fairmilehead extension church 1938; Caledonian Insurance Company, St Andrew Square (1939); nursing home Inverness; YMCA Castle Street and Stock Exchange—never built. Council member of the RIAS; joint Honorary Secretary of the APRS with Frank Mears. **20, 24, 54, 82, 106, 127–8, 129, 153, 174, 176.**

Wylie, Edward Grigg
Born c.1885, pupil of W Forsyth MacGibbon. Close friend of Professor Eugene Bourdon, and very interested in France, early style close to Burnet's. Formed partnership with Alex Wright who had been in Canada, dissolved c.1930. Died 1954. Firm Wylie Wright and Wylie, later joined by George Shanks to become Wylie Shanks. Buildings include Lennox Castle Hospital; Scottish Legal Life Building, Bothwell Street—largest office in Glasgow won in competition 1928; Anderson and Robertson factory 1933; dental hospital, Glasgow 1932; Weir's Welfare Building (1937); Messrs McKean, Port Dundas (1935); Hillington Industrial Estate from 1937; Carfin and Larkhall Industrial Estates from 1938; Cathkin Golf Club 1935; Scottish Widows, West George Street 1932; Hillhead School—double Y-plan—1931; school Mansel Street Springburn—E-plan. **36, 38, 61, 101, 110–12, 120, 122.**

INDEX